Study Guide and
Student Solutions Manual

W9-AGK-665

MATHEMATICAL ANALYSIS

for Business, Economics, and the Life and Social Sciences

THIRD EDITION

Jagdish C. Arya/Robin W. Lardner

Department of Mathematics, Simon Fraser University

Prentice Hall, Englewood Cliffs, New Jersey 07632

Editorial/production supervision and
   interior design: Leeann Tucker
Manufacturing buyer: Paula Massenaro

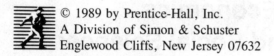 © 1989 by Prentice-Hall, Inc.
A Division of Simon & Schuster
Englewood Cliffs, New Jersey 07632

All rights reserved. No part of this book may be
reproduced, in any form or by any means,
without permission in writing from the publisher.

Printed in the United States of America

10   9   8   7   6   5   4   3   2

ISBN 0-13-561333-7

Prentice-Hall International (UK) Limited, *London*
Prentice-Hall of Australia Pty. Limited, *Sydney*
Prentice-Hall Canada Inc., *Toronto*
Prentice-Hall Hispanoamericana, S.A., *Mexico*
Prentice-Hall of India Private Limited, *New Delhi*
Prentice-Hall of Japan, Inc., *Tokyo*
Simon & Schuster Asia Pte. Ltd., *Singapore*
Editora Prentice-Hall do Brasil, Ltda., *Rio de Janeiro*

CONTENTS

A note to the students

This manual is a supplement to the book 'Mathematical Analysis for Business, Economics and Life and the Social Sciences by J.C. Arya and R.W. Lardner. It is designed primarily for use by the student.

For each chapter of the book, the manual contains the following items.

1. A list of the main objectives that you should have achieved after studying the chapter and a list of the important terms that you should have become familiar with.

2. Complete solutions to every alternate odd question in the Exercises (that is, questions 1, 5, 9, etc. in each exercise set).

3. A review test consisting generally of about thirty questions that can be answered usually in your head. These questions are based on our experience of the mistakes or misunderstandings that students commonly have.

You may find it useful to use this manual in the following way.

1. Read the objectives quickly before studying the chapter so that you have some idea where you are going.

2. After finishing each chapter, study the objectives and the list of important terms carefully. If you are not confident about any objective or if you have forgotten any of the terms then review the relevant material.

3. The solutions to exercises can be used in the obvious way when you cannot get the right answer yourself. However don't turn automatically to the solutions, but make a real effort to solve the problem yourself first, perhaps using a worked example in the textbook as a model. The exercises are there to help you learn, not to give you nightmares!

4. Check that your ideas are straight by working through the review test after each chapter.

Finally, we wish you success.

CHAPTER - 1

Natural number, integer, rational number, real number, the number line.

Commutative, associative and distributive laws of real numbers.

Additive inverse, multiplicative inverse.

LCD (least common denominator) of two or more fractions.

Exponent or power, base. The laws of exponents.

The n-th root and principal n-th root of a real number.

Radical. Fractional power.

Algebraic expression, term, literal part, coefficient, constant term.

Monomial, binomial, multinomial. Like terms. Polynomial.

Divisor, dividend, quotient, remainder, factor.

OBJECTIVES

AFTER READING THIS CHAPTER YOU SHOULD BE ABLE TO DO THE FOLLOWING:

1. To use the commutative, associative and distributive properties of real numbers to simplify algebraic expressions.

2. To multiply and divide fractions and to simplify fractions by cancellation of common factors.

3. To add or subtract fractions by changing them to their lowest common denominator.

4. To know and be able to use the five laws of exponents in simplifying algebraic expressions involving both integer powers and fractional powers.

5. To add or subtract and simplify expressions by combining like terms.

6. To multiply expressions using the distributive property or equivalently by the method of arcs.

7. To divide an expression by a monomial.

8. To divide one polynomial by another using long division.

9. To factor expressions by (a) extracting common monomial factors (b) using standard formulas for the difference of two squares and the sum and difference of two cubes (c) using the grouping method.

10. To factor expressions of the type $mx^2 + px + q$.

11. To simplify an algebraic fraction by rationalizing its denominator.

12. To add, subtract, multiply, divide and simplify complicated algebraic fractions.

SOLUTIONS TO ALTERNATE ODD PROBLEMS

EXERCISES - 1.1

1. See answer in the text book.   5. $(-3)(-7) = +21$

9. $-(-4-3) = -(-7) = +7$ 13. $2(-2-3) = 2(-5) = -10$

17. $-(-x-3) = +x+3 = x+3$ 21. $-4(x-6) = -4x+24$

25. $(-x)(-y)(-z) = -xyz$ 29. $(-3p)(2q)(q-p) = (-6pq)(q-p) = -6pq^2+6p^2q$

33. $3x-t-2(x-t) = 3x - t - 2x + 2t = 3x-2x - t + 2t = x+t.$

37. $x\{3(x-2) - 2x + 1\} = x(3x - 6 - 2x + 1) = x(x-5) = x^2 - 5x$

41. $x^{-1}(2x-1) = \frac{1}{x}(2x-1) = \frac{2x}{x} - \frac{1}{x} = 2 - \frac{1}{x}$

45. $(-xy)^{-1}(2x-3y) = \frac{1}{-xy}(2x-3y) = \frac{2x}{-xy} - \frac{3y}{-xy} = \frac{-2}{y} + \frac{3}{x}$

EXERCISES - 1.2

1. See answers in the text book.   5. $\frac{2}{5} \cdot \frac{3}{6} \cdot \frac{10}{7} \cdot \frac{2\cdot\cancel{3}\cdot\cancel{10}}{\cancel{5}\cdot\cancel{6}\cdot7} = \frac{2}{7}$

9. $(\frac{-2x}{3y})(-5xy) = \frac{2x \cdot 5xy}{3y} = \frac{10x^2y}{3y} = \frac{10x^2}{3}$

13. $(\frac{12}{25} \cdot \frac{15}{7}) \div \frac{20}{7} = \frac{\cancel{12}^3}{\cancel{25}_5} \cdot \frac{\cancel{15}^3}{\cancel{7}} \cdot \frac{\cancel{7}}{\cancel{20}_5} = \frac{9}{25}$

17. $(\frac{3}{8x}) \div (\frac{4x}{15}) = \frac{3}{8x} \cdot \frac{15}{4x} = \frac{45}{32x^2}$

21. $(\frac{2xt}{3} \div \frac{x}{4t}) \div \frac{2t}{3} = (\frac{2xt}{3} \cdot \frac{4t}{x}) \div \frac{2t}{3} = \frac{2xt}{3} \cdot \frac{4t}{x} \cdot \frac{3}{2t} = 4t$

25. L.C.D. of 10 and 15 is 30.   Thus,

   $\frac{1}{10} + \frac{1}{15} = \frac{3}{30} + \frac{2}{30} = \frac{3+2}{30} = \frac{5}{30} = \frac{1}{6}$

29. $\frac{y}{2x} + \frac{1}{3x} = \frac{3y}{6x} + \frac{2}{6x} = \frac{3y+2}{6x}$ 33. $\frac{3y}{10x^2} - \frac{1}{6x} = \frac{9y}{30x^2} - \frac{5x}{30x^2} = \frac{9y-5x}{30x^2}$

37. $(\frac{x}{2} + \frac{2}{x}) \div \frac{6}{x} = \frac{x^2+4}{2x} \div \frac{6}{x} = \frac{x^2+4}{2x} \cdot \frac{x}{6} = \frac{x^2+4}{12}$

41. $(\frac{1}{2} - \frac{1}{3}) / (\frac{1}{4} + \frac{1}{5}) = (\frac{3}{6} - \frac{2}{6}) / (\frac{5}{20} + \frac{4}{20}) = (\frac{3-2}{6}) / (\frac{5+4}{20}) = \frac{1}{6} \div \frac{9}{20} = \frac{1}{6} \cdot \frac{20}{9} = \frac{10}{27}$

45. $(\frac{a}{b} + \frac{2a}{3b}) \div (\frac{3x}{8} \div \frac{x}{9} + \frac{1}{4}) = (\frac{3a}{3b} + \frac{2a}{3b}) \div (\frac{3x}{8} \cdot \frac{9}{x} + \frac{1}{4})$

$\quad = \frac{5a}{3b} \div (\frac{27}{8} + \frac{2}{8}) = \frac{5a}{3b} \div \frac{29}{8} = \frac{5a}{3b} \cdot \frac{8}{29} = \frac{40a}{87b}$

EXERCISES - 1.3

1. $(2^5)^2 = 2^{5 \cdot 2} = 2^{10} = 1024$

5. $(x^2yz)^3 \cdot (xy)^4 = x^6 \cdot y^3 \cdot z^3 \cdot x^4 y^4 = x^6 \cdot x^4 \cdot y^3 \cdot y^4 \cdot z^3 = x^{6+4} \cdot y^{3+4} \cdot z^3 = x^{10}y^7z^3$

9. $(xy^2z^3)^{-1}(xyz)^3 = x^{-1}y^{-2}z^{-3} \cdot x^3y^3z^3 = x^{-1} \cdot x^3 \cdot y^{-2} \cdot y^3 \cdot z^{-3} \cdot z^3$

$\quad = x^{-1+3} \cdot y^{-2+3} \cdot z^{-3+3} = x^2y^1z^0 = x^2y$

13. $(\frac{1}{3})^{-2} \div 3^{-4} = (3^{-1})^{-2} \div 3^{-4} = 3^2 \div 3^{-4} = 3^2/3^{-4} = 3^{2-(-4)} = 3^6 = 729$

17. $\frac{(-2xy)^3}{x^3y} = \frac{(-2)^3 x^3 y^3}{x^3y} = -8y^2$

21. $x^2(x^4-2x) = x^2 \cdot x^4 - x^2 \cdot 2x = x^{2+4} - 2 \cdot x^{2+1} = x^6 - 2x^3$

25. $x^4(2x^2-x-3x^{-2}) = x^4 \cdot 2x^2 - x^4 \cdot x - x^4 \cdot 3x^{-2} = 2x^6 - x^5 - 3x^2$

29. $(xy)^{-1}(x^{-1}+y^{-1})^{-1} = (xy)^{-1}(\frac{1}{x} + \frac{1}{y})^{-1} = (\frac{1}{xy})(\frac{y+x}{xy})^{-1} = \frac{1}{xy} \cdot \frac{xy}{x+y} = \frac{1}{x+y}$

33. $\frac{3y}{10x^3} + \frac{2}{15xy} = \frac{(3y)(3y)}{30x^3y} + \frac{2(2x^2)}{30x^3y} = \frac{9y^2+4x^2}{30x^3y}$

37. $\frac{x^{-3}}{4x} - \frac{x}{6x^5} = \frac{1}{4x} \cdot \frac{1}{x^3} - \frac{1}{6x^4} = \frac{1}{4x^4} - \frac{1}{6x^4} = \frac{3}{12x^4} - \frac{2}{12x^4} = \frac{1}{12x^4}$

EXERCISES - 1.4

1. $2^m = 8^3\sqrt{2} = 2^3 \cdot 2^{1/3} = 2^{3+1/3} = 2^{10/3}$ gives m = 10/3

5. $\sqrt{\sqrt{2}} = 4^m$ or $(2^{1/2})^{1/2} = (2^2)^m$ or $2^{1/4} = 2^{2m}$ gives 2m = 1/4 or m = 1/8

9. $\sqrt{1\frac{9}{16}} = \sqrt{\frac{25}{16}} = 5/4$ 13. $\sqrt{(-3)^2} = \sqrt{9} = 3$

17. $(0.16)^{-1/2} = (\frac{16}{100})^{-1/2} = (\frac{4}{25})^{-1/2} = (\frac{25}{4})^{1/2} = \frac{\sqrt{25}}{\sqrt{4}} = 5/4$

21. $(32\ x^5\ y^{-10})^{1/5} = (2^5 \cdot x^5 \cdot y^{-10})^{1/5} = 2^{5(1/5)} \cdot x^{5(1/5)} \cdot y^{-10(1/5)} = 2xy^{-2}$

$$= \frac{2x}{y^2}$$

25. $(9^{-3} \cdot 16^{3/2})^{1/6} = \{(3^2)^{-3} \cdot (2^4)^{3/2}\}^{1/6} = (3^{-6} \cdot 2^6)^{1/6} = 3^{-1} \cdot 2^1 = 2/3$

29. $\frac{(x^{a+b})^2 (y^{a+b})^2}{(xy)^{2a-b}} = \frac{x^{2a+2b} \cdot y^{2a+2b}}{x^{2a-b} \cdot y^{2a-b}} = x^{2a+2b-(2a-b)} \cdot y^{2a+2b-(2a-b)} = x^{3b} \cdot y^{3b}$

33. $2\sqrt{18} - \sqrt{32} = 2\sqrt{9 \cdot 2} - \sqrt{16 \cdot 2} = 2\sqrt{9} \cdot \sqrt{2} - \sqrt{16}\sqrt{2} = 2 \cdot 3\sqrt{2} - 4\sqrt{2} = 6\sqrt{2} - 4\sqrt{2} = 2\sqrt{2}$

37. $(x^{1/2} \cdot x^{-1/3})^2 = (x^{1/2\ -\ 1/3})^2 = (x^{1/6})^2 = x^{2/6} = x^{1/3}$

EXERCISES - 1.5

1. $(5a+7b-3) + (3b-2a+9) = (5a-2a) + (7b+3b) + (-3+9) = 3a + 10b + 6$

5. $(7t^2+6t-1) - (3t-5t^2+4-t^3) = 7t^2+6t-1-3t+5t^2-4+t^3 = t^3+12t^2+3t-5$

9. $x(2x^2+3xy+y^2) - y(5x^2-2xy+y^2) = 2x^3+3x^2y+xy^2-5x^2y+2xy^2-y^3$

$$= 2x^3 - 2x^2y + 3xy^2 - y^3$$

13. $(x+3)(2x^2-5x+7) = x(2x^2-5x+7) + 3(2x^2-5x+7) = 2x^3-5x^2+7x+6x^2-15x+21$

$$= 2x^3 + x^2 - 8x + 21.$$

17. $(x+y-z)(x+y+z) = \{(x+y)-z\}\{(x+y)+z\} = (x+y)^2 - z^2 = x^2 + 2xy + y^2 - z^2$

21. $(\sqrt{2}x - \sqrt{3y})^2 = (\sqrt{2}x)^2 - 2(\sqrt{2}x)(\sqrt{3y}) + (\sqrt{3y})^2 = 2x^2 - 2x\sqrt{6y} + 3y$

25. $3\{x^2 -5\{x+2(3-5x)\}\} = 3\{x^2 - 5\{x+6-10x\}\} = 3\{x^2 - 5(6-9x)\}$

$$= 3(x^2 - 30 + 45x) = 3x^2 + 135x - 90$$

29. $\dfrac{x^3+7x^2-5x+4}{x^2} = \dfrac{x^3}{x^2} + \dfrac{7x^2}{x^2} - \dfrac{5x}{x^2} + \dfrac{4}{x^2} = x + 7 - \dfrac{5}{x} + \dfrac{4}{x^2}$

33.
$$\begin{array}{r}
x-3 \\
x-2 \overline{\smash{)}x^2-5x+6} \\
\underline{x^2-2x} \\
-3x+6 \\
\underline{-3x+6} \\
0
\end{array}$$
Thus, $(x^2-5x+6) \div (x-2) = x-3$

37.
$$\begin{array}{r}
x^2+1 \\
x+2 \overline{\smash{)}x^3+2x^2+x+5} \\
\underline{x^3+2x^2} \\
x+5 \\
\underline{x+2} \\
3
\end{array}$$
Thus, $(x^3+2x^2+x+5) \div (x+2)$

$= x^2 + 1 + 3/(x+2)$

41.
$$\begin{array}{r}
x^2-2x+3 \\
2x+1 \overline{\smash{)}2x^3-3x^2+4x+6} \\
\underline{2x^3+x^2} \\
-4x^2+4x \\
\underline{-4x^2-2x} \\
6x+6 \\
\underline{6x+3} \\
3
\end{array}$$
Thus, $(2x^3 - 3x^2 + 4x + 6) \div (2x+1)$

$= x^2 - 2x + 3 + 3/(2x+1)$

EXERCISES - 1.6

1. $3a + 6b = 3(a + 2b)$

5. $2u + av - 2v - au = 2u - au + av - 2v = u(2-a) - v(2-a) = (2-a)(u-v)$

9. $x^2 - 16 = x^2 - 4^2 = (x-4)(x+4)$ 13. $x^2 + 5x + 6 = (x+2)(x+3)$

17. $2x^2 + 5x + 3 = 2x^2 + 2x + 3x + 3 = 2x(x+1) + 3(x+1) = (x+1)(2x+3)$

21. $x^3y - 25xy^3 = xy(x^2-25y^2) = xy(x-5y)(x+5y)$

25. $x^3 - 27 = x^3 - 3^3 = (x-3)(x^2+3x+3^2) = (x-3)(x^2+3x+9)$

29. $6x^3y + 4x^2y - 10xy = 2xy(3x^2+2x-5) = 2xy\left[(3x^2+5x)-3x-5\right]$

$= 2xy\left[x(3x+5) - 1(3x+5)\right] = 2xy(3x+5)(x-1)$

33. $(x^2z^2 - 4z^2) + (x^4-4x^2) = z^2(x^2-4) + x^2(x^2-4) = (x^2-4)(z^2+x^2)$

$= (x-2)(x+2)(z^2+x^2)$

37. $2(x+y)^2 + 5(x+y) + 2 = 2a^2 + 5a + 2 = 2a^2 + 4a + a + 2$ $\quad | a = x+y$

$\qquad = 2a(a+2)+1(a+2) = (a+2)(2a+1) = (x+y+2)\{2(x+y) + 1\}$

$\qquad = (x+y+2)(2x+2y+1)$

41. $(x^2)^3 - (2y^2)^3 = (x^2 - 2y^2)(x^4 + 2x^2y^2 + 4y^4)$

$\qquad\qquad = (x^2-2y^2)\{(x^2+2y^2)^2 - (\sqrt{2}xy)^2\}$

$\qquad\qquad = (x-\sqrt{2}y)(x+\sqrt{2})(x^2+2y^2-\sqrt{2}xy)(x^2+2y^2+\sqrt{2}xy).$

45. $x^4 + 4y^4 = (x^2+2y^2)^2 - (2xy)^2 = (x^2+2y^2-2xy)(x^2+2y^2+2xy)$

EXERCISES - 1.7

1. $4x/(2x+3) + 6/(2x+3) = (4x+6)/(2x+3) = 2(2x+3)/(2x+3) = 2.$

5. $(2x+1)/(x+2) + 3 = (2x+1)/(x+2) + 3(x+2)/(x+2) = \{2x+1+3(x+2)\}/x+2 = \dfrac{5x+7}{x+2}.$

9. $1/(x^2-5x+6) - 1/(x^2-3x+2) = \dfrac{1}{(x-2)(x-3)} - \dfrac{1}{(x-2)(x-1)}$

$\qquad\qquad\qquad = \dfrac{(x-1) - (x-3)}{(x-1)(x-2)(x-3)} = \dfrac{2}{(x-1)(x-2)(x-3)}$

13. $\dfrac{1}{(x+1)(x+3)} + \dfrac{3}{(x+1)(x-1)} - \dfrac{2}{x+3} = \dfrac{(x-1) + 3(x+3) - 2(x-1)(x+1)}{(x-1)(x+1)(x+3)}$

$\qquad\qquad\qquad = \dfrac{(10+4x-2x^2)}{(x-1)(x+1)(x+3)}$

17. $\left(3 + \dfrac{1}{x-1}\right)\left(1 - \dfrac{1}{3x-2}\right) = \dfrac{3x-3+1}{x-1} \cdot \dfrac{3x-2-1}{3x-2} = \dfrac{3x-2}{x-1} \cdot \dfrac{3(x-1)}{3x-2} = 3$

21. $\left(\dfrac{x^2+x-2}{2x+3}\right) \Big/ \left(\dfrac{x^2-4}{2x^2+5x+3}\right) = \dfrac{(x+2)(x-1)}{2x+3} \Big/ \dfrac{(x-2)(x+2)}{(2x+3)(x+1)} = \dfrac{(x+2)(x-1)}{2x+3} \cdot \dfrac{(2x+3)(x+1)}{(x-2)(x+2)}$

$\qquad\qquad\qquad = \dfrac{(x-1)(x+1)}{x-2} = \dfrac{x^2-1}{x-2}$

25. $\dfrac{1}{3+\sqrt{7}} \cdot \dfrac{3-\sqrt{7}}{3-\sqrt{7}} = \dfrac{3-\sqrt{7}}{3^2-(\sqrt{7})^2} = \dfrac{3-\sqrt{7}}{9-7} = \dfrac{3-\sqrt{7}}{2}$

29. $\dfrac{3}{3+\sqrt{3}} \cdot \dfrac{3-\sqrt{3}}{3-\sqrt{3}} = \dfrac{3(3-\sqrt{3})}{9-3} = \dfrac{3 - \sqrt{3}}{2}$

1. See answers in the text book.

5. $(\dfrac{x^a}{x^b})^c \cdot (\dfrac{x^b}{x^c})^a (\dfrac{x^a}{x^c})^b = (x^{a-b})^c \cdot (x^{b-c})^a \cdot (x^{a-c})^b$

$$= x^{c(a-b)} \cdot x^{a(b-c)} \cdot x^{b(a-c)} = x^{c(a-b)+a(b-c)+b(a-c)} = x^0 = 1$$

9. $\dfrac{2}{(x+1)(x+1)} - \dfrac{1}{(x+1)(x+3)} + \dfrac{3}{(x-2)(x+1)}$

$$= \dfrac{2(x+3)(x-2) - (x+1)(x-2) + 3(x+1)(x+3)}{(x+1)(x+1)(x+3)(x-2)} = \dfrac{4x^2 + 15x - 1}{(x+1)^2(x+3)(x-2)}$$

13. $\dfrac{(a+b)\,\cancel{(a+b)}}{\cancel{(x+2)}(x+3)} \cdot \dfrac{(x-3)\,\cancel{(x+2)}}{(a-b)\,\cancel{(a+b)}} = \dfrac{(a+b)(x-3)}{(x+3)(a-b)}$

17. $3x^2 - 75y^2 = 3\{x^2 - (5y)^2\} = 3(x-5y)(x+5y)$

21. $(a+4)(a-3) + (2a+3)(a+1) = (a^2+a-12) + (2a^2+5a+3)$

$$= 3a^2 + 6a - 9 = 3(a^2+2a-3) = 3(a+3)(a-1)$$

25. $x^3 + (2/x)^3 = (x + 2/x)(x^2 - x \cdot 2/x + 4/x^2) = (x + 2/x)(x^2 - 2 + 4/x^2)$

REVIEW TEST ON CHAPTER - 1

FILL IN THE BLANKS:

1. The number $\sqrt{x}$ is a real number only if x is a _____ number.

2. The number $1/\sqrt{-x}$ is a real number only if x is a _____ number.

3. $x/x = $ _____ only if x _____.

4. The number $1/p$ is defined only if p _____.

5. $(a^{-1})^{-1} = $ _____ is true if a _____.

6. $a \cdot a^{-1} = $ _____ only if a _____.

7. $(3x)^{-1}(6x^2) = $ _____   8. $p/q \div r = $ _____.

9. $x \div y/z = $ _____.   10. $a/b \div a/d = $ _____.

11. $5/x + 3/x = $ _____.   12. $a/5 + a/3 = $ _____.

13. $a/c - b = $ _____.   14. $a/b + c/d = $ _____.

15. $p/(q+r) = $ _____.   16. $\sqrt{a^2} = $ _____ for all a.

17. $\sqrt{x^2} = \underline{\hspace{1cm}}$ if $x < 0$.

18. $a^0 = \underline{\hspace{1.5cm}}$ for all a $\underline{\hspace{0.7cm}}$.

19. $(2x^{-1})^{-1} = \underline{\hspace{1.5cm}}$.

20. $(5^{72})^0 = \underline{\hspace{1.5cm}}$.

21. $(2/3)^0 = (3/2)^{\underline{\hspace{0.5cm}}}$.

22. $1/(5a^3) = \underline{\hspace{1.5cm}} a^{-3}$.

23. $(a^{-1}b^{-1})^{-2} = \underline{\hspace{1.5cm}}$.

24. $(-a^2 b^3)/(-a^{-1}b)^2 = \underline{\hspace{1.5cm}}$.

25. $(2^{-1} - 3^{-1})^{-1} = \underline{\hspace{1.5cm}}$.

26. $(3^{-1} + 2^{-1})^{-2} = \underline{\hspace{1.5cm}}$.

27. $(32)^{3/5} = \underline{\hspace{1.5cm}}$.

28. $\sqrt[3]{-0.008} = \underline{\hspace{1.5cm}}$.

29. $(x+y)^2 = \underline{\hspace{1.5cm}}$.

30. $(a-b)^2 = \underline{\hspace{1.5cm}}$.

31. $(x+y)(x-y) = \underline{\hspace{1.5cm}}$.

32. $(a+b)(b-a) = \underline{\hspace{1.5cm}}$.

33. $(2x-3)(3+2x) = \underline{\hspace{1.5cm}}$.

34. $(2a-3b)^2 = \underline{\hspace{1.5cm}}$.

35. $9x^2 - y^2 = (\underline{\hspace{1cm}})(\underline{\hspace{1cm}})$.

36. $4x^2 - 9y^2 = (\underline{\hspace{1cm}})(\underline{\hspace{1cm}})$.

37. $x^2 + 4x + 3 = (\underline{\hspace{1cm}})(\underline{\hspace{1cm}})$.

38. $x^2 - 3x + 2 = (\underline{\hspace{1cm}})(\underline{\hspace{1cm}})$.

39. $x^2 - 5x - 6 = (\underline{\hspace{1cm}})(\underline{\hspace{1cm}})$.

40. $x^2 + x - 2 = (\underline{\hspace{1cm}})(\underline{\hspace{1cm}})$.

41. $a^3 - b^3 = (\underline{\hspace{1cm}})(\underline{\hspace{1cm}})$.

42. $x^3 + y^3 = (\underline{\hspace{1cm}})(\underline{\hspace{1cm}})$.

43. $x^3 - 8 = (\underline{\hspace{1cm}})(\underline{\hspace{1cm}})$.

44. $1 + 27a^3 = (\underline{\hspace{1cm}})(\underline{\hspace{1cm}})$.

45. $3y(x-2)/\{2x(x-2)\} = \underline{\hspace{1.5cm}}$ only if $\underline{\hspace{1.5cm}}$.

46. $(x^2-4)/(x+2) = \underline{\hspace{1.5cm}}$ only if $\underline{\hspace{1.5cm}}$.

47. $(2x)^4 \underline{\hspace{1.5cm}} 2x^4$ $\qquad$ ($=$, $\neq$)

48. $(x^{-2} + y^{-2})^{-1} \underline{\hspace{1cm}} x^2 + y^2$ $\qquad$ ($=$, $\neq$)

49. $3(2x)^3 \underline{\hspace{1.5cm}} (6x)^3$ $\qquad$ ($=$, $\neq$)

50. To rationalize the denominator of $1/(\sqrt{3}-\sqrt{2})$, we multiply the top and bottom by $\underline{\hspace{1.5cm}}$ to obtain the answer $\underline{\hspace{1.5cm}}$.

SEE ANSWERS AT THE END OF THIS BOOK.

CHAPTER - 2

YOU SHOULD BE FAMILIAR WITH THE FOLLOWING TERMS:

Equation, right side, left side.

Solution of an equation.

Addition and multiplication principles.

Polynomial equation, degree, quadratic equation, linear equation.

Quadratic formula.

Completing the square.

Revenue, cost profit.

OBJECTIVES

AFTER READING THIS CHAPTER YOU SHOULD BE ABLE TO DO THE FOLLOWING:

1. Use the addition and multiplication principles to solve a linear equation or an equation that is equivalent to a linear equation.

2. To solve quadratic equations by

    (a) the method of factoring when applicable

    (b) completing the square

    (c) using the quadratic formula.

3. To formulate appropriate types of word **problems** in terms of equations and hence to solve them. Study carefully the procedure outlined at the beginning of section 2.3 and try to follow it.

SOLUTIONS TO ALTERNATE ODD PROBLEMS

EXERCISES - 2.1

1. Yes, because on putting x=1 in $3x + 7 = 12 - 2x$, we get $3(1) + 7 = 12 - 2(1)$ or $3+7 = 12 - 2$ which is true.

5. Putting x=2 in $x^2 = 5x-6$ gives $4 = 10-6$ which is true. Thus x=2 is a solution. Putting x=5 in $x^2 = 5x - 6$ gives $25 - 25-6$, which is not true. Thus, 5 is <u>not</u> a solution.

9. No, because on putting x=1 makes the first term in the given equation undefined.

13. $y^2 + 7 = (y^2-2y+1) + 3y$ or $7 = y+1$ or $y-6 = 0$; degree 1.

17. $4(x-3) = 8-x$ or $4x-12 = 8-x$ or $5x = 20$ or $x=4$.

21. $3z - 2 + 4 - 4z = 5 - 10z - 12$ or $9z = -9$ or $z = -1$.

25. $\frac{3x+7}{2} = \frac{1+x}{3}$ or $3(3x+7) = 2(1+x)$ or $7x = -19$ or $x = -19/7$

29. $\frac{1}{3}(2y+1) + \frac{1}{2} y = \frac{2}{5}(1-2y) - 4$. Multiply through out by 30.
    $10(2y+1) + 15y = 12(1-2y) - 120$ or $59y = -118$ or $y = -2$.

33. $x^2 + (x^2+2x+1) = 2x^2 + 5x-3$ or $-3x = -4$ or $x = 4/3$

37. $x(x^2+6x+8) + x^3 = 2(x^3 + 3x^2 + 3x + 1)$
    or $x^3 + 6x^2 + 8x + x^3 = 2x^3 + 6x^2 + 6x + 2$ or $2x = 2$ or $x=1$.

EXERCISES - 2.2

1. $(x+2)(x+3) = 0$ gives $x = -2$, -3.   5. $(x+2)^2 = 0$ gives $x = -2$.

9. $(x-1)(x+1) = 0$ gives $x = 1, -1$.

13. Multiplying by 4 (l.c.d) gives: $24x^2 + 10x + 1 = 0$ or $(6x+1)(4x+1)=0$
    i.e. $x = -1/6$ or $x = -1/4$.

17. $(3x+2)(2x-1) = 0$ gives $x = -2/3$ or $1/2$.

21. $2x^2 + 3x - 4 = 0$ gives $x = \dfrac{-3 \pm \sqrt{9-4(2)(-4)}}{4} = \dfrac{-3 \pm \sqrt{41}}{4}$.

25. $4x^2 + 20x + 25 = 0$ gives $x = \dfrac{-20 \pm \sqrt{400-400}}{8} = \dfrac{-20 \pm 0}{8} = -5/4$.

29. $x^2+2x+1 = 2(x^2-2x+1)$ or $x^2 - 6x + 1 = 0$ gives

$$x = \dfrac{6 \pm \sqrt{36 - 4}}{2} = \dfrac{6 \pm 4\sqrt{2}}{2} = 3 \pm 2\sqrt{2}$$

33. $x^2 - 3x_2 - 1 = 0$ or $x^2 - 3x + (3/2)^2 = 9/4 + 1$ or
    $(x-3/2)^2 = 13/4$ or $x - 3/2 = \pm \sqrt{13}/2$ or $x = (3 \pm \sqrt{13})/2$

41. $6x^2 = 11$ or $x^2 = 11/6$ or $x = \pm\sqrt{11/6}$.

45. $15x^2 = 40(x+2)$ or $3x^2 = 8(x+2)$ or $3x^2 - 8x - 16 = 0$

or $x = \dfrac{8 \pm \sqrt{64 + 192}}{6} = \dfrac{8 \pm 16}{6} = 4, -4/3$

49. $x^2 = 2(x^2+x-2)$ or $x^2 + 2x - 4 = 0$ gives $x = (-2 \pm \sqrt{4+16})/2$

$\qquad = \dfrac{-2 \pm 2\sqrt{5}}{2} = -1 \pm \sqrt{5}.$

53. $\dfrac{x^2}{3} = \dfrac{11}{6} x + 1$ or $2x^2 = 11x + 6$ or $2x^2 - 11x - 6 = 0$ or

$\qquad (2x+1)(x-6) = 0$ or $x=6, -1/2$.

EXERCISES - 2.3

1. $x+4$ 5. $1 + (x+x-4)/2 = x-1$

9. Let x = number of girls, then number of boys = $52 - x$. Now $52-x = 7+2x$
   or $3x = 45$ or $x = 15$ = number of girls in class.

13. Let x = number of quarters. Then number of dimes I have = $2x$.
    We are given that (value in cents): $10(2x-4) + 25(x+3) = 260$ or
    $x = 5$. Thus I have $x=5$ quarters and $2x = 10$ dimes in my pocket.

17. Let x=number of items produced and sold. Cost of producing x items
    = $(2000 + 0.6x)$ dollars and the revenue from sale of x items is
    $\$ 0.9x$. Since the profit is \$1000, we have: $0.9x - (2000 + 0.6x)$
    = 1000 or $x = 10,000$.

21. Let cost = $\$ x$. Then profit is x%. Since revenue = cost + profit,
    $75 = x + x\%$ of x or $75 = x + x^2/100$ or $x^2 + 100x - 7500 = 0$ or
    $(x+150)(x-50) = 0$ or $x = 50$ or -150. The negative value is
    meaningless. Thus $x=50$ dollars.

25. Let x=number of \$3 increments in rent. Then, rent per
    suite = $\$(150 + 3x)$ and the number of suites rented = $60 - x$.
    Total revenue = (no. of suites rented). (rent per suite) = $(60-x)(150+3x)$
    Total costs = $5000 + 50(60-x) + 20x = 8000 - 30x$. Thus, revenue - cost
    = profits gives $(60-x)(150+3x) - (8000-30x) = 1225$ or $x = 5, 15$.
    Thus, the rent per suite is $\$(150 + 3x)$ or $\$(150 + 15) = \$165$
    or $\$(150 + 45) = \$195$.

REVIEW EXERCISES ON CHAPTER - 2

1. See answer in the text.

5. $3x^2 - 11x + 10 = 0$ or $(3x-5)(x-2) = 0$ gives $x = 5/3$, 2.

9. $4x^2 - 4x + 1 = 3x^2 + (x^2-3x+2)$ or $-x = 1$ or $x = -1$.

13. $1 + (3x^2-2x-8) = 2x^2-5x-3$ or $x^2+3x-4 = 0$ or $(x+4)(x-1) = 0$
    gives $x = -4, 1$.

17. $\sqrt{x+5} = x-1$. Squaring gives: $x+5 = x^2-2x+1$ or $x^2 - 3x - 4 = 0$
    or $(x-4)(x+1) = 0$ or $x = 4, -1$. $x = -1$ does not satisfy the
    original equation, whereas $x=4$ does. Thus, the solution is $x=4$.

21. $(2^2)^x = (2^3)^{3-x}$ or $2^{2x} = 2^{9-3x}$ or $2x = 9 - 3x$ or $x = 9/5$

25. Let \$x be invested at 8% so that \$(100,000 - x) is invested at 10%. The annual return is 0.08x + 0.10(100,000 - x) = 8500 given. This gives x = 75,000. Thus \$75,000 is invested at 8% and 100,000 - 75,000 = \$25,000 is invested at 10%.

29. Weekly profit = (p-3)x = (p-3)300(6-p) = 300(p-3)(6-p). For weekly profit of 600, we have 300(p-3)(6-p) = 600 or
$p^2 - 9p + 20 = 0$ or   (p-4)(p-5) = 0   i.e.   p = \$4   or   \$5.

REVIEW TEST ON CHAPTER - 2

1. An equation of the form ax + b = 0, where a, b are constant is called a <u>linear</u> equation in the variable x only if a _____.

2. x = 2 ____ (is or is not) a solution of the equation $x^2 + 12 = 7x$.

3. If 2x = 6, then x = _____.   4. If 3x/2 = 6, then x = _____.

5. If 9 = 7 - x, then x = _____   6. If x + x/5 = 0, then x = _____.

7. If x + x/3 = 4, then x = _____.   8. If $(x+3)^2 = (x-3)^2$, then x = ___.

9. The equation $ax^2 + bx + c = 0$, where a, b, c are constants, is called a quadratic equation in x only if a _____.

10. A linear equation always has only ____ solution(s).

11. A quadratic equation has either _____ real root or _____ real root or _____ different roots.

12. If (x-2)(2x+3) = 0, then x = _____.

13. If $x^2 = 9$, then x = _____.

14. If $x^2 = 5x$, then x = _____.

15. If $y^4 = 9y^2$, then y = _____.

16. If $x^2 + 9 = 0$, then x = _____.

17. If $x^2 + x - 12 = 0$, then (_____)(_____) = 0 or x = _____.

18. If (x+2)(x+7) = 14, then x^2 + _____ = 14 or x = _____.

19. If $ax^2 + bx + c = 0$, then by the quadratic formula, x = _____.

*20. The discriminant of the equation $ax^2 + bx + c = 0$ is given by D = _____.

*21. If the discriminant D of the quadratic equation is zero, then the equation has _____ real root(s).

22. If the discrimnant D of the quadratic equation is negative, then the roots of the equation are _____.

23. If Sue has x books and Joe has 3 more books than Sue, then Joe has _____ books.

24. If Jane has x dollars and Jack has $5 less than Jane, then Jack has _____ dollars.

25. If Bob is x years old and Sue is 3 years more than half the age of Bob, then Sue is _____ years old.

SEE ANSWERS AT THE END OF THE BOOK.

CHAPTER - 3

YOU SHOULD BE FAMILIAR WITH THE FOLLOWING TERMS:

Inequality symbols, an inequality, a strict inequality

A set, elements or members.

Listing method and rule method for specifying a set.

Subset, proper subset, equality of two sets.

Open, closed and semi-open (or semi-closed) intervals. End points of an interval.

A linear inequality, a quadratic inequality, the solution set of an inequality.

Absolute value of a real number.

OBJECTIVES

AFTER READING THIS CHAPTER YOU SHOULD BE ABLE TO DO THE FOLLOWING

1. To specify a set by the listing or rule method as appropriate.

2. To determine if one set is a subset of another or if two sets are equal.

3. To simplify and solve a linear equality by application of the addition and multiplication rules.

4. To solve a quadratic inequality by factoring the quadratic expression and examining the signs of the two linear factors on appropriate intervals.

5. To formulate simple word problems in terms of linear or quadratic inequalities and hence to solve them.

6. To solve equations and inequalities involving the absolute value of a linear expression.

SOLUTIONS TO ALTERNATE ODD PROBLEMS

EXERCISES - 3.1

1, 5, 9, 13, 17 see answers in the text book.

21. $\{x \mid x^2 - x - 6 = 0\} = \{3, -2\}$ is <u>not</u> a subset of natural numbers because -2 is not a natural number.

EXERCISES - 3.2

1. 5 + 3x < 11 or 3x < 11-5 or 3x < 6 or x < 2.

5. 6x-3 > 4 + 5x - 5 or 6x-5x > 4 - 5 + 3 or x > 2.

9. $\frac{y+1}{4} - \frac{y}{3} > 1 + \frac{2y-1}{6}$. Multiply both sides by 12 (l.c.d.)

    3(y+1) - 4y > 12 + 2(2y-1) or 3y + 3 - 4y > 12 + 4y - 2 or -5y > 7
    or y < -7/5.

13. 5 < 2x+7 < 13 or 5-7 < 2x+7-7 < 13-7 or -2 < 2x < 6 or -1 < x < 3.

17. 3x+7 > 5-2x ≥ 13-6x implies 3x+7 > 5-2x and 5-2x ≥ 13-6x.
     3x+7 > 5-2x or 5x > -2 gives x > -2/5. 5-2x ≥ 13-6x gives 4x ≥ 8 or
     x ≥ 2. **Now** x > -2/5 and x ≥ 2 together imply x ≥ 2.

21. If x units are produced and sold, revenue = $30x and cost = $(12000+22x)
     To realize a profit, we must have revenue > cost or 30x > 12,000 + 22x
     or x > 1500 i.e. x = 1501 or more.

25. Let x copies be published to realize a profit of at least $1000.
     Revenue = 0.30x + 0.20{0.30(x-2000)} = 0.36x - 120 and
     cost = 0.35x. Profit = 0.36x - 120 - 0.35x. Profit > $1000 implies
     0.01x - 120 ≥ 1000 or 0.01x ≥ 1120 or x ≥ 112,000.

EXERCISES - 3.3

> __IMPORTANT RESULT.__   If a < b, then
>
> (x-a)(x-b) < 0 implies   a < x < b   .... (A)
>
> and (x-a)(x-b) > 0 implies either x < a or x > b ... (B)

1. (x-2)(x-5) < 0 implies 2 < x < 5   (Result (A) above).

5. x^2 - 7x + 12 ≤ 0 or (x-3)(x-4) ≤ 0 implies 3 ≤ x ≤ 4 (Result (A)).

9. y(2y+1) > 6 or $2y^2$ + y - 6 > 0 or (2y-3)(y+2) > 0 or
    2(y-3/2)(y+2) > 0 or (y-3/2)(y+2) > 0 implies either y < -2 or y > 3/2,
    because -2 < 3/2   (Result (B)).

13. x^2 ≥ 4 or x^2 - 4 ≥ 0 or (x-2)(x+2) ≥ 0 implies either
     x ≤ -2 or x ≥ 2.   (Result (B)).

17. x^2 - 6x + 9 ≤ 0 or $(x-3)^2$ ≤ 0 implies $(x-3)^2$ = 0 or x=3
     because $(x-3)^2$ < 0 can never be true for any value of x.

21. $x^2 + 13 < 6x$ or $x^2 - 6x + 13 < 0$ or $(x-3)^2 + 2^2 < 0$ has
no solution, because the left side being the sum of **squares**
can never be negative i.e. < 0.

25. From exercises 23, revenue = $px = x(600-5x) = 600x-5x^2$.
Cost = 8000 + 75x , so that profit = revenue − cost
= $600x - 5x^2 - (8000 + 75x) = 525x - 5x^2 - 8000$. Now,
profit $\geq$ 5500 gives $525x - 5x^2 - 8000 \geq 5500$ or $5x^2-525x+13500 \leq 0$
or $x^2 - 105x + 2700 \leq 0$ or $(x-60)(x-45) \leq 0$ or $45 \leq x \leq 60$.

29. Let the dimensions of the rectangular
field be x yds. and y yds. Then
2(x+y) = 200 or y = 100 − x
Area = xy = x(100−x) $\geq$ 2100 implies
$x^2 - 100x + 2100 \leq 0$ or $(x-30)(x-70) \leq 0$.
Thus $30 \leq x \leq 70$.

33. Let the charge per customer be increased by x increments of 50¢.
Thus, new charge per customer = $(4 + 0.5x) and the number of
people who will have hair cut at this price = 120 − 8x.
The weekly revenue is given by
Revenue = (charge per customer)(No. of customers)
$$= (4 + 0.5x)(120 - 8x) = 4(120 + 7x - x^2)$$
Revenue $\geq$ 520 implies $4(120 + 7x - x^2) \geq 520$
or $x^2 - 7x + 10 \leq 0$ or $(x-2)(x-5) \leq 0$
Thus $2 \leq x \leq 5$ or $1 \leq x/2 \leq 5/2$ or $4+1 \leq 4 + x/2 \leq 4 + 5/2$ or
$5 \leq 4 + 0.5x \leq 6.5$ Thus charge p per hair cut must be given by
$5 \leq p \leq $6.50.

EXERCISES − 3.4

1. $|3-7x| = 4$ implies $3 - 7x \pm 4$. $3-7x = 4$ gives x = −1/7 and
3−7x = −4 gives x=1. Ans. x = 1, −1/7.

5. $|3x-2| = 4-x$ implies $3x-2 = \pm(4-x)$. Now 3x−2 = 4−x
gives x = 3/2 and 3x−2 = −(4−x) gives x = −1. Ans. 3/2, −1.

9. No solution because the left side is always $\geq$ 7.

13. $|1/x - 3| = 4$ gives $1/x - 3 = \pm 4$ or $1/x = 3 \pm 4 = 7, -1$ i.e. $x = \frac{1}{7}, -1$.

17. $|2 - 5x| \geq 3$ implies either $2-5x \leq -3$ i.e. $x \geq 1$ or
$2-5x \geq 3$ i.e. $x \leq -1/5$. Ans. $x \leq -1/5$ or $x \geq 1$; $(-\infty,-1/5]$ or
$[1,\infty)$.

21. $7 + |3x-5| \leq 5$ gives $|3x-5| \leq -2$. The left side being always
non-negative cannot be less than or equal to −2. Thus no solution.

25. $|2x-3| = 2x-3$ if $x \geq 3/2$ and $-(2x-3)$ if $x \leq 3/2$. If $x \geq 3/2$, then
$|2x-3| < x-4$ implies 2x−3 < x−4 or x < −1. But $x \geq 3/2$ and x < −1

gives no solution.   If $x \leq 3/2$ then $|2x-3| < x-4$ implies $-(2x-3) < x-4$ or $x > 7/3$.   But x cannot be $<3/2$ and $>7/3$ at the same time.   Hence no solution.   29.   See answers in the text book.

REVIEW EXERCISES ON CHAPTER - 3

1.   See answers in the text book.

5. $2x^2 < 3x + 5$ or $2x^2 - 3x - 5 < 0$ or $(2x-5)(x-1) < 0$
     or $2(x - 5/2)(x-1) < 0$ or $1 < x < 5/2$.

9. $(x+1)(2x+5) \geq -3$ or $2x^2 - 3x - 2 \geq 0$ or $(2x+1)(x-2) \geq 0$ or
     $2(x + 1/2)(x-2) \geq 0$ i.e. $x \leq -1/2$ or $x \leq 2$.

13. $|5-3x| = x+2$ gives $5-3x = \pm(x+2)$ or $x = 7/2, 3/4$.

17.   Since x is in hundred of thousands, the revenue is $R = px = p(24-2p)$
      hundred thousands $= p(24-2p) \cdot 10^5$.   We want the revenue to be $7
      million.   Thus, $R = p(24-2p) \cdot 10^5 = 7(10^6)$ or $p(24-2p) = 70$ i.e.
      $p = \$5$ or $\$7$.   Since the cost per bottle is $2, the profit per
      bottle is $(p-2)$, where p is selling price per bottle.   Thus,
      profit $= (p-2)(24-2p) \cdot 10^5 > (4.8)10^6$ gives $(p-2)(12-p) \geq 24$ or
      $p^2 - 14p + 48 \leq 0$ or $(p-6)(p-8) \leq 0$.   Thus, $\$6 \leq p \leq \$8$.

21.   Revenue $= px = x(60-x)$; for revenue to be at least $800, we have:
      $x(60-x) \geq 800$ or $x^2 - 60x + 800 \leq 0$ or $(x-20)(x-40) \leq 0$.
      Thus $20 \leq x \leq 40$.

25.   Refer to #21.   Profit = Revenue - Cost $= x(60-x) - (260+8x) \geq 400$
      gives: $x^2 - 52x + 660 \leq 0$ or $(x-22)(x-30) \leq 0$
      Thus $22 \leq x \leq 30$ or $-22 \geq -x \geq -30$ or
      $-22 + 60 \geq 60 - x \geq 60 - 30$ or $38 \geq p \geq 30$.
      Thus price p per unit is $30 \leq p \leq \$38$.

REVIEW TEST ON CHAPTER - 3

FILL IN THE BLANKS:

1.   By definition, $x < y$ if $x-y$ is ___ and $x > y$ if $x-y$ is ___.

2. $a \geq b$ implies that either a ___ b or a ___ b.

3.   The double inequality $x < y < z$ implies $x<y$ and $y<z$.

4.   A well-defined collection of objects is called a set ___.

5.   The objects constituting the set are called the $elements$ of the set.

6.   By the listing method, the set of all

     (a)   natural numbers less than 10 can be written as $\{x | x < 10\}$
     (b)   English alphabets is written as $\{x | a...z\}$
     (c)   vowels in the English alphabet can be written as $\{x | a \, e \, i \, o \, u \, s\}$

7. Using the rule method, we can write

    (a) {1, 3, 5, 7, ...} = {x| _is a positive odd integer._ }

    (b) {1/2, 2/3, 3/4, ...} = {x| _____ } $x = \frac{n}{n+1}$ when n is a natural number

    (c) {..., −6, −3, 0, 3, 6, ...} = {x| _____ } $x = -3y$ when y is any integer

8. x ∈ A means that x is a _element_ of A.

9. A set with no elements is called a(n) _empty_ and is denoted by _∅_ .

10. If each element of a set P is in the set Q, then P is called a _subset_ of set Q and is denoted by P _⊆_ Q.

11. An empty set ∅ is a _subset_ of any set A.

12. If A = {1,2,3} and B = {−2,−1,0,1,2,3,4} , then A _⊆_ B.

13. If P is a subset of Q and Q is a subset of P, then P _=_ Q.

14. If a > b, then a+c _≥_ b+c, a·c _≥_ b·c if c > 0 and

    a·c _≤_ b·c if c < 0.

15. If −2x > −8, then x _<_ 4.   divide reverse sign wrong $x < 4$ 2+−2   1+−2 = 0 > 1

16. The solution of the inequality 2x+7 < 3x+2 is given by _x > 5_ .

17. The solution of the inequality (x+2)² > (x+1)² is given by _x > −3/2_ .

18. The solution of the inequality (x−2)(x−7) < 0 is _2 < x < 7_ .

19. The solution of the inequality (x+3)(x−4) < 0 is given by _3 < x < 4_ .

20. If (x−1)(x+3) > 0, then either x < _−3_ or x > _1_ .

21. If (x+2)(x−5) ≥ 0, then either x ≥ _5_ or x ≤ _−2_ .

22. The solution of the inequality (x−2)² + 5 > 0 is given by _all x_ .

23. The solution of x²−6x+9 ≥ 0 is given by _all x_ .   nests any term² is ≥ 0

24. The solution of (x−2)² < 0 is given by _no x_ .

25. The solution of (x+5)² ≤ 0 is given by _−5_ .

26. By definition, the absolute value of x, denoted by |x|, is   note this one

    |x| = _x_ if x ≥ 0 and |x| = _−x_ if x < 0.

27. |x| _≥_ 0 for all real numbers x.   hate this one

28. |x| > x only if x _≤ 0_ and |x| ≤ x only if x _≥ 0_ .

29. |x|/x = _−1_ if x < 0 and |x|/x = _1_ if x > 0.

x < 0
|−7| > −7
7 > −7

|x| = x
if x ≥ 0
not ever less than

18

30. $\sqrt{x^2} =$ _____ for all real numbers x.

(handwritten: I remember this one)

(handwritten answer: |x|)

(handwritten: $\sqrt{(a-b)^2} = |a-b|$)

31. $|x-y|$ _____ $|y-x|$. (= , ≠)

(handwritten answer: =)

32. If $c > 0$, then $|x| = c$ implies $x =$ _____

(handwritten answer: ± c)

(handwritten: $c<0$ $|x|=c$ no solution $|-7|=$)

33. If $|a| = |b|$, then $a =$ _____ .

(handwritten answer: ± b)

34. If $|2x-3| = |x+5|$, then $2x-3 =$ _____ or $x =$ _____ .

(handwritten answer: ± x+5   -2/3, 8)

35. The solution of $|3x-5| + 7 = 0$ is given by _____ .

(handwritten answer: no x)

(handwritten: whether this one ↓)

36. If $c > 0$, then $|x| < c$ implies _____

(handwritten answer: -c < x < c)

37. If $c > 0$, then $|x| > c$ implies _____ .

(handwritten answer: x < -c or x > c)

(handwritten: -2 <   > 1   How to figure mathematically)

38. The solution of $|x+3| + 7 > 0$ is given by _____ .

(handwritten answer: all x)

39. The solution of $|x+5| < -3$ is given by _____ .

(handwritten answer: no x)

40. The solution of $|x-2| > 0$ is given by _____ .

(handwritten answer: all x ≠ 2)

41. The solution of $|2x-5| \geq 0$ is given by _____ .

(handwritten answer: all x)

42. The solution of $|x-3| < 0$ is given by _____ .

(handwritten answer: no x)

43. The solution of $|x+2| \leq 0$ is given by _____ .

(handwritten answer: -2)

44. The inequality $x^2 < 4$ is equivalent to _____ < 2.

(handwritten answer: |x|)

45. The inequality $x^2 \geq 9$ is equivalent to _____ ≥ 3.

(handwritten answer: |x|)

SEE ANSWERS AT THE END OF THE BOOK.

CHAPTER - 4

YOU SHOULD BE FAMILIAR WITH THE FOLLOWING TERMS:

Cartesian plane (xy-plane), co-ordinate axes, 1st quadrant etc.

Cartesian co-ordinates, abscissa (or x-co-ordinate), ordinate (or

y-co-ordinate).

Distance formula.

Graph of an equation.

Rise, run, slope, x-intercept, y-intercept.

Point-slope formula, slope-intercept formula, general linear equation.

System of linear equations.

Method of substitution, method of addition.

Point of intersection of two lines (or of two graphs).

Linear cost model, fixed costs, variable costs.

Break-even point ; profitability.

Straight line depreciation.

Demand curve, supply curve, market equilibrium.

Additive tax, subsidy.

OBJECTIVES

AFTER READING THIS CHAPTER YOU SHOULD BE ABLE TO DO THE FOLLOWING:

1. Calculate the distance between two points. Express in algebraic terms
   a statement that involves distances.

2. Plot the graph of an equation.

3. Calculate the equations of a line if you are given

   (a) its slope and one point on it

   (b) two points on it

   (c) its slope and y-intercept.

4. Calculate the slope and intercepts if you are given any linear equation.

5. Graph a linear equation using either its two intercepts or one intercept and the slope.

6. Solve systems consisting of two linear equations by the method of addition and the method of substitution. Interpret the solution in terms of a graph.

7. Solve systems of three linear equations.

8. Understand and use the linear cost model.

9. Carry out a break-even analysis for a linear cost model and for simple nonlinear models.

10. Compute the depreciated value of an asset using straight-line depreciation.

11. Determine the market equilibrium for linear supply and demand equation and also for simple nonlinear cases.

12. Determine the effect of a tax or a subsidy on the market equilibrium.

SOLUTIONS TO ALTERNATE ODD PROBLEMS

EXERCISES - 4.1

1. See answers in the text book.

5. Distance $= \sqrt{(-2 - 1/2)^2 + (1-2)^2} = \sqrt{25/4 + 1} = \sqrt{29}/2$.

9. $\sqrt{(7-a)^2 + (6-1)^2} = 13$ gives $(7-a)^2 + 25 = 169$ or $(a-7)^2 = 144$
   or $a - 7 = \pm 12$ or $a = \pm 12 + 7 = 19, -5$.

13. If P is (x,y) then $\sqrt{(x+1)^2 + (y-3)^2} = 3$ gives $(x+1)^2 + (y-3)^2 = 9$
    or $x^2 + y^2 + 2x - 6y + 1 = 0$.

17.   21.

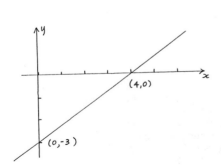

(4,0)

(0,-3)

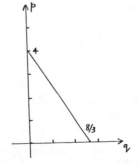

8/3

1. m = (7-1)/(5-2) = 2   5. (4-2)/{-3-(-3)} = 2/0, undefined i.e.

    no slope.   9. y-4 = 0(x-3) or y = 4.

13. m = $\frac{7-(-2)}{3-3}$ = $\frac{9}{0}$ = undefined i.e. no slope. Thus, the line is vertical.
    Equation of the vertical line through (3,-2) is x = x-co-ordinate
    or x = 3.

17. The given line 3x+y-2 = 0 or y = -3x + 2 has the slope m = -3. Since
    the required line is parallel to the given line, it also has the slope
    m = -3. Thus, the line through (2,-1) with slope m = -3 is given by
           y - (-1) = -3(x-2) or y = -3x + 5.

21. x=2 is a vertical line. A line perpendicular to it is a horizontal
    line. Thus, the horizontal line through (3,4) has the equation
    y = y-co-ordinate of the given point i.e. y = 4.

25. 3x-2y = 6 or y = (3/2)x - 3 gives m = 3/2 , b = -3.

29. 2y-3 = 0 or y = 0x + 3/2 gives m=0, b = 3/2.

33. y = 2x+3 gives m_1 = 2 and x = 2y+3 or y = x/2 - 3/2 gives m_2 = 1/2.
    Since neither $m_1 m_2$ = -1 nor m_1 = m_2, the lines are neither perpendicular
    nor parallel.

37. y-3 = 0 is a horizontal line whereas x+5 = 0 is a vertical line.
    Thus the given lines are perpendicular.

41. (a) If t=1, y = 650 - 25 = 625, if t=2, y = 625 - 25 = 600.
         Thus, equation of line through (1,625) and (2,600) is given by
         y = 650 - 25t.

    (b) y = 0 gives 650 - 25t = 0 or t = 26 days

    (c) y = 125 gives 125 = 650 - 25t or t = 21.
         Thus, new order must be placed at the end of 21st day.

45. Total intake of thiamine per day is 0.05x + 0.08y = 1 or 5x+8y = 100.

EXERCISES - 4.3

1. x - y = 1   ... (i)   2x + 3y = -8   ... (ii)
    Adding 3 times (i) to (ii) gives 5x = -5 or x = -1. Then from
    (i), we have -1 - y = 1 or y = -2. Thus, x = -1, y = -2.

5. 3x+5t = 12   ... (i)   4x - 3t = -13   ... (ii)
    Multiplying (i) by 3 and (ii) by 5 and adding, we have:
    3(3x+5t) + 5(4x-3t) = 36-65 or 29x = -29 or x = -1.
    Using this, (i) gives -3 + 5t = 12 or 5t = 15 or t = 3.
    Thus, x = -1, t = 3.

9. $x/4 + y/5 + 1 = 23$ or $5x + 4y = 440$ ... (i)
    $x/5 + y/4 = 23$ or $4x + 5y = 460$ ... (ii)

    Multiplying (i) by 5 and (ii) by 4 and subtracting, we get:
    $5(5x+4y) - 4(4x+5y) = 5(440) - 4(460)$ or $9x = 360$ or $x = 40$.
    Using this value of x, (i) gives $200 + 4y = 440$ or $y = 60$. Thus,
    $x = 40$, $y = 60$.

13. $x + 2y = 4$ ... (i) $3x + 6y = 12$ ... (ii)
    (ii) $- 3\{(i)\}$ gives $3x + 6y - 3(x+2y) = 12 - 3(4)$ or $0 = 0$.
    Thus, the system has an infinite number of solutions given by all
    the coordinates of points on the line $x + 2y = 4$.

17. $x + y + z = 6$ ... (i) $2x-y+3z = 9$ ...(ii)
    $-x + 2y + z - 6$ ... (iii)
    (i) + (iii) gives $3y + 2z = 12$ ... (iv) and (ii) + 2{(iii)}
    gives $3y + 5z = 21$ ... (v). Now (v) $-$ (iv) gives $3z = 9$ or $z=3$.
    Then (iv) gives $3y + 6 = 12$ or $y=2$. Using $y=2$, $z=3$ in (i) we have
    $x + 2 + 3 = 6$ or $x = 1$. Thus, $x = 1$, $y = 2$, $z = 3$.

21. $x+3y+4z = 1$ ...(i), $2x+7y+z = -7$ ...(ii), $2x+10y+8z = -3$ ...(iii)
    (ii) $- 2(i)$ gives $y - 7z = -9$ ...(iv). Now (iii) $- 3(i)$ gives
    $y - 4z = -6$ ... (v). Now (v) $-$ (iv) gives $3z = 3$ or $z = 1$. Now,
    (iv) gives $y-7 = -9$ or $y = -2$. Using $y = -2$, $z=1$ in (i) gives
    $x-6+4 = 1$ or $x=3$. Thus, $x=3$, $y = -2$, $z=1$.

25. Let x pounds of ore I and y pounds of ore II be required.
    Then, $0.03x + 0.04y = 72$ and $0.05x + 0.025y = 95$
    This gives $x = 1600$, $y = 600$. Thus 1600 lbs. of ore I and 600 lbs.
    of ore II is required.

29. Let x gallons of 25% acid solution and y gallons of 15% acid
    solution be mixed. Then $x+y = 200$ and $0.25x + 0.15y = 0.18(200)$ or
    $x = 60$, $y = 140$ i.e. 60 gallons of 25% acid solution and 140
    gallons of 15% acid solution.

33. Let x tons of type A, y tons of type B and z tons of type C be
    produced. Then $0.25x + 0.15y = 1.5$,
    $0.45x + 0.50y + 0.75z = 5$ and $0.3x + 0.35y + 0.25z = 3$.
    Solution gives: $x = 45/14$, $y = 65/14$ and $z = 23/14$.

EXERCISES - 4.4

1. $y = 7x + 150$. If $x = 100$, $y = \$850$.

5. Let $\$y_c$ be cost of manufacturing x units.

    $y_c = mx + b$. Here $b = 300$ and we are given that if $x=20$, $y_c = 410$.
    This gives $410 = 20m + b = 20m + 300$ or $m = 5.5$. Thus, $y_c = 5.5x + 300$.
    If $x = 30$, $y_c = 5.5(30) + 300 = 465$ dollars.

9. Let x items be produced. Cost $= 0.90x + 240$ and revenue $= 1.20x$.
    To have no profit or loss, we have revenue $=$ cost or
    $1.20x = 0.90x + 240$ or $x = 800$.

13. Revenue = cost gives $1.10x = 0.70x + 350$ or $x = 875$ items. Since this break-even point of $x = 875$ items is less than the break-even point of $x = 1120$ items in question 12 , it is advantageous to the firm.

17. Revenue = cost gives $20x = 1000 + 20\sqrt{x} + 8x$ or $3x - 250 = 5\sqrt{x}$. Squaring gives: $9x^2 - 1500x + 62500 = 25x$. Solving this gives, $x = 100$ or $625/9$. But $x = 625/9$ does not satisfy the original equation, whereas $x = 100$ does. Thus $x = 100$.

21. If the equipment depreciates by an amount D each year, then $P = S + ND$ or $D = (P-S)/N$. The value V after t years is given by $V = P - Dt = P - (P-S)t/N$.

EXERCISES - 4.5

1. Using $x = 10,000$, $p = 1.20$ and $x = 12,000$, $p = 1.10$ in $p = mx + b$ gives $1.20 = 10,000m + b$ and $1.10 = 12000m + b$. Subtraction gives $0.10 = -2000m$ or $m = -1/20000 = -0.00005$ Then, $1.20 = 10,000(-0.00005) + b$ gives $b = 1.70$.

5. Using $p = x/10 + 2$ in $2p + 3x = 100$ gives $2(x/10 + 2) + 3x = 100$ or $x/5 + 3x = 96$ or $x = 30$. Then $p = x/10 + 2 = 30/10 + 2 = 5$. Thus, $x = 30$, $p = 5$.

9. $p = x + 1$ in $p^2 + x^2 = 25$ gives $(x+1)^2 + x^2 = 25$ or $x^2+x-12 = 0$ or $(x+4)(x-3) = 0$ i.e. $x = -4, 4$. But $x \neq -4$. Thus, $x = 3$. Then $p = x+1 = 3+1 = 4$. Therefore, $x = 3$, $p = 4$.

13. $p = x+5$ and $3p + 4x = 12$ give the solution $x = -3/7$, $p = 32/7$. Since x can't be negative, the market equilibrium occurs at $x=0$ (that is no goods are being produced and sold).

17. $xp = 5$ or $p = 5/x$ in $3x + 4p = 30$ gives $3x + 20/x = 30$

or $3x^2 - 30x + 20 = 0$ or $x = \dfrac{30 \pm \sqrt{900-240}}{6} = 9.28$, 0.72

When $x = 9.28$, $p = 5/x = 5/9.28 = 0.54$ and when $x = 0.72$, $p = 5/x = 5/0.72 = 6.96$. Thus, we have: $x = 9.28$, $p = 0.54$ and $x = 0.72$, $p = 6.96$.

REVIEW EXERCISES ON CHAPTER - 4

1. See answers in the text book.

5. No slope means the line is vertical. The equation of a vertical line through $(2,-1)$ is given by x = x-coordinate i.e. $x = 2$.

9. $x + y - 2z = -1$ ...(i) $2x-3y+z = 13$ ...(ii) $-3x+2y+5z = -8$ ..(iii)
(i) + 2(ii) gives $5x - 5y = 25$ or $x-y = 5$ ... (iv). Now (iii) - 5(ii) gives: $-13x + 17y = -73$ ... (v). Now (v) + 17(iv) gives $4x = 12$ or $x = 3$. Then (iv) gives $3 - y = 5$ or $y = -2$. Using $x = 3$, $y = -2$ in (ii) gives: $6+6+z = 13$ or $z = 1$. Thus, $x=3$, $y = -2$, $z=1$.

24

13. If x units of A and y units of B are produced, then $5x + 8y = 640$.

17. Let the first kind be $x per lb. and the second kind be $y per lb.
Then $8x + 5y = 35$ and $10x + 8y = 49$, i.e. $x = 2.50$ and $y = 3$.
Thus the rates are $2.50 per lb. and $3.00 per lb.

21. (a) $p = 50$, $x = 4500$ and $p = 60$, $x = 4400$ gives the linear
demand equation as D: $p = 500 - 0.1x$ ....(i)
$p = 50$, $x = 3300$ and $p = 60$, $x = 4200$ gives the linear
supply equation as S: $p = x/90 + 40/3$ ....(ii)

(b) Solving (i) and (ii) gives $p = \$62$ and $x = 4380$

(c) New supply equation is: $p_1 = (1/90)x_1 + 40/3 + 2$ ....(iii)
The demand equation (i) remains the same i.e. $p_1 = 500 - 0.1x_1$
Solving for p_1 and x_1 gives $p_1 = \$63.80$ and $x_1 = 4362$. Thus,
increase in price $= p_1 - p = \$1.80$ and decrease in demand
$= 4380 - 4362 = 18$ tons.

25. Let x belts be required to justify manufacturing. Then
$6000 + 1.30x < 2.50x$ or x 5000 i.e. over 5000 belts.

29. Let x units be produced and sold. Then $C = 40,000 + 6x$ and
$R = 10x$ and profit $= P = R - C = 4x - 40,000 = 0.15(40,000)$
gives $x = 11,500$ units.

33. R = revenue obtained by selling x units = 30x dollars.
C_1 = cost of producing x units by first method = $10x + 20,000$
C_2 = cost of producing x units by second method = $15x + 9000$.
(a) If $x = 800$, then $R = \$24,000$, $C_1 = \$28,000$, $C_2 = \$21,000$
Since $C_2 < C_1$, second method should be used.
(b) If $x = 2500$, then $R = \$75,000$, $C_1 = \$45,000$, $C_2 = 46,500$
Since $C_1 < C_2$, first method should be used.
(c) If $x = 1500$, then $R = \$45,000$, $C_1 = 35,000$ and $C_2 = \$31,500$
Since $C_2 < C_1$, second method should be used.

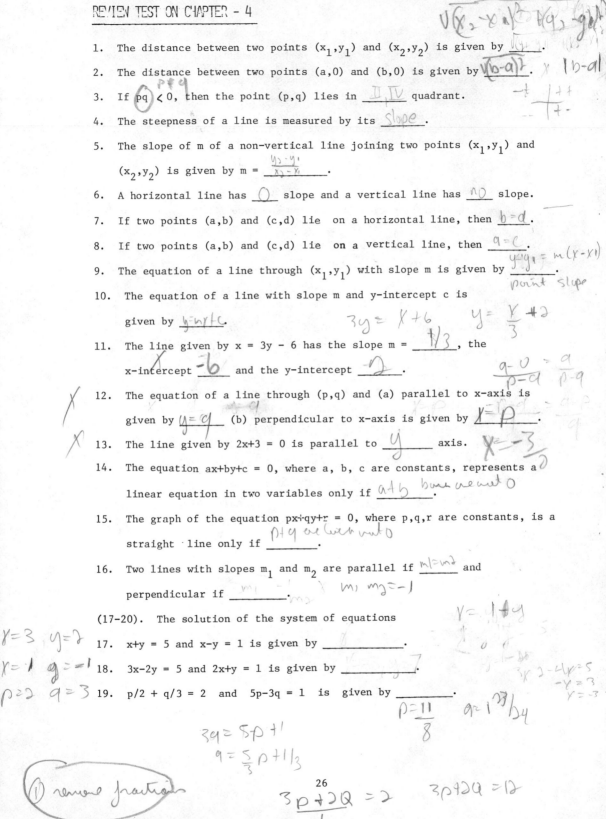

REVIEW TEST ON CHAPTER - 4

1. The distance between two points (x_1, y_1) and (x_2, y_2) is given by _____.

   [margin: $\sqrt{(x_2-x_1)^2+(y_2-y_1)^2}$]

2. The distance between two points $(a,0)$ and $(b,0)$ is given by $\sqrt{(b-a)^2}$. $|b-a|$

3. If pq < 0, then the point (p,q) lies in $\underline{II, IV}$ quadrant. *[margin: $p+q$]*

4. The steepness of a line is measured by its $\underline{slope}$.

5. The slope of m of a non-vertical line joining two points (x_1, y_1) and (x_2, y_2) is given by m = $\underline{\dfrac{y_2-y_1}{x_2-x_1}}$.

6. A horizontal line has $\underline{0}$ slope and a vertical line has $\underline{no}$ slope.

7. If two points (a,b) and (c,d) lie on a horizontal line, then $\underline{b=d}$.

8. If two points (a,b) and (c,d) lie on a vertical line, then $\underline{a=c}$.

9. The equation of a line through (x_1, y_1) with slope m is given by $\underline{y-y_1 = m(x-x_1)}$. *[below: point slope]*

10. The equation of a line with slope m and y-intercept c is given by $\underline{y = mx+c}$. *[right: $3y = x+6 \qquad y = \dfrac{x}{3}+2$]*

11. The line given by x = 3y – 6 has the slope m = $\underline{1/3}$, the x-intercept $\underline{-6}$ and the y-intercept $\underline{2}$.

12. The equation of a line through (p,q) and (a) parallel to x-axis is given by $\underline{y=q}$ (b) perpendicular to x-axis is given by $\underline{x=p}$.

    [right margin: $\dfrac{q-0}{p-a} = \dfrac{q}{p-q}$]

13. The line given by 2x+3 = 0 is parallel to $\underline{y}$ axis. $x=-3$

14. The equation ax+by+c = 0, where a, b, c are constants, represents a linear equation in two variables only if $\underline{a+b}$ $\underline{both\ are\ not\ 0}$

15. The graph of the equation px+qy+r = 0, where p,q,r are constants, is a straight line only if $\underline{p+q\ are\ both\ not\ 0}$.

16. Two lines with slopes m_1 and m_2 are parallel if $\underline{m_1=m_2}$ and perpendicular if $\underline{m_1 m_2 = -1}$.

(17-20). The solution of the system of equations

[left margin: $x=3, y=2$]
17. x+y = 5 and x-y = 1 is given by _____.

[left margin: $x=1\ y=-1$]
18. 3x-2y = 5 and 2x+y = 1 is given by _____. *[right: $3x-4y=5$, $-y=3$, $y=-3$]*

[left margin: $p=2\ q=3$]
19. p/2 + q/3 = 2 and 5p-3q = 1 is given by _____. *[right: $p = \dfrac{11}{8}$ $q = 1^{7}/24$]*

[bottom working:]

$3q = 5p+1$

$q = \dfrac{5}{3}p + 1/3$

[circled, bottom left: ① remove fractions]

$\dfrac{3p+2q}{6} = 2 \qquad 3p+2q = 12$

26

X *20. x+y+z = 4, x+y-2z = 1 and x-y+2z = 1 is given by ___x=1, y=2 z=1___.

X 21. The system of equations 2x-3y = 7 and 9y = 6x-20 has ___NO___ X
(one, no or infinite) solution(s). How determine? first plug into Solve the bigone

22. The system of equations 2p+3q = 6 and p/3 = 1 - q/2 has ___Infinte___ X
(one, no or infinite) solution(s). Same equations

23. In a linear cost model, if the total cost y_c of producing x units is
given by y_c = mx + b, then m represents the _variable_ and b the _fixed_
costs. cost/unit

24. If the cost y_c of producing x units of a certain commodity is given
by y_c = 3x+500, then the fixed costs are ___500___ and the variable
cost per unit is ___3___. profit=0 total cost

25. When a certain business breaks even, then total revenue = _total cost_. X

26. If x = x_o is the break-even point for a firm, then the firm makes a
profit if x ___>___ x_o and a loss if x _<_ x_o. Substitute or set equal

(27 - 29) The demand and supply equations of a certain product are
D: p + 2x = 38 ; S = p = 3 + 0.5x
X 38-2x = 3+.5x
35 = 2.5x

27. Then the market equilibrium price and quantity are given by
p = ___10___ and x = ___14___. $p_1 = p + t$

28. If a tax of 1 per unit is imposed, then the new supply and demand
equations are _4+.5x_ and _38-2x_. p= 4+.5x p=38-2x
The market equilibrium is now given by _p=10.8_. X=13.6 2.5x=34

29. If a subsidy of 0.5 per unit is given, then the new demand and supply
equations are _p+2x=38_ and _p=2.5+0.5x_. $p_1 = p$ - Subsidy
and the equilibrium point is _p=9.6_. x=14.2 38-2x=2.5+0.5x
-2.5x=-35.5

30. In a linear cost model, the y-intercept of the line represents $y_c = mx + b$
fixed and the slope of the line determines the _variable cost/unit_
costs

SEE ANSWERS AT THE END OF THIS BOOK.

x=y-6

y=9

27

CHAPTER - 5

YOU SHOULD BE FAMILIAR WITH THE FOLLOWING IMPORTANT TERMS:

Function, function value, domain, range.

Independent variable, argument, dependent variable.

Vertical line test.

Constant function, polynomial function of degree n, linear function, quadratic function, rational function, algebraic function.

Parabola, vertex.

Power function.

Rectangular hyperbola, asymptote.

Circle, center, radius. Centre-radius formula.

Product-transformation curve.

Absolute value function.

Sum, difference, product, quotient of two functions.

The composite function fog.

Implicit relation, implicit function.

The inverse of a function.

OBJECTIVES

AFTER READING THIS CHAPTER YOU SHOULD BE ABLE TO DO THE FOLLOWING:.

1. Evaluate a function at a given value of its argument.

2. Determine the domain of a given algebraic function.

3. Use the vertical line test.

4. Construct a function from verbal information in an applied problem.

5. Determine the vertex and sketch the graph of a quadratic function.

6. Use the properties of parabolas to solve certain maximum and minimum problems.

7. Sketch the graph of any power function $y = ax^n$.

8. Find the equation of a circle given the center and radius. Calculate the center and radius from a given equation in general form.

9. Sketch the graph of the absolute value function and related functions.

10. Form the sum, difference, product or quotient of two given functions and compute their domains.

11. Form the composition of two functions and compute its domain.

12. Calculate the inverse of a function, by restricting the domain if necessary.

SOLUTIONS TO ALTERNATE ODD PROBLEMS

EXERCISES - 5.1

1. $f(x) = 3x+2$ gives $f(1) = 3 \cdot 1 + 2 = 5$, $f(-2) = 3(-2) + 2 = -4$,

   $f(x^2) = 3x^2 + 2$, $f(x+h) = 3(x+h) + 2$.

5. $f(x) = x^2$ gives $f(3) = 3^2 = 9$, $f(-2) = (-2)^2 = 4$, $f(a) = a^2$,

   $f(\sqrt{x}) = (\sqrt{x})^2 = x$, $f(x+h) = (x+h)^2$

9. $g(x) = \sqrt{x}$ gives $f(4) = \sqrt{4} = 2$, $f(x^2) = \sqrt{x^2} = |x|$, $f(a^2+h^2) = \sqrt{a^2+h^2}$.

13. $f(x) = 2x-3$ if $x \geq 5$ and $f(x) = 6-3x$ if $x < 5$ gives

    (a) $f(0) = 6-3(0) = 6$, (b) $f(7) = 2(7)-3 = 11$,

    (c) $f(-2) = 6-3(-2) = 12$ (d) $f(5+h) = 2(5+h)-3 = 7+2h$ and

    $f(5-h) = 6 - 3(5-h) = -9 + 3h$.

17. $g(2) = 4-1 = 3$ and $f\{g(2)\} = f(3) = 9+1 = 10$.

21. $f(x) = 7$ gives $f(x+h) = 7$, so that

    $\{f(x+h) - f(x)\}/h = (7-7)/h = 0/h = 0$.

25. $f(x) = 2x+3$, domain is all x.

29. $f(x) = \dfrac{x+1}{x^2-3x+2} = \dfrac{x+1}{(x-1)(x-2)}$; domain is all $x \neq 1,2$.

33. $f(y) = -\sqrt{3y-2}$. Domain is given by $3y - 2 \geq 0$ or $y \geq 3/2$.

37. $f(x)$ is defined for all $x > 5$, $x < 5$ but not for $x=5$. Thus, the domain is all $x \neq 5$.

41.

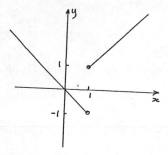

45. (a) A(0) = 3.9   (b) A(1) = 4.0   (c) A(5/2) = 3.775

49. A = x(100-x) = 100x - x², where x is one side of the rectangle.

53.
$$C(x) = \begin{cases} 25x & \text{if } x \le 50 \\ 20x & \text{if } x > 50 \end{cases}$$
where C is the cost in cents. For graph, see the answer in the text.

57. If x ≤ 12, C(x) = 500. Total cost for a group x > 12 is the cost

($6000) of the first 12 plus the extra (x-12) at $450 each, i.e.

${6000 + 450(x-12)} = $(450x + 600). Therefore C(x) = 450 + 600/x

if x > 12.
$$C(x) = \begin{cases} 500 & \text{if } 6 \le x \le 12 \\ 450 + 600/x & \text{if } x > 12 \end{cases}$$

61. No.

EXERCISES - 5.2

1. y = 2x² - 3. Comparing with y = ax² + bx + c, we have: a=2, b=0, c=-3

The x-coordinate of vertex is: x = -b/2a = -0/4 = 0. Then y-coordinate

is given by y = 2x² - 3 = 2(0)² - 3 = -3. Thus, the vertex is (0,-3).

5. y = 2 - x - 2x². Here a = -2, b = -1, c = 2. The vertex is given by
x = -b/2a = 1/(-4) = -1/4 and y = 2 - x - 2x² = 2 - (-1/4) - 2(-1/4)²
= 17/8   i.e. (-1/4, 17/8).

9. y = 2x² + 3x - 1. For vertex, x = -b/2a = -3/4 and

y = 2(-3/4)² + 3(-3/4) - 1 = -17/8. i.e. the vertex is at (-3/4,-17/8).
(See graph in the book).

13. y = f(x) = -x²-x+1. Since the coeff. of x² = -1 < 0, the graph of
f(x) is a parabola which opens downwards. It has a maximum value at
the vertex. The x-coordinate of vertex is : x = -b/2a = -(-1)/2(-1)
= -1/2. The maximum value is y = f(-1/2) = -(-1/2)² -(-1/2) + 1 = 5/4.

17. (a) $C(x) = 25x + 2000$

    (b) $R(x) = 60x - 0.01x^2$ is maximum when
$x = -b/2a = -60/2(-0.01) = 3000$ units are sold.
$R_{max.} = R(3000) = 60(3000) - 0.01(3000)^2 = \$90,000.$

    (c) If $P(x)$ denotes the profit function, then
$$P(x) - R(x) - C(x) - 35x - 0.01x^2 - 2000$$

Maximum of $P(x)$ occurs at the vertex of parabola which is the graph of $P(x)$. The x-coordinate of vertex is

$x = -b/2a = -35/2(0.01) = 1750.$
$P_{max.} = P(1750) = 35(1750) - 0.01(1750)^2 - 2000 = \$28,625.$

21. $y = $ yield $= x(10 - 0.5x) = 10x - 0.5x^2$
$x = -b/2a = -10/2(-0.5) = 10.$ <u>Ans</u>. x=10.

25. Let the rent per suite be increased by x increments of \$5, i.e. the new rent is $\$(150 + 5x)$. Then $(40 - x)$ suites can be rented at this new rate. If $R(x)$ is the total monthly revenue, then

$R(x) = (150 + 5x)(40 - x) = 6000 + 50x - 5x^2.$
For maximum R, $x = -b/2a = -50/2(-5) = 5$
Thus, the rent per suite $= \$(150 + 5x) = \$(150 + 25) = \$175.$
$R_{max.} = R(5) = (175)(35) = \$6125.$

EXERCISES - 5.3

1. $y = f(x) = \sqrt{4-x^2}$ implies $y \geq 0$ and $y^2 = 4 - x^2$ or $x^2 + y^2 = 4$.

Thus the graph of $y = \sqrt{4-x^2}$ is the upper half (because $y \geq 0$) of the circle given by $x^2 + y^2 = 4$ whose center

is at (0,0) and the radius is 2. The

graph is as shown in the figure. The

domain is the set of all possible values

of x on the graph which is $-2 \leq x \leq 2$.

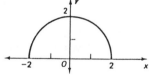

5.

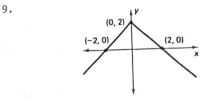

$D_f = \{x \mid x \neq 0\}$

9.

$D_f = \{x \mid x \text{ is real}\}$

31

13. If $x > 3$, $f(x) = |x-3|/(x-3)$
    $= (x-3)/(x-3) = 1$ and if $x < 3$,
    $f(x) = -(x-3)/(x-3) = -1$. The
    domain of $f(x)$ is all $x \neq 3$.

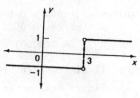

$$D_f = \{x \mid x \neq 3\}$$

17. $(x-2)^2 + (y-5)^2 = 3^2$ or $x^2 + y^2 - 4x - 10y + 20 = 0$.

21. radius = distance between $(-2,1)$ and $(0,4) = 13$.
    Equation: $(x+2)^2 + (y-1)^2 = 13$ or $x^2 + y^2 + 4x - 2y - 8 = 0$.

25. Max. Coronado $(x_m) = 4.48$

    Max. Eastern star $(y_m) = 3.49$

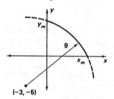

29. $y = f(x) = |2x+1| + 2$. The graph
    of $y = f(x)$ is as shown in the figure.
    Clearly the graph has a minimum at
    $x = -1/2$ and the minimum value is
    $f(-1/2) = 2$. There is no maximum in
    this case.
    ALITER : $y = f(x) = |2x+1| + 2$. Since $|2x+1| \geq 0$ for all x,
    $y = 2 + |2x+1| \geq 2$ for all x i.e. y has a minimum value of 2 which
    occurs when $|2x+1| = 0$ or $x = -1/2$.

33. $y = 1 + 2\sqrt{1-x}$. The domain is all $x \leq 1$. Since $2\sqrt{1-x} \geq 0$ for all
    x in the domain, it follows that $y = 1 + 2\sqrt{1-x} \geq 1+0$ i.e. $y \geq 1$.
    Thus y has a minimum value of 1 which occurs when $2\sqrt{1-x} = 0$ i.e. $x=1$.

EXERCISES - 5.4

1. $(f \pm g)(x) = x^2 \pm (x-1)^{-1}$; $(fg)(x) = x^2(x-1)^{-1}$; $(f/g)(x) = x^2(x-1)$;
   $(g/f)(x) = \{x^2(x-1)\}^{-1}$; $D_{f+g} = D_{f-g} = D_{f/g} = \{x \mid x \neq 1\}$;
   $D_{g/f} = \{x \mid x \neq 0, 1\}$.

5. $(f \pm g)(x) = (x+1)^2 \pm (x^2-1)^{-1}$; $(fg)(x) = (x+1)/(x-1)$;
   $(f/g)(x) = (x+1)^2(x^2-1)$; $(g/f)(x) = \{(x^2-1)(x+1)^2\}^{-1} = \{(x-1)(x+1)^3\}^{-1}$
   $D_{f+g} = D_{f-g} = D_{fg} = D_{f/g} = D_{g/f} = \{x \mid x \neq \pm 1\}$.

9. $g \circ f(-2) = g\{f(-2)\} = g(4) = \sqrt{4-1} = \sqrt{3}$.

13. $(g \circ f)(1) = g\{f(1)\} = g(1) = \sqrt{1-1} = 0.$

17. $f \circ g(4) = f\{g(4)\} = f(-2) = -1/3.$

21. $g \circ f(-1/2) = g\{f(-1/2)\} = $ undefined, because $f(-1/2) = 1/0$ is undefined.

25. $(f \circ g)(x) = 2 + |x-2| \; ; \; (g \circ f)(x) = x.$

29. $(f \circ g)(x) = f(1/x) = x^{-1} - 1 \; ; \; (g \circ f)(x) = g\{f(x)\} = g(x-1) = (x-1)^{-1}$

33. $f\{g(x)\} = (x^2+1)^3.$ Let $u = g(x) = x^2+1$, then we have $f(u) = u^3$ or $f(x) = x^3.$ Thus, $f(x) = x^3$, $g(x) = x^2 + 1$ is the simplest answer.

37. $x = 2000 - 15p$ gives $p = (2000 - x)/15.$ Using this value of p in
$R = 2000p - 15p^2 = p(2000-15p)$ gives
$R = \left[(2000-x)/15\right](x) = (1/15)(2000x - x^2).$

EXERCISES - 5.5

1. $3x + 4y = 12$ gives $4y = 12-3x$ or $y = 3 - (3/4)x.$

5. $x^2 - y^2 + x + y = 0$ or $(x-y)(x+y) + (x+y) = 0$ or $(x+y)(x-y+1) = 0$
gives $y = -x$ or $y = x+1.$

9. $4x^2 + 9y^2 = 36$ or $y^2 = (4/9)(9 - x^2)$ gives $y = \pm(2/3)\sqrt{9-x^2}.$

13. Solving $xy^2 + (x^2-1)y - x = 0$ as a quadratic in y gives:

$y = \{-(x^2-1) \pm \sqrt{(x^2-1)^2 + 4x^2}\}/(2x) = \{(1-x^2) \pm (x^2+1)\}/2x = 1/x \; , \; -x.$
Thus, $y = 1/x, \; y = -x.$

17. $x = f^{-1}(p) = 10 - 5p/2.$

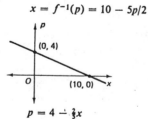

$x = f^{-1}(p) = 10 - 5p/2$

(0, 4)

O (10, 0)

$p = 4 - \tfrac{2}{5}x$

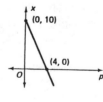

(0, 10)

(4, 0)

O

$x = 10 - \tfrac{5}{2}p$

21. $x = f^{-1}(y) = y^{1/5}$

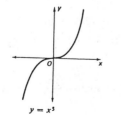

$y = x^5$

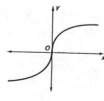

$x = y^{1/5}$

25. $x = f^{-1}(y) = -1 + \sqrt{y}$; if $x \geq -1$; $x = f^{-1}(y) = -1 - \sqrt{y}$; if $x \leq -1$.

29. $y = |x-1|$ implies $y \geq 0$. If $x \geq 1$, $y = |x-1| = x-1$ gives $x = f^{-1}(y)$
$= 1+y$, $(y \geq 0)$. If $x \leq 1$, $y = |x-1| = -(x-1)$ gives $x = f^{-1}(y) = 1-y$
$(y \geq 0)$.

REVIEW EXERCISES ON CHAPTER - 5

1. See answers in the text.

5. The equation of circle of radius 5 and center at $(p, -1)$ is:
$(x-p)^2 + (y+1)^2 = 25$. Since this circle passes through the point
$(1,2)$ we have: $(1-p)^2 + (2+1)^2 = 25$ or $(1-p)^2 = 16$ or $p = 5, -3$.

9. $(fog)(x) = (gof)(x) = x^2$.

13.
$$E = \begin{cases} 1000 & \text{if } 0 < x \leq 6000 \\ 1000 + 0.8(x-6000) & \text{if } x \geq 6000 \end{cases}$$
   (a) Domain = all $x \geq 0$.

   (b) \$1000; \$1160.

17. If the rent is increased by x increments of \$5, then new rent per
    suite = \$(120+5x) and the number of suites rented at this rate
    = $(60-2x)$.
    R = monthly revenue = (Rent per suite)·(No. of suites rented)
       = $(120 + 5x)(60 - 2x)$ ..... (i)

   (a) If \$p denotes the monthly rent per unit, then $p = 120 + 5x$
       or $x = 0.2p - 24$. Substituting this value of x in (i) we get:
       $R = (120 + 5x)(60 - 2x) = p\{(60 - 2(0.2p - 24)\} = 108p - 0.4p^2$.

   (b) If q denotes the number of suites rented, then $q = 60 - 2x$
       or $x = 30 - 0.5q$. Using this value of x in (i) we get:
       $R(q) = \{120 + 5(30 - 0.5q)\}q = 270q - 2.5q^2$.

21. $C(x) = $ Cost of producting x units $= 0.70x + 200$
    $2p = 5 - 0.01x$ gives $p = 2.5 - 0.005x$
    $R = px = x(2.5 - 0.005x) = 2.5x - 0.005x^2$

   (a) R is maximum when $x = -2.5/2(-0.005) = 250$ units.

   (b) If P denotes the profit, then
       $P = R - C = (2.5x - 0.005x^2) - (200 + 0.7x) = 1.8x - 0.005x^2 - 200$
       P is maximum when $x = -1.8/2(-0.005) = 180$ units.

25. $y = \pm\sqrt{x-1}$.

29. $p(0) = 3000 - \dfrac{2000}{(1+0)} = 1000$, $p(1) = 3000 - \dfrac{2000}{(1+1)} = 2000$,

    $p(2) = 3000 - 2000/(1+4) = 2600$.

FILL IN THE BLANKS:

1. If $f(x) = 2x+3$, then $f(x^2) =$ _____ and $f(x+h) =$ _____.

2. If $f(x) = 5$, then $f(x^2) =$ _____, $f(1/x) =$ _____, $f(x+2) =$ _____.

3. If $f(x) = (x-2)(x+3)/(x-2)(x+1)$, then $f(3) =$ _____ and $f(2) =$ _____.

4. If $f(x) = -|-x|$, then $f(3) =$ _____.

5. The domain of $f(x) = (x^2+1)/(x^2-4)$ is given by $D_f =$ _____.

6. The domain of $f(x) = (x^2-1)/(x^2+4)$ is given by $D_f =$ _____.

7. The domain of $f(x) = \sqrt{2x-3}$ is given by $D_f =$ _____.

8. The domain of $f(x) = \sqrt{3-2x}/(x-2)$ is given by $D_f =$ _____.

9. The graph of $y = x^2-4x+1$ is a _____ which opens _____ (up or
    down) with vertex at _____.

10. $y = 3 + 8x - 2x^2$ has a _____ (maximum/minimum) at the point _____.

11. If $y = f(x) = :x^2-6x+8$, then the domain is $D_f =$ _____ and the range
    is $R_f =$ _____.

12. By **definition**, $|x| =$ _____ if $x \leq 0$ and $=$ _____ if $x \geq 0$.

13. If $y = f(x) = |x-3|/(x-3)$, then the domain is $D_f =$ _____ and the
    range is $R_f =$ _____.

14. The equation of a circle of radius r and center at (a,b) is given
    by _____.

15. The equation of a circle of radius 3 units and which touches the
    coordinate axes and lies in the second quadrant is given by _____.

16. By definition, $f \circ g(x) =$ _____.

17. If $f(x) = 3$ and $g(x) = 7$, then $f \circ g(x) =$ _____ and $g \circ f(x) =$ _____.

18. If $f(x) = 2x+3$ and $g(x) = x^2$, then $f \circ g(x) =$ _____ and $g \circ f(x) =$ _____

19. If $f(x) = x^2$ and $g(x) = \sqrt{x}$, then $f \circ g(x) =$ _____ and $g \circ f(x) =$ _____.

20. If $f(x) = 1/x$, then $f \circ f(x) =$ _____.

21. If $f(x) = 9$ and $g(x) = \sqrt{x}$, then $f \circ g(x) =$ _____ and $g \circ f(x) =$ _____.

22. If f(x) = 3, then f∘f(x) = _____ and f∘f(7) = _____.

23. In general, f∘g(x) _____ g∘f(x)   (= , ≠)

24. If p+2x = 70 is the demand equation, where x units can be sold at a price of p each, then the revenue R as a function of

    (i) x is R(x) = _____ and (ii) p is R(p) = _____.

25. If x units are sold at a price of p each where 3p+2x = 60 and cost function is C(x) = 70 + 3x, then the revenue R and the profit P as functions of

    (i) x are given by R(x) = _____ and P(x) = _____.

    (ii) p are given by R(p) = _____ and P(p) = _____.

26. y = f(x) has a unique inverse if to each value of y in the range of f, there is _____ value of x in the domain.

27. y = f(x) has a unique inverse, if any _____ line meets the graph of f(x) in _____ points.

28. If y = f(x) has a unique inverse, then x = _____.

29. If f(x) = 3x+7, then $f^{-1}(x)$ = _____.

30. If f(x) = $\sqrt[5]{x}$, then $f^{-1}(x)$ = _____.

31. If f(x) = 3 + x^2 , (x ≤ 0), then $f^{-1}(x)$ = _____.

32. If f(x) = 7, then $f^{-1}(x)$ = _____.

33. The graph of y = $f^{-1}(x)$ is the reflection of the graph of y = f(x) in the line given by _____.

34. If f(x) = 1/x , then $f^{-1}(x)$ _____ f(x)   (= , ≠)

35. In general, $f^{-1}(x)$ _____ f(x)   (= , ≠)

36. A given curve represents the graph of some function if any _____ line meets the curve in _____ point.

37. If C(x) = 500 - 30x + x^2, then the cost C is minimum when x = _____.

38. If P(x) = 20x - x^2 - 300, then the profit P is maximum when x = _____.

39. If f(x) = x^2-1 and g(x) = (x-1)/(x-2), then

(i) $(f \pm g)(x) = $ _____, $(f/g)(x) = $ _____.

(ii)   domain of $(f + g)(x)$ is _____.

(iii)   domain of $(f \cdot g)(x)$ is _____.

(iv)   domain of $(f/g)(x)$ is _____.

40.   The explicit function corresponding to the implicit relation

$\sqrt{x} + \sqrt{y} = 1$ is _____.

SEE ANSWERS AT THE END OF THIS BOOK.

CHAPTER - 6

YOU SHOULD BE FAMILIAR WITH THE FOLLOWING TERMS:

Exponential function, base.

Natural exponential function, the number e.

Compound interest, interest rate, nominal interest rate.

Logarithm of a number, base, logarithm function.

Logarithmic form and exponential form.

Common logarithm, natural logarithm.

The properties of logarithms.

Present value.

Base change formulas for exponentials and logarithms.

Specific growth rate, specific decay rate.

Continuous compounding.

Logistic model.

OBJECTIVES

AFTER READING THIS CHAPTER YOU SHOLULD BE ABLE TO DO THE FOLLOWING:

1. Sketch the graph of a given exponential function.

2. Calculate values of the natural exponential function using either a table or a calculator.

3. Solve problems involving exponential growth or decay, for example population growth problems.

4. Solve compound interest problems involving either annual compounding or compounding k times per year.

5. Sketch the graph of a given logarithm function.

6. Transform a given statement from exponential form to logarithmic form or vice versa.

7. Calculate the value of a given common logarithm or natural logarithm.

8. Use the four properties of logarithms to simplify expressions or solve logarithmic equations.

9. Apply logarithms to solve equations when the unknown is in the exponent.

10. Calculate present values and use them to decide between alternative investment strategies.

11. Use the base change formulas to transform either exponential functions or logarithm functions to a different base, expecially to and from base e or base 10.

12. Compute the growth of an investment using continuous compounding. Calculate an effective annual interest rate for continuous compounding.

13. Use the logistic growth model in appropriate problem involving restricted growth.

SOLUTIONS TO ALTERNATE ODD PROBLEMS

EXERCISES - 6.1

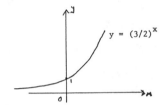

$y = (3/2)^x$

1. $y = (3/2)^x$

$x =$	-3	-2	-1	0	1	1	...
$y =$	8/27	4/9	2/3	1	3/2	9/4	...

Plotting these points, we get the graph as shown.

5. From the Appendix A 3.3, we have $e^{0.41} = 1.5068$.

9. From the Appendix A 3.3, we have: $e^{-0.68} = 0.5066$.

13. Value $= \$100(1.08)^5 = \$146.93$

17. Here $i = 0.12$, $k = 2$, $n=4$. Value $= \$2000(1.06)^8 = \$3187.70$.

21. $100 invested at 12% compounded monthly for 1 year becomes $100(1.01)^{12}$ = \$112.68. The effective rate of interest is $(112.68 - 100) = 12.68\%$.

25. If R% is the nominal rate of interest, then $100 invested for 1 year, when the compounding is monthly, becomes $\$100(1 + R/1200)^{12} = \$110$.

This gives, $1 + R/1200 = (1.1)^{1/12} = 1.007974$ or $R = 1200(1.007974 - 1) = 9.57$ i.e. 9.57%.

29. $100 invested at 8.2% compounded annually becomes $108.20 whereas $100 invested at 8% compounded quarterly becomes $\$100(1.02)^4 = \$108.24$. Since, we get more by quarterly compounding at 8%, it is better.

33. $P_o(1.03)^5(1 + R/100)^4 = 2P_o$ or $(1 + R/100)^4 = 2(1.03)^{-5} = 1.7252$ or

$1 + R/100 = (1.7252)^{1/4} = 1.1461$ or $R = 14.61$.

37. (a) In 1980, t=10. Now t=10 in $P = 500,000e^{-0.02t}$ gives

$P = 500,000\ e^{-0.2} = 409,365$. In the year 2000, $t = 30$. Then

$P = 500,000\ e^{-0.02(30)} = 500,000e^{-0.6} = 274,406$.

41. (a) $V = 10,000 \, e^{-0.2(8)} = \$2018.97.$

(b) If the value declines by R% per year, then
$$1 - R/100 = e^{-0.2} = 0.8187 \quad \text{or} \quad R = 18.13 \quad \text{i.e.} \quad 18.13\%.$$

EXERCISES - 6.2

1. $(27)^{-4/3} = (3^3)^{-4/3} = 3^{3(-4/3)} = 3^{-4} = 1/3^4 = 1/81.$

   $(27)^{-4/3} = 1/81$ in the logarithmic form gives $\log_{27}(1/81) = -4/3.$

5. $(8/27)^{-1/3} = \{(2/3)^3\}^{-1/3} = (2/3)^{3(-1/3)} = (2/3)^{-1} = 3/2.$

   Now $(8/27)^{-1/3} = 3/2$ in the log form becomes $\log_{8/27}(3/2) = -1/3$

9. $\log_4(1/2) = -1/2$ gives $4^{-1/2} = 1/2$ or $(2^2)^{-1/2} = 1/2$ or $2^{-1} = 1/2$

   which is true.

13. Let $\log_{\sqrt{2}} 16 = x.$ Then $(\sqrt{2})^x = 16$ or $(2^{1/2})^x = 2^4$ or $2^{x/2} = 2^4$ or

    $x/2 = 4$ or $x = 8$ i.e. $\log_{\sqrt{2}} 16 = 8.$

17. Since $a^{\log_a y} = a$ (See formula on page 206) , we have: $10^{\log 100}$

    $= 10^{\log_{10} 100} = 100.$

21. Let $\log_{1/2}(3) = x.$ then $(1/2)^x = 3$ or $1/2^x = 3$ or $2^x = \frac{1}{3}$ or

    $2^{\log_{1/2} 3} = \frac{1}{3}$ Ans.

25. $\log 12 = \log (2^2 \cdot 3) = 2 \log 2 + \log 3 = 2 \log(10/5) + \log(9^{1/2})$

    $\qquad = 2(\log 10 - \log 5) + (1/2)\log 9 = 2(1 - 0.6990) + (1/2)(0.9542)$

    $\qquad = 1.0791.$

29. $\log (x+1) - \log x = \log \left(\frac{x+1}{x}\right) .$

33. $2 \log x + x \log 3 - (1/2)\log (x+1) = \log x^2 + \log 3^x - \log (x+1)^{1/2}$

    $\qquad = \log \{x^2 \cdot 3^x/(x+1)^{1/2}\} .$

37. $\log_2(x+3) = -1$ gives $2^{-1} = x+3$ or $x = 3 - 1/2 = 5/2.$

41. $\log_x(6-5x) = 2$ gives $x^2 = 6 - 5x$ or $x^2 + 5x - 6 = 0.$

    or $(x+6)(x-1) = 0$ i.e. $x = 1, -6.$ We reject both values of x,

    because the base of log is always $> 0, \neq 1.$ Thus, no solution.

45. $\log x = \log 3 + 2 \log 2 - (3/4)\log 16 = \log 3 + \log 2^2 - \log 16^{3/4}$

$= \log 3 + \log 4 - \log 8 = \log(3 \cdot 4/8) = \log(3/2)$ or $x = 3/2$.

49. $\ln 3.41 = 1.2267$ (from Table A.3.2 in Appendix).

53. $\ln 0.341 = \ln(3.41/10) = \ln 3.41 - \ln 10 = 1.2267 - 2.3026 = -1.0759$.

57. $C_1(x) = C_2(x)$ gives $3.5 + \log(2x+1) = 2 + \log(60x + 105)$ or

$\log\left(\frac{60x+105}{2x+1}\right) = 1.5$ or $\frac{60x+105}{2x+1} = 10^{1.5} = 31.62$. This gives

$x = 22.61$. For larger x, $C_2(x) < C_1(x)$ and so the second design is

cheaper.

EXERCISES - 6.3

1. $10^x = 25$. Taking logs, we have: $\log 10^x = \log 25$ or

$x \log 10 = \log 25$ or $x = \log 25 = 1.3979$, because $\log 10 = 1$.

5. $3^x = 2^{2-x}$. Taking logs, we have: $x \log 3 = (2-x) \log 2$ or

$x(\log 3 + \log 2) = 2 \log 2$ or $x = 2 \log 2/(\log 3 + \log 2) = 0.7737$.

9. $a^x = cb^x$. Taking logs gives: $x \log a = \log(cb^x) = \log c + x \log b$

or $x(\log a - \log b) = \log c$ or $x = (\log c)/(\log a - \log b)$.

13. Let it be t years after 1976 (i.e. $t+6$ years after 1970). Then

$(0.75)(1.04)^{t+6} = (1/2)(4)(1.02)^t$ or $(0.75)(1.04)^6(1.04)^t = 2(1.02)^t$

or $(1.04/1.02)^t = 2/0.75(1.04)^6$. Taking logs and solving for t

gives $t = 38.4$ i.e. 38.4 years after 1976.

17. $3000 = 1000(1.08)^t$ gives $(1.08)^t = 3$, or $t \log(1.08) = \log 3$ or

$t = \log 3/\log(1.08) = 14.27$ years.

21. Present value $= \$1000(1.08)^{-1} + \$1000(1.08)^{-2} + \$1000(1.08)^{-3} = \$2577.10$.

25. $y = 5(1.04)^t = 5 \, e^{t \ln 1.04} = 5e^{(0.0392)t}$.

29. (a) $196 = 121(1 + i)^5$ or $1 + i = 1.10127$ or $R = 100i = 10.13\%$.
    (b) $I = 121(1.10127)^5 = 121 \, e^{5 \ln 1.10127} = 121 \, e^{(0.0965)t}$
    (c) $250 = 121(1.10127)^t$ gives $t = 7.52$ yrs. after Jan. 1975.

33. $V(t) = (2/3)V(0)$ gives $750(1.3)^{-t} = (2/3)(750)$ or $(1.3)^{-t} = 2/3$

or $-t \log(1.3) = \log(3/2)$ or $t = 1.55$ months.

37. When t=5, $R = 4(1.2)^5 = 9.95$.

$4(1.2)^t = 20$ gives $(1.2)^t = 5$ or $t \log 1.2 = \log 5$

or $t = 8.83$ years i.e. during Sept. of 1990.

41. For Venus, we have $M = -3.9$. This gives $M = (-5/2)\log (B/B_o) = -3.9$

or $B/B_o = $ antilog $\left[\frac{2}{5}(3.9)\right] = 36.3$. For Polaris, taking the

brightness as B', we have $M = (-5/2)\log (B'/B_o) = 2.1$. This gives

$B'/B_o = $ antilog$\left[-2/5(2.1)\right] = $ antilog $(-0.84) = 0.1445$.

Thus, $\frac{B}{B'} = \frac{(B/B_o)}{(B'/B_o)} = \frac{36.3}{0.1445} = 251.13$. Hence Venus is 251 times as

bright as Polaris.

45. $y = 10^5 \cdot 2^{t/19}$ where t is in minutes. Here $y = 10^7$. Thus,

$10^7 = 10^5 \cdot 2^{t/19}$ or $2^{t/19} = 10^2 = 100$ or $(t/19) \log 2 = \log 100 = 2$

or $t = \frac{38}{\log 2} = 126.23$ i.e. after 126 minutes.

EXERCISES - 6.4

1. $\$500 \cdot e^{(0.06)3} = \$5000\, e^{0.8} = \$598.61$.

5. Value $= \$100\, e^{2(0.09)} \cdot e^{5(0.11)} = \$100\, e^{0.18} \cdot e^{0.55} = \$100\, e^{0.18 + 0.55}$

$= \$100\, e^{0.73} = \$207.51$.

9. $150 = 100\, e^{4i}$ gives $4i = \ln 1.5$ or $i = (\ln 1.5)/4 = 0.1014$

i.e. $R = 100i = 10.14\%$.

13. \$100 invested at 4.5% continuous compounding for one year becomes

$\$100\, e^{0.045} = \$104.60$ i.e. the effective rate of interest is 4.60%.

17. \$100 invested at 8% continuous compounding for one year becomes

$\$100\, e^{0.08} = 108.33$ whereas \$100 invested at 8.2% compounded

quarterly for one year will become $\$100(1.0205)^4 = \$108.46$. Thus,

quarterly compounding is better for the investor.

21. $P(x) = 30 - 15e^{-0.02x}$ gives $P(0) = 30 - 15e^0 = 30 - 15 = 15$ and

$P(100) = 30 - 15e^{-2} = 27.97 \approx 28$. As x gets larger and larger,

$e^{-0.02x}$ gets closer and closer to zero and $P(x)$ gets closer and closer to 30. Thus in the long run, the rate of production is 30 items per hour.

25. $t = 1$, $y = 10$ and $t=2$, $y = 15$ in $y = A(1 - e^{-kt})$ gives

$10 = A(1 - e^{-k})$ and $15 = A(1 - e^{-2k})$. Dividing the two equations,

$15/10 = (1 - e^{-2k})/(1 - e^{-k})$ or $1.5 = 1 + e^{-k}$ or $k = 0.6931$. Then

$10 = A(1 - e^{-k}) = A(1 - 0.5) = A/2$ gives $A = 20$. Thus

$y = 20(1 - e^{-0.6931t})$. When $t=4$, we get $y = 20(1 - e^{-0.6931(4)})$

$= 18.75$ nuts per 5 minute period.

29. At $t=0$, $y = pe^{-ce^{-kt}}$ gives $y = pe^{-ce^{0}} = pe^{-c}$, because $e^{0} = 1$.

As t becomes larger, e^{-kt} gets closer and closer to zero. Thus, y gets

closer and closer to value $pe^{-c(0)} = pe^{0} = P$.

REVIEW EXERCISES ON CHAPTER - 6
_____

1. See answers in the text book.

5. $\log_{12}\sqrt{108} = (1/2) \log_{12} 108 = (1/2) \log_{12}(12 \cdot 9) = 1/2(\log_{12}12 + \log_{12}9)$

$= (1/2)(1 + 2 \log_{12}3) = (1/2)\{1 + 2\log_{12}(12/4)\}$

$= 1/2 \{1 + 2(\log_{12}12 - \log_{12}4)\} = 1/2 + (1 - 2\log_{12}2)$

$= 3/2 - 2x = (3-4x)/2$.

9. $2^{x+1} = 3^{2-2x}$ gives $(x+1) \log 2 = (2-2x) \log 3$ or

$x(\log 2 + 2 \log 3) = 2 \log 3 - \log 2$ or $x = \dfrac{2 \log 3 - \log 2}{\log 2 + 2 \log 3} = 0.5204$.

13. (a) $p = 62.50$ gives $(62.50) \ln (x+1) = 500$ or $(x+1) = e^{500/62.5} = e^{8}$

or $x = e^{8} - 1 = 2980$ units.

(b) $x = 5000$ gives $p \ln (5001) = 500$ or $p = \$58.70$.

17. If $\$x$ is the value of each installment, then

$1000 = x(1.1)^{-1} + (1.1)^{-2}$ or $x = \$576.19$.

21. Let $\$100$ be invested for 1 year. Then after 1 year, its value with

bank A is $\$100(1.061)^{2} = \$112.57$ whereas with bank B it will be

worth $\$100(1.01)^{12} = \$112.68$. Clearly the bank B gives a better

return.

25. If R% is the nominal rate of interest, then $3P_0 = P_0 e^{(R/100)(10)}$
gives $3 = e^{R/10}$ or $\ln 3 = R/10$ i.e. $R = 10 \ln 3 = 10.99$.

29. (a) Effective rate $= 100(1.03)^2 - 100 = 6.09$ i.e. 6.09%.

(b) Effective rate $= 100(1.015)^4 - 100 = 6.14$ i.e. 6.14%.

(c) Effective rate $= 100(1.005)^{12} - 100 = 6.17$ i.e. 6.17%.

(d) Effective rate $= 100\, e^{0.6(1)} - 100 = 6.18$ i.e. 6.18%.

33. (a) If R is the average percentage growth per annum for B,

then $1.5 = 1(1 + R/100)^{10}$ or $1 + R/100 = (1.5)^{1/10}$ or $R = 4.14$.

(b) $y = $ G.N.P. after t years $= 1(1 + R/100)^t = (1.0414)^t = e^{t\ln(1.0414)}$

$$= e^{0.04055t}.$$

(c) Let G.N.P. of nation A overtake that of nation B after t years.

Then using (b) parts of #32, 33, we have: $(0.5)e^{0.079t}$

$= e^{0.04055t}$ or $t = 18.1$ i.e. 18.1 years from 1970.

REVIEW TEST ON CHAPTER - 6

$\left[D_f = \text{domain of f} \; ; \; R_f = \text{range of function f} \right]$

FILL IN THE BLANKS: (Do not simplify your answers).

1. A function of the form $f(x) = a^x$ is called an exponential function
if a _____ .

2. The graph of $f(x) = a^x$ rises to the right if a _____ and falls to the
right if a _____ .

3. If $y = f(x) = 2^{-x}$, then $D_f = $ _____ and $R_f = $ _____

4. If $y = f(x) = 3 - 2^x$, then $D_f = $ _____ and $R_f = $ _____ .

5. The growth of $y = a^x$ always passes through the point _____ for all
values of a.

6. If a sum of P is invested at a nominal rate of R% and $i = R/100$, then
the value of the investment after n years is given by the expression

(a) _____ , if the compounding occurs every year.

(b) _____ , if the compounding occurs every six months.

(c) _____ , if the compounding occurs every three months.

44

(d) $P(1+\frac{i}{K})^{nK}$, if the compounding occurs k times a year.

(e) Pe^{in}, if the compounding occurs continuously.

7. If $y = a^x$, $(a > 0, \neq 1)$, then $x = \underline{\log_a y}$.

8. If $y = 10^x$, then $x = \underline{\log_{10} y}$
   $p^u = x$

9. If $x = e^t$, then $t = \underline{\ln x}$.

10. If $\log_p x = u$, then $x = \underline{\quad}$

11. $\log_a 1 = \boxed{0}$ for all $a \underline{> 0 \neq 1}$

12. $\log_a a = \underline{1}$ for all $a \underline{> 0 \neq 1}$.

13. $\ln e = \underline{1}$ and $\ln 1 = \underline{0}$.

14. $\log x + \log y = \log (\underline{xy})$.

15. $\log x - \log y = \log (\underline{\frac{x}{y}})$.

16. $e^{\ln x} = \underline{x}$.

17. $\ln (e^x) = \underline{x}$.

parentheses

18. $(\ln x^3)/(\ln x^2) = \underline{\frac{3\ln x}{2\ln x}} = \frac{3}{2}$

19. $(\log x)^n = \underline{\text{cannot be simplified}}$ not $\neq n \log x$

20. $\log x^n = \boxed{n} \log x$

21. $a^{\log_a x} = \underline{x}$.
    $10^{\log_{10} x} = 1$
    $e^{\ln x}$

22. $\log_a x$ is defined only if $x \underline{> 0}$ and $a \underline{> 0 \neq 1}$.

Study there

23. If $y = f(x) = 2^x$, then $f^{-1}(y) = \underline{\log_2 y}$.

24. If $g(x) = 3^{-x}$, then $g^{-1}(x) = \underline{-\log_3 x}$. notebase $= r$

25. If $f(x) = \ln x$, then $f^{-1}(x) = \underline{e^x}$. $\ln e^r = r$

*26. If $f(t) = \log(3t-2)$, then $f^{-1}(t) = \underline{\quad}$ $\frac{10^r}{3} \cdot \frac{3x}{}$

27. If $\log_{27} 81 = x$, then $81 = \underline{27}$ or $3^4 = 3^{3x}$ or $x = \underline{4/3}$.
    need a common base $81 = 27^x$ $3^4 = 3^{3x}$
    $\log 81 = x \log 27$
    $x = \frac{\log 81}{\log 27}$

28. If a sum P invested at 10% compounded continuously doubles in x years, then x is given by the equation $2P = \underline{Pe^{.1x}}$ or $x = \underline{10 \ln 2}$.
    $2 = e^{.01x}$

29. If a nominal rate of R% compounded continuously is equivalent to 12% interest compounded yearly, then R is given by the equation $e^{r/(100 = 1.12}$ or $R = \underline{100 \ln 1.12}$ $P(1.12)^n = Pe^{in}$

30. If a nominal rate of R% compounded yearly is equivalent to 8% interest compounded quarterly, then R is given by the equation $1 + \frac{R}{100} = 1.02^4$ or $R = \underline{100(1.02^4 - 1)}$.

$3r = 4$
$r = 4/3$
$\log 3^4 = \log 3^r$

31. If $y = 3/\{1 + 2(3^{-t})\}$, then $3^{-t} = \underline{\quad}$ and $t = \underline{\quad}$.

32. If $P = (1 + ce^{-kt})^{-1}$, then $e^{-kt} = \underline{\frac{1-P}{Pc}}$ and $t = \underline{\quad}$.
    $4 \log 3 = x \log 3$

(33 – 36) By the base change formula of logs,

$3r = 4$
$x = 4$

33. $\log_y x = (\log_a x)/(\underline{\log_a y}) = (\log x)/(\underline{\log y}) = (\ln x)/(\underline{\ln y})$

34. $\log x = (\ln x)(\underline{\log e}) = (\ln x)/(\underline{\ln 10})$ $\ln x (\log e) = \frac{\ln x}{\ln e 10}$

35. $(\log_b a)(\log_a b) = \underline{1}$

36. $(\ln x)(\log e) = \underline{\log x}$.

$\log e^x (\log_{10} e) = 1$ $\ln x = \ln \log y$
$\log_y r = \frac{\log_a r}{\log_{450} y}$

$\ln r (\log e) = \frac{\ln r}{\ln 10}$ $\log e = \frac{1}{\ln 10}$ $\log_{10} e \log_e 10 =$

37. $(1 + P)^{1/P} \to$ ____ $\underline{1}$ ____ as $p \to \infty$.

38. If a sum P invested at R% compounded continuously for 5 years doubles in value, then the rate R is given by the equation $2P = \underline{Pe^{5R/100}}$ or R = _____.

$P2 = e^{1/20 R}$ $\ln 2 = R/20$ $R = 20\ln 2$

39. If a sum P invested at R% compounded yearly for 7 years doubles in value, then R is given by the equation $2P =$ _____ or R = _____

40. If a sum P invested at R% compounded quarterly for 10 years triples in value, then R is given by the equation $3P =$ _____ or R = _____.

SEE ANSWERS AT THE END OF THIS BOOK.

39)

$$2P = P\left(1 + R/100\right)^7$$

$$2 = \left(1 + R/100\right)^7$$

$$2^{1/7} = 1 + R/100$$

$$2^{1/7} - 1 = R/100$$

$$R = \left(2^{1/7} - 1\right)100$$

46

CHAPTER - 7

YOU SHOULD BE FAMILIAR WITH THE FOLLOWING TERMS:

Sequence, first term, nth term (or general term)

Arithmetic progression, common difference.

Simple interest.

Sum of n terms.

Geometric progression, common ratio.

Compound interest, geometric depreciation.

Sum of n terms of a G.P. Sum of an infinite G.P.

Savings plan, annuity, mortgage.

The notation $s_{\overline{n}|\,i}$ and $a_{\overline{n}|\,i}$.

The sigma (or summation) notation.

OBJECTIVES

AFTER READING THIS CHAPTER YOU SHOULD BE ABLE TO DO THE FOLLOWING:

1. Calculate the general term in an arithmetic progression given any two terms or any one term and the common difference.

2. Calculate the sum of a given number of terms in an A.P.

3. Use properties of arithmetic progressions to solve problems of simple interest and straight line depreciation.

4. Calculate the general term of a geometric progression.

5. Calculate the sum of a given number of terms in a G.P.

6. Use geometric progressions to solve problems involving compound interest and geometric depreciation; in particular to calculate the value of a savings plan after a given number of payments.

7. Use either the formula or the tabulated value of $s_{\overline{n}|\,i}$ to calculate the future value of a savings plan.

8. Use either the formula or the tabulated value of $a_{\overline{n}|\,i}$ to calculate the present value of an annuity.

9. Solve problems related to mortgages using either calculated or tabulated values of $a_{\overline{n}|\,i}$.

10. Express sums using the sigma notation and evaluate expressions involving the sigma notation.

11. Use the formulas for $\sum\limits_{k=1}^{n} k$, $\sum\limits_{k=1}^{n} k^2$, $\sum\limits_{k=1}^{n} k^3$ and properties of the sigma notation to evaluate appropriate expressions involving sums.

SOLUTIONS TO ALTERNATE ODD PROBLEMS

EXERCISES - 7.1

1. $T_{10} = a + 9d = 3 + 9(4) = 39$, $T_{15} = a + 14d = 3 + 14(4) = 59$.

5. Let the sequence in A.P. be a, a+d, a+2d, ...

    Then T_3 = a+2d = 18 and T_7 = a+6d = 30 give
    a = 12, d=3. Thus T_{15} = a + 14d = 12 + 42 = 54.

9. $S_n = \frac{n}{2} \{2a + (n-1)d\} = \frac{30}{2} \{2(1) + (30-1)3\} = 1335$.

13. Let there be n terms in the sequence. Then
    $18 = T_n = 51 + (n-1)(-3)$ or n = 12.
    $S_n = (n/2)(a + \ell) = 6(51 + 118) = 414$.

17. Let \$d be the annual depreciation. The value of the machine after
    0,1,2, ... 9 years is then 1500, 1500-d, 1500-2d, ... 1500-9d.
    We are given that at the end of 9th year, the value of the machine
    is \$420. Thus, 420 = 1500-9d or d = 120.

21. (a) From #19, we have: a = 125 and d = 4. Now, we have
        S_n = 5490 (given) and we want to find n.
        $S_n = (n/2) \{2a + (n-1)d\}$ gives $5490 = (n/2) \left[250 + 4(n-1)\right]$
        or $2n^2 + 123n - 5490 = 0$ or $(2n + 183)(n-30) = 0$
        i.e. n = 30 or -183/2. The negative value is not admissible
        and so n=30=number of payments.
    (b) Last payment = T_n = a + (n-1)d = 125 + 29(4) = 241 dollars.

25. $P = \$100\{ (1 - \frac{12}{100} \cdot \frac{1}{12}) + (1 - \frac{12}{100} \cdot \frac{2}{12}) + \dots + (1 - \frac{12}{100} \cdot \frac{12}{12})\}$

    $= \$100\{12 - \frac{1}{100}(1 + 2 + 3 + \dots + 12)\} = \$1122$.

29. (a) Value = Principal + Interest = \$200 + \$200(0.1)(n) = \$(200+20n)
    (b) n = 5 in (a) gives, value = \$300.

33. N = 3, D = 500,000 - 200,000 = 300,000 = $\frac{1}{2}$ N(N+1)d = $\frac{1}{2}$ (3)(4) d;
    thus, d=50,000. The 3 depreciations are 150,000, 100,000, 50,000.

48

1. $a=3$, $r=2$. $T_9 = ar^8 = 3 \cdot 2^8 = 768$.

5. Let 3/16 be nth term of the series. Here $a = 96$, $r = 1/2$.

$3/16 = T_n = ar^{n-1} = 96 \cdot (1/2)^{n-1}$ gives $(1/2)^{n-1} = (3/16)(1/96)$
$= 1/512 = (1/2)^9$ or $n-1 = 9$ or $n = 10$.

9. $a=2$, $r=3$, $n=12$ gives $S_n = \dfrac{a(r^n-1)}{r-1} = \dfrac{2(3^{12}-1)}{3-1} = 3^{12} - 1$.

13. $a=1$, $r=1/2$ gives $S_\infty = a/(1-r) = 1/(1 - 1/2) = 2$.

17. $v + v^2 + v^3 + \ldots \cdots = v/(1-v) = \left(1/(1+i)\right)/\left(1 - 1/(1+i)\right) = 1/i$.

21. The value of the machine in any year is 90% of its value during the preceding year. Thus, $a = \$10,000$, $r = 90\% = 0.9$ and $T_n = \$5314.41$.

The formula,

$T_n = a \, r^{n-1}$ gives: $5314.41 = 10,000(0.9)^{n-1}$ or
$(0.9)^{n-1} = 0.531441 = (0.9)^6$ i.e. $n-1 = 6$ or $n=7$. Thus, effective life = 7 years.

25. (a) $\$4000(1.005)^{12} = \$4246.71$
    (b) $\$4000(1.005)^{48} = \$5081.96$.

29. $\$1,000,000 = \$P\{(1.08)^6 + (1.08)^5 + (1.08)^4 + \ldots + (1.08)\}$
    $= \$P(1.08)\{(1.08)^6 - 1\}/(1.08 - 1) = \$P(7.922803)$ gives

$P = 126,217.96$.

33. Present value of 1st payment $= \$300(1.01)^{-1}$
    Present value of 2nd payment $= \$300(1.01)^{-2}$

Present value of 48th payment $= \$300(1.01)^{-48}$
Total present value = sum of P with a $300(1.01)^{-1}$, $r = (1.01)^{-1}$, $n=48$

$$= \dfrac{300(1.01)^{-1}\{1 - (1.01)^{-48}\}}{1 - (1.-1)^{-1}} = \$11,392.19$$

Sum of 96 terms = $\$18,458.31$; sum of 144 terms = $\$22,841.15$.

EXERCISES - 7.3
----

1. 7.335929.   5. 9.471305.

9. $S = P \; s_{\overline{n}|\,i} = (\$1000)s_{\overline{10}|\,0.08} = (\$10,000)(14.486562) = \$14,486.56$

13. $S = P \; s_{\overline{n}|\,i} = (\$200) \; s_{\overline{36}|\,0.01} = \$8615.38.$

17. $P = S/s_{\overline{n}|\,i} = \$20,00/s_{\overline{16}|\,0.02} = (\$20,000)/(18.639285) = \$1073.00.$

21. (a) $S = (\$2000) \; s_{\overline{5}|\,0.08} = (\$2000)(5.866601) = \$11,733.20.$

   (b) $S = (\$2000)s_{\overline{n}|\,0.08} = \$2000\{(1.08)^{n} - 1\}/(0.08)$

   $= (\$20000/3)\{(1.08)^{n} - 1\}.$

25. Accumulated value of first 8 payments

   $= \$11,855.41 \; s_{\overline{8}|\,0.06} = \$117,338.54.$

   Four years later, this value $= \$117,338.54(1.08)^{4} = \$159,637.79$

   Remaining amount needed $= \$(200,000 - 159,637.79) = \$40,362.21$

   Remaining annual payments $= \$40,362.21/s_{\overline{4}|\,0.08}$

   $= \$8957.21.$

29. $A = P \; a_{\overline{n}|\,i} = (\$750)a_{\overline{12}|\,0.02} = (\$750)(10.575341) = \$7931.51.$

33. $A = (\$8000) \; a_{\overline{15}|\,0.06} = \$8000(9.712249) = \$77,698.00.$

37. $A = P \; a_{\overline{n}|\,i}$ gives $10,000 = P \; a_{\overline{10}|\,0.06} = P(7.360087)$ or $P = \$1358.68.$

41. $5000 = Pa_{\overline{18}|\,0.01} = P(16.398269)$ gives $P = \$304.91.$

45. See at the end of this chapter on page 54.

49. After 24th payment, present **value** of remaining payments $= 300a_{\overline{24}|\,0.01}$

   $= \$6373.02.$ Monthly interest on this $= \$6373.02(0.01) = \$63.73.$

   Alternatively: Present value after the next payment $= 300 \; a_{\overline{23}|\,0.01}$

   $= \$6136.70.$ Therefore principal reduction $= \$6373.02 - \$6136.75$

   $= \$236.27$, so interest $= 300 - 236.27 = \$63.73.$

EXERCISES - 7.4
_____

1. $\sum\limits_{k=1}^{4} (2k-3) = (2-3) + (4-3) + (6-3) + (8-3) = 8.$

5. $\sum\limits_{i=2}^{4} \frac{i}{i-1} - 2/1 + 3/2 + 4/3 - 29/6.$

9. $\sum\limits_{k=1}^{n} (2k-1) = 2 \sum\limits_{k=1}^{n} k - n = 2 \cdot \frac{1}{2}n(n+1) - n = n^2.$

13. $\sum\limits_{k=1}^{n} (k+1)(2k-1) = \sum\limits_{k=1}^{n} (2k^2+k-1) = 2 \cdot \frac{1}{6} n(n+1)(2n+1) + \frac{1}{2} n(n+1) - n$

$= \frac{1}{6} n(4n^2 + 9n + 4).$

17. $\sum\limits_{p=1}^{n} (p^2+7p-6) = \frac{n(n+1)(2n+1)}{6} + 7 \cdot \frac{n(n+1)}{2} - 6n.$ Put n=20.

$\sum\limits_{p=1}^{20} (p^2+7p-6) = \frac{20(21)(41)}{6} + 7 \cdot \frac{20(21)}{2} - 6(20) = 3220.$

21. $\sum\limits_{k=11}^{50} k^2 = \sum\limits_{k=1}^{50} k^2 - \sum\limits_{k=1}^{10} k^2 = \frac{50(50+1)(101)}{6} - \frac{10(11)(21)}{6} = 42,540.$

25. (a) $\sum\limits_{p=1}^{5} (2x_p - 3) = (2x_1-3) + (2x_2-3) + (2x_3-3) + (2x_4-3) + (2x_5-3)$

$= (-1) + (-7) + (3) + (11) + (5) = 11.$

(b) $\sum\limits_{p=1}^{5} (x_p+2)^2 = (x_1+2)^2 + (x_2+2)^2 + (x_3+2)^2 + (x_4+2)^2 + (x_5+2)^2$

$= (1+2)^2 + (-2+2)^2 + (3+2)^2 + (7+2)^2 + (4+2)^2 = 164.$

REVIEW EXERCISES ON CHAPTER - 7
_____

1. See answers in the text book.

5. Let the sequence be a, ar, ar^2, ...

Then $T_3 = ar^2 = 2$ and $T_6 = ar^2 = 0.25 = 1/4$ give r = 1/2 and a = 8.

The six terms of the G.P. are a, ar, ar^2, ... , ar^5 or

8, 4, 2, 1, 0.5 and 0.25.

9. The given sequence is in G.P. with a=3, r=2.

$$S_n = a(r^n-1)(r-1) = 3(2^n-1)/(2-1) = 3(2^n-1).$$

13. Here $S_n = 1530$, a = 100, n = 12 and d = ? $1 = T_n = ?$

$$S_n = (a/2)(a+\ell) \quad \text{gives} \quad 1530 = 6(1000 + \ell) \quad \text{or} \quad \ell = \$155.$$

$$\ell = a + (n-1)d \quad \text{gives} \quad 155 = 100 + 11d \quad \text{or} \quad d = \$5.$$

17. (a) $A = Pa_{\overline{n}|i} = 12,000 \, a_{\overline{20}|0.06} = 12,000(11.469921) = \$13,7639.05.$

(b) $A = Pa_{\overline{n}|i} = 12,000 a_{\overline{20}|0.08} = 12,000(9.818147) = \$117817.76.$

REVIEW TEST ON CHAPTER - 7

FILL IN THE BLANKS:

1. A given sequence T_1, T_2, T_3, T_4, ... is in

    (a) A.P. if _____ .

    (b) G.P. if _____ .

2. If a is the first term, d the common difference of an A.P., then

    (a) the nth term is given by T_n = _____ .

    (b) the sum to n terms is given by S_n = _____

    or S_n = _____ , where ℓ is the

    last term.

3. If a is the first term, r the common ratio of a G.P., then

    (a) the nth term is given by T_n = _____ .

    (b) the sum to n terms is given by S_n = _____ .

    (c) the sum to infinity is given by S = _____ , provided $|r|$ _____ .

4. For the sequence 2, 5, 8, ... the

    (a) 9th term is T_9 = _____ and the nth term is T_n = _____ .

    (b) sum to 15 terms is S_{15} = _____ .

    (c) sum to p terms is S_p = _____ .

5. The sequence 85 + 82 + 79 + ... + 13 has _____ terms and the sum of

    the sequence is given by S = _____ .

6. For the sequence 1, -2, 4, -8, ... , the

    (a) 9th term is T_9 = _____ and the pth term is T_p = _____.

    (b) sum to 10 terms is S_{10} = _____.

    (c) sum to p terms is S_p = _____.

7. The sequence 192 + 96 + 48 + ... + 6 has _____ terms and the sum of sequence is S = _____.

8. If the nth term of the sequence is T_n = 20 - 3n, then

    (a) the successive terms of the sequence are _____.

    (b) the sum to p terms of the sequence is _____.

9. If the nth term of a sequence is $3 \cdot 2^{2-n}$, then

    (a) the successive terms of the sequence are _____.

    (b) the sum to n terms of the sequence is S_n = _____.

    (c) the sum to infinite terms is S = _____.

10. If the sum to n terms of a sequence is $S_n = n^2 + 3n$, then

    (a) the nth term is given by T_n = _____.

    (b) the successive terms of the sequence are _____.

    (c) the sequence _____ (is or is not) in A.P.

11. If the sum to n terms of a sequence is $S_n = n^2 + 2^n - 1$, then the

    (a) nth term of the sequence is T_n = _____.

    (b) the successive terms of the sequence are _____.

    (c) the sequence is _____ (A.P., G.P., neither)

12. The sum of infinite geometric progression 2 - 1 + 0.5 - 0.25 + ... is given by S = _____.

13. If the first term and the sum of infinite terms of a G.P. are 2 and 3 respectively, the common ratio is given by r = _____.

14. If the common ratio and the sum to infinity of a G.P. are 2/3 and 15 respectively, then the first term of the G.P. is a = _____.

15. If $500 is deposited at the end of each year into a savings plan earning 6% interest per annum, the value of the plan at the end of 8 years is given by S = _____.

16. If John uses his savings of $150,000 to buy an annuity for 15 years from an insurance company which pays 8% interest per annum, then the amount John will receive each year is given by P = _____.

17. $\sum\limits_{k=1}^{n} k$ = _____ and $\sum\limits_{k=1}^{n} k^2$ = _____.

18. $\sum\limits_{k=5}^{27} x_k$ has _____ terms in the expansion.

19. If 4, a, b, c, -18 form A.P., the values of a, b, c are given by _____

20. If 54, p, q, 2 form a G.P., then p = _____ and q = _____.

SEE THE ANSWERS AT THE END OF THIS BOOK

EXERCISES 7.3

45. (a) The amount A owed on the mortgage after 5 years is the present value of P = $335.68 per month for the remaining 20 years or n = 240 months. Thus,

$A = P\{1-(1+i)^{-n}\}/i = (\$335.68)\{1 - (1.0075)^{-240}\}/(0.0075)$

$= \$37,309.14.$

(b) Here P = $335.68, n = 10 years = 120 (months remaining)

$A = P\{1 - (1+i)^{-n}\}/i = (\$335.68)\{1 - (1.0075)^{-120}\}/(0.0075)$

$= \$26,499.15.$

CHAPTER - 8

YOU SHOULD BE FAMILIAR WITH THE FOLLOWING TERMS:

Sample space, sample point, event, impossible event, certain event.

Venn diagram.

Union and intersection of two events.

Mutually exclusive events.

Complement of an event.

Probability of an outcome ; probabolity of an event.

Equally likely outcomes.

The probability formulas.

Conditional probability ; independent events, the multiplcation rule.

Bayes theorem.

Permutation, combinations, factorials.

The notatation $n!$, $_nP_r$ and $\binom{n}{r}$

Bernoulli trials, the binomial probability formula.

Binomial theorem, binomial coefficients.

OBJECTIVES

AFTER READING THIS CHAPTER YOU SHOULD BE ABLE TO DO THE FOLLOWING

1. Construct the sample space for a given experiment using either set
    notation or a Venn diagram.

2. Express an event, the complement of an event or the union or intersection
    of two events using either set notation or a Venn diagram.

3. Calculate probabilities of events in experiments with outcomes that
    are equally likely.

4. Use the probability formulas relating the probabilities of an event
    and its complement and relating the probabilities of the intersection
    and union of two events to the probabilities of the two events
    themselves.

5. Compute conditional probabilities ; use the multiplication rule to
    test whether two events are independent.

6. Use Bayes theorem to compute the posterior probabilities $P(B_k|A)$ given the prior probabilities $P(A|B_k)$.

7. Calculate the numbers of permutations or combinations of a given size from a given set of objects. Use these quantities to count the numbers of outcomes for given events and experiments and hence to compute probabilities.

8. Use the binomial probability formula to compute probabilities related to the numbers of successes and failures in a sequence of Bernoulli trials. Solve applied problems involving binomial probabilities, in particular opinion poll problems.

9. Use the binomial theorem to expand an integer power of a binomial expression or to calculate any term in such an expansion.

SOLUTIONS TO ALTERNATE ODD PROBLEMS

EXERCISES - 8.1

1. {A, B, C, D, E} , where A, B, ... , E are the names of the five candidates.

5. {ABC, ACB, BCA, BAC, CAB, CBA} where A, B, C are the names of the sales people.

9. The sample space consists of 13 points, one for each spade card in the deck.

13. See sample space in solved Example 7 of section 8.2. The events that make the sum 7 **are** {(6,1), (5,2), (4,3), (3,4), (2,5),(1,6)}.

17. $E_1 \cup E_3$ = {x|x is a heart or is of denomination less than 7 or both} is the event that the drawn card is either a heart or is of denomination less than 7.

21. E_2' = {x|x is a red card}is the event that the drawn card is <u>not</u> black.

25. The given events are not mutually exclusive, because the card can be a 4 as well as a spade.

29. (a) $F' \cap U$ (b) $U' \cap E'$ (c) $(U \cap E') \cap F$ (d) $(U' \cap E) \cap F'$.

EXERCISES - 8.2

1. A card can be drawn out of a deck of 52 cards in 52 ways and a heart can be drawn out of 13 in 13 ways. Thus n=52, k=13 and P(heart) = k/n = 13/52 = 1/4.

5. Let A = the event that the drawn card is a 4 or a 5.
   and H = event that the drawn card is a heart.
   P(A) = 8/52, P(H) = 13/52 and P(A $\cap$ H) = 2/52.
   P(A $\cup$ H) = P(A) + P(H) - P(A $\cap$ H) = 8/52 + 13/52 - 2/52 = 19/52.

9. If B = boy, G = girl, then the sample space is
{BBB, BBG, BGB, GBB, BGG, GBG, GGB, GGG}, where BGB implies that
first child is a boy, second a girl and the third is a boy.
Here n=8. The event 'at least one boy' consists of 7 sample points.
Thus, P(at least one boy) = 7/8.

13. Refer to sample space for solved example 7 of this section.
E_1 = sum 6 = {(5,1), (4,2), (3,3), (?,4), (1,5)} and
E_2 = sum 8 = {(6,2), (5,3), (4,4), (3,5), (2,6)} . Thus $P(E_1)$ = 5/36.
$P(E_2)$ = 5/36. Also $E_1 \cap E_2$ = $\emptyset$, i.e. $P(E_1 \cap E_2)$ = 0
P(sum 6 or 8) = $P(E_1 \cup E_2)$ = $P(E_1) + P(E_2) - P(E_1 \cap E_2)$ = 5/36+5/56-0

17. From the Venn diagram, we have: = 5/18.

(a) $P(E_2')$ = 1 - $P(E_2)$ = 1 - 0.45 = 0.55

(b) $P(E_1 \cup E_2)$ = $P(E_1) + P(E_2)$ = 0.3 + 0.45 = 0.75

(c) $P(E_1 \cap E_2)$ = 0

(d) $P(E_1 \cap E_2')$ = $P(E_1)$ = 0.3

(e) $P(E_1' \cap E_2')$ = 1 - $P(E_1)$ - $P(E_2)$ = 0.25

(f) $P(E_1' \cup E_2')$ = P(S) = 1 , where S is the whole sample space.

21. The event 9 or more consists of the 10 sample points, namely:

(3,6), (4,5), (5,4), (6,3), (4,6), (5,5), (6,4), (5,6), (6,5) and (6,6)
Thus, P(9 or more) = 10/36 = 5/18 and P(not 9 or more) = 1 - 5/18
= 13/18.

25. P(5,6,7) = 7/10 and P(0,1,2,3,4,5) = 2/5.

(a) P(0,1,2,3,4) = 1 - P(5,6,7) = 1 - 7/10 = 3/10.

(b) Thus, P(5) = P(0,1,2,3,4,5) - P(0,1,2,3,4) = 2/5 - 3/10 = 1/10.

(c) P(6,7) = P(5,6,7) - P(5) = 7/10 - 1/10 = 6/10 = 3/5.

(d) Not sufficient information to calculate P(7).

29. (a) $E_1 \cap E_2$ = is the shaded region

$E_1 \cap E_2'$ = is the region where
lines are drawn.

Clearly E_1 = $(E_1 \cap E_2) \cup (E_1 \cap E_2')$

Also the events $E_1 \cap E_2$ and $E_1 \cap E_2'$ are mutually exclusive.

Thus, $P(E_1)$ = $P[(E_1 \cap E_2) \cup (E_1 \cap E_2')]$ = $P(E_1 \cap E_2) + P(E_1 \cap E_2')$
.... (i).

(b) From the formula in (a) part, it follows that

$$P(E_2' \cap E_1) + P(E_2' \cap E_1') = P(E_2') = 1 - P(E)$$

from which the result follows.

33. Here $P(T) = 180/200 = 0.9$, $P(C) = 150/200 = 0.75$, $P(C \cap T') = 14/200$
= 0.07.

	T	T'	
C		0.07	0.75
C'			
	0.09		1

$\Rightarrow$

	T	T'	
C	0.68	0.07	0.75
C'	0.22	0.03	0.25
	0.90	0.10	1

(a) $P(T' \cap C') = 0.03$ (b) $P(T \cap C) = 0.68$ (c) $P(T \cap C') = 0.22$

(d) $P(T \cup C') = P(T) + P(C') - P(T \cap C') = 0.9 + 0.25 - 0.22 = 0.93$

(e) $P(T' \cup C) = P(T') + P(C) - P(T' \cap C) = 0.1 + 0.75 - 0.07 = 0.78$

(f) $P(T' \cup C') = P(T') + P(C') - P(T' \cap C') = 0.1 + 0.25 - 0.03 = 0.32$.

EXERCISES - 8.3

1. S = second coin falls heads, A = both coins fall alike = {HH, TT};
           $P(S \, / \, A) = 1/2$.

5. First dice shown 5 spots consists of x is sample points;

   (5,1), (5,2), (5,3), ... , (5,6). But these 3 sample points have sum
   9 or more. These points are (5,4), (5,5), (5,6). Thus the prob. is
   3/6 = 1/2.

9. Look at the sample space listed on page 277 of the text. There are
   26 sample points where the sum of the scores is 6 or more and out of
   these 26 there are 20 sample points where at least one of the dice
   shows 5 or 6. Thus the prob. is 20/26.

13. First coin falls head = {HHH, HHT, HTH, HTT} Reqd. prob. 3/4.

17. (a) (150/500)(149/499)   (b) (350/500)(349/499).

21. A = the customer lives in the urban
   area; B = customer spends over $200
   on the credit card. Then
   $P(A) = 0.40$, $P(B) = 0.30$ and $P(A \cap B)$
   = 0.10. Complete the table on the right
   as shown.

	A	A'	
B	0.1	0.2	0.25
B'	0.3	0.4	0.7
	0.4	0.6	1

   $P(A \mid B') = P(A \cap B')/P(B') = (0.3)/(0.7) = 3/7$.

25. $P(S) = 3/5$ $P(C) = 1/20$ $P(S \cap C) = 1/25$.
   Since $P(S \cap C) \neq P(S) \cdot P(C)$ the events C and S are not independent.

EXERCISES - 8.4

1. P(B & E training) = 0.3. P(Becoming manager) = 0.45

P(Becoming manager | B & E training) = 0.7.

therefore P(Becoming manager | B & E training) = (0.7)(0.3) = 0.21

P(B & E training | Becoming manager) = (0.21)/(0.45) = 7/15.

5.

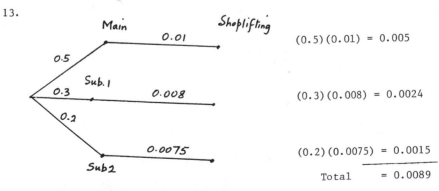

$$P(\text{Old line} \mid \text{Rejected}) = \frac{0.04}{0.04 + 0.024} = \frac{5}{8}.$$

9.

$$P(3B,5W \mid \text{Chosen ball is black}) = \frac{3/24}{3/24 + 4/24 + 5/24} = \frac{1}{4}$$

$$P(4B, 4W \mid \text{Chosen ball is black}) = \frac{4/24}{3/24 + 4/24 + 5/24} = \frac{1}{3}$$

$$P(5B,3W \mid \text{Chosen ball is black}) = \frac{5/24}{3/24 + 4/24 + 5/24} = \frac{5}{12}.$$

13.

Proportion at main store = 0.005/0.0089 = 50/89 = 0.56.

59

EXERCISES - 8.5

1. $_{10}P_2 = 10 \cdot 9 = 90$ 5. $_nP_2 = n(n-1)$ 9. $\binom{15}{0} = 1$

13. $(20!)/(18!) = 20 \cdot 19 \cdot (18!)/(18!) = 20 \cdot 19 = 380.$

17. $(n+1)! = 20n$ gives $(n+1) \cdot (n!) = 20n!$ or $n+1 = 20$ or $n = 19$.

21. P(king) = 13/52 , P(queen) = 13/52. Since the first card is replaced before the second is drawn, the events drawing of a king, drawing of a queen are independent. Thus, P(king, queen) = P(king)·P(queen) = 13/52 · 13/52 = 1/16.

25. 6 persons can be selected from a group of 30 persons (20 smokers and 10 non-smokers) in $\binom{30}{6}$ ways. Thus, $n = \binom{30}{6}$. We want the sample to contain 4 smokers (and 2 non-smokers). Now 4 smokers out of 20 and 2 non-smokers out of 10 can be selected in $\binom{20}{4}\binom{10}{2}$ ways. Thus, $k = \binom{20}{4}\binom{10}{4}$, and prob. $= \binom{20}{4}\binom{10}{2}/\binom{30}{6} = 969/2639.$

29. Here 3 drivers out of 5 can be selected in $\binom{5}{3} = 10$ ways and 3 cabs out of 4 can be selected in $\binom{4}{3} = 4$ ways. Assuming any drivers can drive any cab, the single request for 3 cabs and 3 drivers can be met in $(10)(4) = 40$ ways.

33. 4 astronauts out of 12 can be selected in $\binom{12}{4}$ ways. Thus, $n = \binom{12}{4}$. There are 7 experienced and 5 non-experienced astronauts. The event of selecting 4 astronauts with at least 2 experienced consists of either 4 experienced, 0 unexperienced or 3 experienced and 1 unexperienced or 2 experienced and 2 unexperienced. These selections can be made in

$$k = \binom{7}{4}\binom{5}{0} + \binom{7}{3}\binom{5}{1} + \binom{7}{2}\binom{5}{2} \text{ ways. Thus,}$$

$$\text{prob.} = k/n = \binom{7}{4}\binom{5}{0} + \binom{7}{3}\binom{5}{1} + \binom{7}{2}\binom{5}{2} / \binom{12}{4} = 28/33.$$

37. There are 11 letters in the word SHAKESPEARE. The prob. of getting each letter correct out of 26 alphabets is 1/26. Thus, the reqd. prob. is $(1/26)^{11} = 26^{-11}$.

41. Total number of selections, $n = \binom{9}{3} = 9 \cdot 8 \cdot 7/1 \cdot 2 \cdot 3 = 84.$

(a) No. of ways of selecting 3 white rats $k = \binom{5}{3} = 10.$
Thus, probability = k/n = 10/84 = 5/42.

(b) No. of ways of selecting 2 white and 1 brown rat,

$$k = \binom{5}{2}\binom{4}{1} = 10 \cdot 4 = 40. \text{ Thus, probability} = k/n = \frac{40}{84} = \frac{10}{21}.$$

(c) No. of ways of selecting 3 brown rats, $k = \binom{4}{3} = 4.$
Thus, probability = k/n = 4/84 = 1/21.

EXERCISES - 8.6

1. p = prob. of head = 1/2, q = 1 - 1/2 = 1/2. Here n=4. r = 1 (one head)

$$P(1) = \binom{n}{r} p^r q^{n-r} = \binom{4}{1} pq^3 = \binom{4}{1} (1/2)(1/2)^3 = 4/16 = 1/4.$$

5. p = prob. of left-handed child = 1/5, q = 1-p = 1 - 1/5 = 4/5.
Here n=5. $P(2) = \binom{5}{2} p^2 q^3 = \binom{5}{2} (1/5)^2 (4/5)^3 = 128/625.$

9. Here p = 0.25, q = 1 - 0.25 = 0.75 , n=8, r > 2.
$P(r < 2) = 1 - P(r \le 2) = 1 - \{P(0) + P(1) + P(2)\}$

$$= 1 - \binom{8}{0}(1/4)^0(3/4) - \binom{8}{1}(1/4)^1(3/4)^7 - \binom{8}{2}(1/4)^2(3/4)^6$$

$$= 1 - 61(3^6/4^8) \approx 0.32.$$

13. $\binom{10}{5} p^5 q^5 = \frac{10}{5} (1/2)^5 (1/2)^5 = 63/256 \approx 0.25$

17. p = prob. of making an error = 1/5, q = 4/5, n = 8.

(a) $P(r=0) = \binom{8}{0} p^0 q^8 = q^8 = (4/5)^8$

(b) $P(r \ge 2) = 1 - P(0) - P(1) = 1 - q^8 - 8pq^7 = 1 - (4/5)^8 - 8(1/5)(4/5)^8.$

21. p = prob. of a defective can = 1/6, q = 5/6

(i) n = 2 ; $P(0) = \binom{2}{0} p^0 q^2 = (5/6)^2 = 25/36$

(ii) n=4 ; $P(r \ge 2) = 1 - P(0) - P(1)$

$$= 1 - \binom{4}{0}(5/6)^4 - \binom{4}{1}(1/6)(5/6)^3$$

$$= 1 - 9(125)/1296 \approx 0.132.$$

25. $\binom{10}{2}(0.02)^2(0.98)^8 = 0.0153.$

29. Prob. of 6, 7 or 8 cures = $\binom{8}{8}(0.75)^8 + \binom{8}{7}(0.75)^7(0.25) +$

$$\binom{8}{6}(0.75)^6(0.25)^2 = 0.679.$$

EXERCISES - 8.7

1. $(a+b)^7 = a^7 + \binom{7}{1}a^6b + \binom{7}{2}a^5b^2 + \binom{7}{3}a^4b^3 + \binom{7}{4}a^3b^4 + \binom{7}{5}a^2b^5 +$

$$\binom{7}{6}ab^6 + \binom{7}{7}b^7$$

$$= a^7 + 7a^6b + 21a^5b^2 + 35a^4b^3 + 35a^3b^4 + 21a^2b^5 + 3ab^6 + b^7.$$

5. $(\frac{2x}{3} + \frac{3}{2x})^5 = (2x/3)^5 + 5(2x/3)^4(3/2x) + 10(2x/3)^3(3/2x)^2$

$$+ 10(2x/3)^2(3/2x)^3 + 5(2x/3)(3/2x)^4 + (3/2x)^5$$

$$= 32x^5/243 + 40x^3/27 + 20x/3 + 15/x + 135/8x^3 + 243/32x^6.$$

9. $(2p-3q)^5 = (2p)^5 + 5(2p)^4(-3q) + 10(2p)^3(-3q)^2 + 10(2p)^2(-3q)^3$

$$+ 5(2p)(-3q)^4 + (-3q)^5$$

$$= 32p^5 - 240p^4q + 720p^3q^2 - 1080p^2q^3 + 810pq^4 - 243q^5.$$

13. $T_7 = T_{6+1} = \binom{9}{6} (3x)^{9-6}(y/2)^6 = 567x^3y^6/16.$

17. 5th term from end = 6th term from beginning $= \binom{9}{5}\left(\frac{x^3}{2}\right)^4\left(\frac{2}{x^2}\right)^5 = 252x^2.$

21. 5th & 6th terms $= \binom{9}{4} (3x)^5(-x^3/6) + \binom{9}{5}(3x)^4(-x^3/6)^5$

$$= \frac{189}{8} x^{17} - \frac{21}{16} x^{19}.$$

25. $(1 + ax)^n = 1 + n(ax) + \frac{n(n-1)}{2} (ax)^2 + \dots$ Therefore, $na = 4$,

$\frac{n(n-1)}{2} a^2 = 7.$ Divide second equation by first: $(n-1)a = 14/4 = 7/2$

Therefore, $a = na - (n-1)a = 4 - 7/2 = 1/2.$ Therefore, $n=8$.

REVIEW EXERCISES ON CHAPTER - 8

1. See answers in the text.

5. $\binom{8}{6} = \binom{8}{8-6} = \binom{8}{2} = \frac{8 \cdot 7}{2 \cdot 1} = 28.$

9. $\binom{15}{4}/\binom{14}{3} = (\frac{15 \cdot 14 \cdot 13 \cdot 12}{4 \cdot 3 \cdot 2 \cdot 1})/(\frac{14 \cdot 13 \cdot 12}{3 \cdot 2 \cdot 1}) = 15/4.$

13. $\frac{6 \cdot 5 \cdot 4}{1 \cdot 2 \cdot 3} \cdot \frac{5 \cdot 4}{1 \cdot 2} + \frac{6 \cdot 5}{1 \cdot 2} \cdot 5 + 6 \cdot 1 = 200 + 75 + 6 = 281.$

17. (a) $\binom{4}{2}/\binom{10}{2} = 2/15$ (b) $\binom{6}{2}/\binom{10}{2} = 1/3$

(c) $\left[\binom{4}{1}\binom{6}{1} + \binom{4}{2}\right]/\binom{10}{2} = 30/45 = 2/3.$

21. S = smoke, D = drink. Then

$P(S \cup D) = P(S) + P(D) - P(S \cap D)$ gives $0.6 = 0.4 + 0.32 - P(S \cap D)$
or $P(S \cap D) = 0.12.$

25.　p = prob. of girl = 1/2, q = 1/2, n = 8.

Reqd. prob. = P(0) + P(1) + P(2) + P(3)

$$= (1/2)^8 + \binom{8}{1}(1/2)^8 + \binom{8}{2}(1/2)^8 + \binom{8}{3}(1/2)^8 = 93/156.$$

29.　S = smoker, L = living to be 75, then we are given that:
P(S) = 0.60, P(S') = 0.40, P(L | S) = 0.25 and P(L | S') = 0.40 and
we want to find P(S' | L).
P(L | S') = 0.4 gives P(L ∧ S') = (0.4)P(S') = (0.4)(0.4) = 0.16
P(L | S) = 0.25 gives P(L ∧ S) = (0.25)P(S) = (0.25)(0.6) = 0.15

P(L) = P(L ∧ S) + P(L ∧ S') = 0.15 + 0.16 = 0.31
Now P(S' | L) = P(S' ∧ L)/P(L) = (0.16)/(0.31) = 16/31.

33.　$_{36}P_{30}$　;　　　$_{30}P_{26}$

37.　Here p = prob. of failing to make a sale = 1/3 ; q = 2/3; n=4

$$P(3) = \binom{4}{3}p^3 q = 4(1/3)^4 (2/3) = 8/81.$$

41.

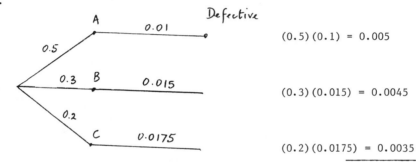

$$P(A \mid \text{Defective}) = \frac{0.005}{0.013} = \frac{5}{13} .$$

63

FILL IN THE BLANKS:

1. The set S of all possible outcomes of an experiment is called a _____ and each outcome of this set is called a _____.

2. If two coins are tossed, then the sample space is given by S = _____.

3. If two dice are rolled, then the sample space consists of _____ points.

4. A subset E of the sample space is called a(an) _____.

5. If E = Ø (empty set), then the event E is called a(an) _____ event.

6. If E = S, the whole sample space, the event E is called a(an) _____ event.

7. If $E_1 \cap E_2$ = Ø, then the two events E_1 and E_2 are _____.

8. $P(E_1 \cup E_2)$ = _____.

9. If $P(E_1 \cap E_2) = P(E_1) \cdot P(E_2)$, then the events E_1 and E_2 are _____.

10. If $P(E_1 \cup E_2) = P(E_1) + P(E_2)$, then the events E_1 and E_2 are _____.

11. $P(E_1 \mid E_2)$ = _____ and $P(E_1 \mid E_2) \cdot P(E_2)$ = _____.

12. If E' is the complement of the event E, then P(E) + P(E') = _____, P(E $\cap$ E') = _____ and P(E $\cup$ E') = _____ .

13. If E_1 and E_2 are two events with $P(E_1)$ = 0.45, $P(E_2)$ = 0.7 and $P(E_1 \cap E_2)$ = 0.3, then $P(E_1 \cup E_2)$ = _____.

14. If $P(E_1)$ = 0.4, $P(E_1 \cap E_2)$ = 0.35 and $P(E_1 \cup E_2)$ = 0.7, then $P(E_2)$ = _____.

15. If $P(E_1)$ = 0.5, $P(E_2)$ = 0.65 and $P(E_1 \cup E_2)$ = 0.9, then $P(E_1 \cap E_2)$ = _____.

16. If E_1 and E_2 are any two events of a sample space , then (by using Venn diagrams),

    (a) $P(E_1 \cap E_2) + P(E_1 \cap E_2')$ = _____

    (b) $P(E_1' \cap E_2) + P(E_2' \cap E_1')$ = _____.

17. If A and B are two events with P(A) = 0.6, P(B) = 0.5 and P(A $\cap$ B)=0.36 then (by completing the adjoining table)

(a) $P(A \cap B') = $ _____

(b) $P(A' \cap B') = $ _____

(c) $P(A' \cup B') = $ _____

(d) $P(A' \cup B) = $ _____

	A	A'
B		
B'		

(e) $P(A \mid B) = $ _____

(f) $P(B \mid A) = $ _____

(g) $P(A \mid B') = $ _____

(h) $P(B \mid A') = $ _____

(i) $P(A' \mid B') = $ _____

(j) $P(B' \mid A) = $ _____ .

*18. If $P(A \cup B) = P(A) + P(B)P(A')$, then the events A and B are _____ (independent, mutually exclusive or neither).

19. If A and B are any two events of a sample space S, then by Bayes Theorem, $P(B \mid A) = P(A \mid B) \cdot$ _____ .

20. If n and r are positive integer and $r \leq n$ then

(a) $n! = $ _____ .

(b) $_nP_r = $ _____

(c) $\binom{n}{r} = $ _____ .

(d) $\binom{n}{r} = \binom{n}{\underline{\quad}}$

(e) $\binom{n}{n} = $ _____

(f) $\binom{n}{0} = $ _____ .

21. (a) $0! = $ _____

(b) $3! = $ _____

(c) $8!/7! = $ _____ .

(d) $_8P_2 = $ _____

(c) $_8P_8 = $ _____

(f) $\binom{8}{2} = $ _____ .

(g) $\binom{20}{18} = \binom{20}{\underline{\quad}}$

(h) $\binom{50}{50} = $ _____ .

22. If p is the probability of success and $q = 1-p$, the probability of failure in a single Bernoulli trial, then the probability of r successes in n trials is given by $P(x=r) = $ _____ .

23. A coin is tossed 5 times. Then $p = $ _____ , $q = $ _____ and the probability of getting (a) 3 heads is $P(x=3) = $ _____ ;

(b) at least 3 heads is $P(x \geq 3) = $ _____ .

24. If n is a positive integer, then by binomial theorem,

(a) $(a+b)^n = $ _____ .

(b) the $(r+1)$th term in the expansion is $T_{r+1} = $ _____ .

(c) the expansion in (a) has _____ terms.

25. Expansion of $(x-y)^5$ is _____ .

SEE ANSWERS AT THE END OF THIS BOOK.

CHAPTER - 9

YOU SHOULD BE FAMILIAR WITH THE FOLLOWING TERMS:

Matrix, elements of a matrix, row, column; size of a matrix

Row matrix (row vector), Column matrix (column vector).

Zero matrix, identity matrix.

Square matrix; diagonal elements.

Scalar multiplication of a matrix ; addition and subtraction of matrices.

Multiplication of matrices (matrix product).

Coefficient matrix (of system of algebraic equations), variable vector, value vector.

Augmented matrix ; row operations ; method of row reduction.

Singular system ; consistent and inconsistent system.

Reduced form of augmented matrix.

OBJECTIVES

AFTER READING THIS CHAPTER YOU SHOULD BE ABLE TO DO THE FOLLOWING:

1. Find the size of a given matrix ; identify particular elements in a matrix ; test two matrix for equality.

2. Multiply a given matrix by a real number.

3. Add or subtract two given matrices (when possible).

4. Arrange appropriate data as a matrix and interpret certain practical questions in terms of matrix operations.

5. Test two matrices to see whether their product can be formed. Multiply two matrices of appropriate sizes.

6. Express a system of linear algebraic equations as the matrix equation $\underline{A}\,\underline{X} = \underline{B}$.

7. Use the method of row reduction to

    (a) determine whether a system of linear equations has a unique solution, no solution or an infinite number of solutions.

    (b) determine the solution if a unique solution exists.

EXERCISES - 9-1

1. See answers in the text book.

5. If $j = i$, then $c_{ij} = -c_{ji}$ implies $c_{ii} = -c_{ii}$ or $c_{ii} = 0$

i.e. $c_{11} = c_{22} = c_{33} = 0$. If $c_{12} = x$, then $c_{21} = -c_{12} = -x$.

Similarly if $c_{13} = y = -c_{31}$, $c_{23} = -c_{32} = z$ (say). Then the matrix

is of the form: $\begin{bmatrix} 0 & x & y \\ -x & 0 & z \\ 0 & -z & 0 \end{bmatrix}$, where x, y, z are any real numbers.

9. $\begin{bmatrix} 2 & 1 & 3 \\ -1 & 4 & 7 \end{bmatrix} + \begin{bmatrix} 0 & -1 & 2 \\ 1 & 2 & -8 \end{bmatrix} = \begin{bmatrix} 2+0 & 1-1 & 3+2 \\ -1+1 & 4+2 & 7-8 \end{bmatrix} = \begin{bmatrix} 2 & 0 & 5 \\ 0 & 6 & -1 \end{bmatrix}$

13. $2\begin{bmatrix} 1 & 2 & 3 \\ 2 & -1 & 0 \\ 4 & 5 & 6 \end{bmatrix} + 3\begin{bmatrix} 0 & -1 & 2 \\ 3 & 2 & -4 \\ -1 & 0 & 3 \end{bmatrix} = \begin{bmatrix} 2 & 4 & 6 \\ 4 & -2 & 0 \\ 8 & 10 & 12 \end{bmatrix} + \begin{bmatrix} 0 & -3 & 6 \\ 9 & 6 & -12 \\ -3 & 0 & 9 \end{bmatrix}$

$= \begin{bmatrix} 2+0 & 4-3 & 6+6 \\ 4+9 & -2+6 & 0-12 \\ 8-3 & 0+0 & 12+9 \end{bmatrix} = \begin{bmatrix} 2 & 1 & 12 \\ 13 & 4 & -12 \\ 5 & 0 & 21 \end{bmatrix}$

17. $\begin{bmatrix} 4 & x & 3 \\ y & -1 & 2 \end{bmatrix} = \begin{bmatrix} y-1 & 2-x & 3 \\ 5 & z+1 & 2 \end{bmatrix}$

gives $y-1 = 4$ or $y = 5$. $x = 2-x$ or $x=1$ and $z+1 = -1$ or $z = -2$.

21. Adding the two matrices on the leftside, we have:

$\begin{bmatrix} x+1 & 3+t & 3 \\ 5 & 3 & y+x \\ 1+u & z+y & -1 \end{bmatrix} = \begin{bmatrix} 2 & 7 & v+1 \\ 5 & w-2 & 3 \\ 0 & 5 & -1 \end{bmatrix}$ This gives: $x+1 = 2$ or $x=1$, $3+t=7$ or $t=4$; $3=v+1$ or $v=2$, $3 = w-2$ or $w=5$, $y+x = 3$.

or $y = 3-x = 3-1 = 2$, $1+u = 0$ or $u = -1$, $z+y = 5$ or $z = 5-y = 5-2=3$. Thus, $x=1$, $y=2$, $z=3$, $u=-1$, $v=2$, $w=5$ and $t=4$.

25. (a)

The new
transport
matrix is
$\begin{bmatrix} 10+1 & 12+1 & 15+1 \\ 13+1 & 10+1 & 12+1 \\ 8+1 & 15+1 & 6+1 \\ 16+1 & 9+1 & 10+1 \end{bmatrix} = \begin{bmatrix} 11 & 13 & 16 \\ 14 & 11 & 13 \\ 9 & 16 & 7 \\ 17 & 10 & 11 \end{bmatrix}$

(b) The new transport matrix is:

$(1.20)\begin{bmatrix} 10 & 12 & 15 \\ 13 & 10 & 12 \\ 8 & 15 & 6 \\ 16 & 9 & 10 \end{bmatrix} = \begin{bmatrix} 12 & 14.4 & 18 \\ 15.6 & 12 & 14.4 \\ 9.6 & 18 & 7.2 \\ 19.2 & 10.8 & 12 \end{bmatrix}$

29. (a) The required matrix is the sum of given two matrices:

$$\begin{bmatrix} 65 & 64 & 46 \\ 97 & 45 & 34 \\ 37 & 50 & 57 \end{bmatrix}$$

(b) The required matrix is given by

$$(1.5)\begin{bmatrix} 30 & 34 & 20 \\ 45 & 20 & 16 \\ 14 & 26 & 25 \end{bmatrix} + (1.25)\begin{bmatrix} 35 & 30 & 26 \\ 52 & 25 & 18 \\ 23 & 24 & 32 \end{bmatrix}$$

$$= \begin{bmatrix} 88.75 & 88.50 & 62.5 \\ 132.5 & 61.25 & 46.5 \\ 49.75 & 69 & 77.5 \end{bmatrix}$$

EXERCISES - 9.2

1, 5. See answers in the text.

9.

$$\begin{bmatrix} 3 & 0 & 1 \\ 2 & 4 & 0 \end{bmatrix}\begin{bmatrix} 4 \\ 5 \\ 6 \end{bmatrix} = \begin{bmatrix} 3\cdot4 + 0\cdot5 + 1\cdot6 \\ 2\cdot4 + 4\cdot5 + 0\cdot6 \end{bmatrix} = \begin{bmatrix} 18 \\ 28 \end{bmatrix}$$

13.

$$\begin{bmatrix} 2 & 3 & 1 \\ -1 & 2 & -3 \\ 4 & 5 & 6 \end{bmatrix}\begin{bmatrix} 1 \\ 2 \\ 3 \end{bmatrix} = \begin{bmatrix} 2 + 6 + 3 \\ -1 + 4 - 9 \\ 4 + 10 + 18 \end{bmatrix} = \begin{bmatrix} 11 \\ -6 \\ 32 \end{bmatrix}$$

17. Given product =

$$\begin{bmatrix} 4 & 1 & -2 \\ -3 & 2 & 1 \end{bmatrix}\begin{bmatrix} 1 & 8 \\ 4 & 1 \\ 0 & 0 \end{bmatrix} = \begin{bmatrix} 8 & 33 \\ 5 & -22 \end{bmatrix}$$

21. (a)

$$\underline{A} + \underline{B} = \begin{bmatrix} 3 & 1 \\ 0 & 2 \end{bmatrix} \text{ and } (\underline{A} + \underline{B})^2 = \begin{bmatrix} 3 & 1 \\ 0 & 2 \end{bmatrix}\begin{bmatrix} 3 & 1 \\ 0 & 2 \end{bmatrix} = \begin{bmatrix} 9 & 5 \\ 0 & 4 \end{bmatrix}$$

(b)

$$\underline{A}^2 + 2\underline{A}\,\underline{B} + \underline{B}^2 = \begin{bmatrix} 1 & 2 \\ 3 & 4 \end{bmatrix}\begin{bmatrix} 1 & 2 \\ 3 & 4 \end{bmatrix} + 2\begin{bmatrix} 1 & 2 \\ 3 & 4 \end{bmatrix}\begin{bmatrix} 2 & -1 \\ -3 & -2 \end{bmatrix}$$

$$+ \begin{bmatrix} 2 & -1 \\ -3 & -2 \end{bmatrix}\begin{bmatrix} 2 & -1 \\ -3 & -2 \end{bmatrix} = \begin{bmatrix} 7 & 10 \\ 15 & 22 \end{bmatrix} + 2\begin{bmatrix} -4 & -5 \\ -6 & -11 \end{bmatrix} + \begin{bmatrix} 7 & 0 \\ 0 & 7 \end{bmatrix} = \begin{bmatrix} 6 & 0 \\ 3 & 7 \end{bmatrix}$$

(c) No; $(\underline{A} + \underline{B})^2 \neq \underline{A}^2 + 2\underline{A}\,\underline{B} + \underline{B}^2$

25. $\underline{A}$ must be of size : 1×2. Let A = [x y]. Then,

$$[5 \ \ 3] = \underline{A}\begin{bmatrix} 2 & 1 \\ 1 & 0 \end{bmatrix} = [x \ \ y]\begin{bmatrix} 2 & 1 \\ 1 & 0 \end{bmatrix} = [2x+y \ \ x \ ]. \text{ Thus,}$$

$2x + y = 5$, x=3 or x=3, y = -1 or $\underline{A} = [x \ \ y] = [3 \ \ -1]$.

29. $\begin{bmatrix} 2 & 3 \\ 1 & 4 \end{bmatrix} \begin{bmatrix} x \\ y \end{bmatrix} = \begin{bmatrix} 7 \\ 5 \end{bmatrix}$

33. $\begin{bmatrix} 2 & 1 & 0 & -1 \\ 0 & 3 & 2 & 4 \\ 1 & -2 & 4 & 1 \end{bmatrix} \begin{bmatrix} x \\ y \\ z \\ u \end{bmatrix} = \begin{bmatrix} 0 \\ 5 \\ 12 \end{bmatrix}$

37. $\underline{A}^2 = \begin{bmatrix} 1 & 0 \\ 0 & 1 \end{bmatrix} \begin{bmatrix} 1 & 0 \\ 0 & 1 \end{bmatrix} = \begin{bmatrix} 1 & 0 \\ 0 & 1 \end{bmatrix} = \underline{A}$; $A^3 = \underline{A} \cdot \underline{A}^2 = \begin{bmatrix} 1 & 0 \\ 0 & 1 \end{bmatrix} \begin{bmatrix} 1 & 0 \\ 0 & 1 \end{bmatrix} = \begin{bmatrix} 1 & 0 \\ 0 & 1 \end{bmatrix} = \underline{A}$

41.

$\begin{bmatrix} 5 & 8 & 4 & 10 \end{bmatrix} \begin{bmatrix} 650 \\ 550 \\ 500 \\ 300 \end{bmatrix} = 12,650.$

45. (a) $\underline{A} = \begin{bmatrix} 0 & 1 & 0 & 0 \\ 1 & 0 & 1 & 1 \\ 0 & 1 & 0 & 1 \\ 0 & 1 & 1 & 0 \end{bmatrix}$, $\underline{A}^2 = \begin{bmatrix} 1 & 0 & 1 & 1 \\ 0 & 3 & 1 & 1 \\ 1 & 1 & 2 & 1 \\ 1 & 1 & 1 & 2 \end{bmatrix}$

For example, the 22-element in $\underline{A}^2$ gives the number of routes from vertex 2 to itself passing through just one intermediate.

(b) $\underline{A} = \begin{bmatrix} 0 & 1 & 0 & 0 & 1 \\ 1 & 0 & 1 & 1 & 0 \\ 0 & 1 & 0 & 1 & 0 \\ 0 & 1 & 1 & 0 & 1 \\ 1 & 0 & 0 & 1 & 0 \end{bmatrix}$, $\underline{A}^2 = \begin{bmatrix} 2 & 0 & 1 & 2 & 0 \\ 0 & 3 & 1 & 1 & 2 \\ 1 & 1 & 2 & 1 & 1 \\ 2 & 1 & 1 & 3 & 0 \\ 0 & 2 & 1 & 0 & 2 \end{bmatrix}$

The ij-element in $\underline{A}^3$ gives the number of routes from vertex i to vertex j passing through exactly 2 intermediate vertices.

EXERCISES - 9.3

1. $\begin{bmatrix} 2 & 3 & | & 7 \\ 3 & -1 & | & 5 \end{bmatrix} \xrightarrow{(1/2)R_1} \begin{bmatrix} 1 & 3/2 & | & 7/2 \\ 3 & -1 & | & 5 \end{bmatrix} \xrightarrow{R_2 - 3R_1} \begin{bmatrix} 1 & 3/2 & | & 3/2 \\ 0 & -11/2 & | & -11/2 \end{bmatrix}$

$\xrightarrow{(2/11)R_2} \begin{bmatrix} 1 & 3/2 & | & 7/2 \\ 0 & 1 & | & 1 \end{bmatrix} \xrightarrow{R_1 - (3/2)R_2} \begin{bmatrix} 1 & 0 & | & 2 \\ 0 & 1 & | & 1 \end{bmatrix}$. Thus, x=2, y=1

5. $\begin{bmatrix} 1 & 1 & 1 & | & 6 \\ 2 & -1 & 3 & | & 9 \\ -1 & 2 & 1 & | & 6 \end{bmatrix} \begin{array}{c} R_2 - 2R_1 \\ \xrightarrow{} \\ R_3 + R_1 \end{array} \begin{bmatrix} 1 & 1 & 1 & | & 6 \\ 0 & -3 & 1 & | & -3 \\ 0 & 3 & 2 & | & 12 \end{bmatrix} \xrightarrow{(-1/3)R_2} \begin{bmatrix} 1 & 1 & 1 & | & 6 \\ 0 & 1 & -1/3 & | & 1 \\ 0 & 3 & 2 & | & 12 \end{bmatrix}$

$\begin{array}{c} R_1 - R_2 \\ \xrightarrow{} \\ R_3 - 3R_2 \end{array} \begin{bmatrix} 1 & 0 & 4/3 & | & 5 \\ 0 & 1 & -1/3 & | & 1 \\ 0 & 0 & 3 & | & 9 \end{bmatrix} \xrightarrow{(1/3)R_3} \begin{bmatrix} 1 & 0 & 4/3 & | & 5 \\ 0 & 1 & -1/3 & | & 1 \\ 0 & 0 & 1 & | & 3 \end{bmatrix}$

$\begin{array}{c} R_1-(4/3)R_3 \\ R_2+(1/3)R_3 \\ \xrightarrow{\hspace{1cm}} \end{array}$ $\begin{bmatrix} 1 & 0 & 0 & | & 1 \\ 0 & 1 & 0 & | & 2 \\ 0 & 0 & 1 & | & 3 \end{bmatrix}$. Thus, $x=1$, $y=2$, $z=3$.

9. Augmented matrix is

$\begin{bmatrix} 1 & -1 & 1 & | & -1 \\ 3 & 0 & -2 & | & -7 \\ 0 & 4 & 1 & | & 10 \end{bmatrix}$ $\xrightarrow{R_2-3R_1}$ $\begin{bmatrix} 1 & -1 & 1 & | & -1 \\ 0 & 3 & -5 & | & -4 \\ 0 & 4 & 1 & | & 10 \end{bmatrix}$ $\xrightarrow{(1/3)R_2}$ $\begin{bmatrix} 1 & -1 & 1 & | & -1 \\ 0 & 1 & -5/3 & | & -4/3 \\ 0 & 4 & 1 & | & 10 \end{bmatrix}$

$\begin{array}{c} R_1+R_2 \\ \hline R_3-4R_2 \end{array}$ $\begin{bmatrix} 1 & 0 & -2/3 & | & -7/3 \\ 0 & 1 & -5/3 & | & -4/3 \\ 0 & 0 & 23/3 & | & 46/3 \end{bmatrix}$ $\xrightarrow{(3/23)R_3}$ $\begin{bmatrix} 1 & 0 & -2/3 & | & -7/3 \\ 0 & 1 & -5/3 & | & -4/3 \\ 0 & 0 & 1 & | & 2 \end{bmatrix}$

$\begin{array}{c} R_1+(2/3)R_3 \\ \hline R_2+(5/3)R_3 \end{array}$ $\begin{bmatrix} 1 & 0 & 0 & | & -1 \\ 0 & 1 & 0 & | & 2 \\ 0 & 0 & 1 & | & 2 \end{bmatrix}$. Thus, $p = -1$, $q=2$, $r=2$.

13. Augmented matrix is:

$\begin{bmatrix} 1 & 1 & 1 & 0 & | & 1 \\ 2 & 3 & 0 & -1 & | & 3 \\ -1 & 0 & 2 & 3 & | & 3 \\ 0 & 2 & -1 & 1 & | & 5 \end{bmatrix}$ $\begin{array}{c} R_2-2R_1 \\ \xrightarrow{\hspace{1cm}} \\ R_3+R_1 \end{array}$ $\begin{bmatrix} 1 & 1 & 1 & 0 & | & 1 \\ 0 & 1 & -2 & -1 & | & 1 \\ 0 & 1 & 3 & 3 & | & 4 \\ 0 & 2 & -1 & 1 & | & 5 \end{bmatrix}$ $\begin{array}{c} R_1-R_2 \\ R_3-R_2 \\ \xrightarrow{\hspace{1cm}} \\ R_4-2R_2 \end{array}$

$\begin{bmatrix} 1 & 0 & 3 & 1 & | & 0 \\ 0 & 1 & -2 & -1 & | & 1 \\ 0 & 0 & 5 & 4 & | & 3 \\ 0 & 0 & 3 & 3 & | & 3 \end{bmatrix}$ $\begin{array}{c} (1/5)R_3 \\ \xrightarrow{\hspace{1cm}} \\ (1/3)R_4 \end{array}$ $\begin{bmatrix} 1 & 0 & 3 & 1 & | & 0 \\ 0 & 1 & -2 & -1 & | & 1 \\ 0 & 0 & 1 & 4/5 & | & 3/5 \\ 0 & 0 & 1 & 1 & | & 1 \end{bmatrix}$ $\begin{array}{c} R_1-3R_3 \\ R_2+2R_3 \\ \xrightarrow{\hspace{1cm}} \\ R_4-R_3 \end{array}$

$\begin{bmatrix} 1 & 0 & 0 & -7/5 & | & -9/5 \\ 0 & 1 & 0 & 3/5 & | & 11/5 \\ 0 & 0 & 1 & 4/5 & | & 3/5 \\ 0 & 0 & 0 & 1/5 & | & 2/5 \end{bmatrix}$ $\xrightarrow{5R_4}$ $\begin{bmatrix} 1 & 0 & 0 & -7/5 & | & -9/5 \\ 0 & 1 & 0 & 3/5 & | & 11/5 \\ 0 & 0 & 1 & 4/5 & | & 3/5 \\ 0 & 0 & 0 & 1 & | & 2 \end{bmatrix}$

$\begin{array}{c} R_1+(7/5)R_4 \\ R_2-(3/5)R_4 \\ \hline R_3-(4/5)R_4 \end{array}$ $\begin{bmatrix} 1 & 0 & 0 & 0 & | & 1 \\ 0 & 1 & 0 & 0 & | & 1 \\ 0 & 0 & 1 & 0 & | & -1 \\ 0 & 0 & 0 & 1 & | & 2 \end{bmatrix}$ Thus, $x=1$, $y=1$, $z = -1$ and $w=2$.

17. The given equations are: $p+2x = 25$ and $p-3x = 5$. The augmented matrix is:

$\begin{bmatrix} 1 & 2 & | & 25 \\ 1 & -3 & | & 5 \end{bmatrix}$ $\xrightarrow{R_2-R_1}$ $\begin{bmatrix} 1 & 2 & | & 25 \\ 0 & -5 & | & -20 \end{bmatrix}$ $\xrightarrow{(-1/5)R_2}$ $\begin{bmatrix} 1 & 2 & | & 25 \\ 0 & 1 & | & 4 \end{bmatrix}$

$\xrightarrow{R_1-2R_2}$ $\begin{bmatrix} 1 & 0 & | & 17 \\ 0 & 1 & | & 4 \end{bmatrix}$ Thus, $p=17$, $x=4$.

21. Let x units of A, y units of B and z units of C be produced. Then
$3x+y+2z = 850$, $x+2y+4z = 1200$ and $2x+y+z = 550$. The augmented
matrix is:

$$\begin{bmatrix} 3 & 1 & 2 & | & 850 \\ 1 & 2 & 4 & | & 1200 \\ 2 & 1 & 1 & | & 550 \end{bmatrix} \xrightarrow{R_1 \leftrightarrow R_2} \begin{bmatrix} 1 & 2 & 4 & | & 1200 \\ 3 & 1 & 2 & | & 850 \\ 2 & 1 & 1 & | & 550 \end{bmatrix} \begin{matrix} R_2 - 3R_1 \\ \xrightarrow{} \\ R_3 - 2R_1 \end{matrix}$$

$$\begin{bmatrix} 1 & 2 & 4 & | & 1200 \\ 0 & -5 & -10 & | & -2750 \\ 0 & -3 & -7 & | & -1850 \end{bmatrix} \begin{matrix} (-1/7)R_2 \\ \xrightarrow{} \\ -R_3 \end{matrix} \begin{bmatrix} 1 & 2 & 4 & | & 1200 \\ 0 & 1 & 2 & | & 550 \\ 0 & 3 & 7 & | & 1850 \end{bmatrix} \begin{matrix} R_1 - 2R_2 \\ \xrightarrow{} \\ R_3 - 3R_2 \end{matrix}$$

$$\begin{bmatrix} 1 & 0 & 0 & | & 100 \\ 0 & 1 & 2 & | & 550 \\ 0 & 0 & 1 & | & 200 \end{bmatrix} \xrightarrow{R_2 - 2R_3} \begin{bmatrix} 1 & 0 & 0 & | & 100 \\ 0 & 1 & 0 & | & 150 \\ 0 & 0 & 1 & | & 200 \end{bmatrix} \begin{matrix} \text{Thus, } x = 100, \ y = 150 \\ \\ \text{and } z = 200. \end{matrix}$$

25. The given equations are: $x+2p = 5$, $-2x + 3p = 11$.
The augmented matrix is:

$$\begin{bmatrix} 1 & 2 & | & 5 \\ -2 & 3 & | & 11 \end{bmatrix} \xrightarrow{R_2 + 2R_1} \begin{bmatrix} 1 & 2 & | & 5 \\ 0 & 7 & | & 21 \end{bmatrix} \xrightarrow{(1/2)R_2} \begin{bmatrix} 1 & 2 & | & 5 \\ 0 & 1 & | & 3 \end{bmatrix} \xrightarrow{R_1 - 2R_2}$$

$$\begin{bmatrix} 1 & 0 & | & -1 \\ 0 & 1 & | & 3 \end{bmatrix}$$
Thus, $x = -1$, $p=3$. Since x cannot be negative, the
market equilibrium occurs at x=0. In practice, there will
be no market , (i.e. x=0).

EXERCISES - 9.4

1. The augmented matrix is:

$$\begin{bmatrix} 1 & 1 & 1 & | & 5 \\ -1 & 1 & 3 & | & 1 \\ 1 & 2 & 3 & | & 8 \end{bmatrix} \begin{matrix} R_2 + R_1 \\ \xrightarrow{} \\ R_3 - R_1 \end{matrix} \begin{bmatrix} 1 & 1 & 1 & | & 5 \\ 0 & 2 & 4 & | & 6 \\ 0 & 1 & 2 & | & 3 \end{bmatrix} \xrightarrow{(1/2)R_2} \begin{bmatrix} 1 & 1 & 1 & | & 5 \\ 0 & 1 & 2 & | & 3 \\ 0 & 1 & 2 & | & 3 \end{bmatrix}$$

$$\begin{matrix} R_1 - R_2 \\ \xrightarrow{} \\ R_3 - R_2 \end{matrix} \begin{bmatrix} 1 & 0 & -1 & | & 2 \\ 0 & 1 & 2 & | & 3 \\ 0 & 0 & 0 & | & 0 \end{bmatrix}$$
The system is equivalent to:
$x-z = 2$ and $y+2z = 3$ i.e.
$x = 2+z$, $y = 3-2z$ and $z = $ arbitraty.

5. The augmented matrix is:

$$\begin{bmatrix} 1 & -1 & 2 & | & 5 \\ 4 & 1 & 3 & | & 15 \\ 5 & -2 & 7 & | & 31 \end{bmatrix} \begin{matrix} R_2 - 4R_1 \\ \xrightarrow{} \\ R_3 - 5R_1 \end{matrix} \begin{bmatrix} 1 & -1 & 2 & | & 5 \\ 0 & 5 & -5 & | & -5 \\ 0 & 3 & -3 & | & 6 \end{bmatrix} \begin{matrix} (1/5)R_2 \\ \xrightarrow{} \\ (1/3)R_3 \end{matrix} \begin{bmatrix} 1 & -1 & 2 & | & 5 \\ 0 & 1 & -1 & | & -1 \\ 0 & 1 & -1 & | & 2 \end{bmatrix}$$

$$\begin{matrix} R_1 + R_2 \\ \xrightarrow{} \\ R_3 - R_2 \end{matrix} \begin{bmatrix} 1 & 0 & 3 & | & 4 \\ 0 & 1 & -1 & | & -1 \\ 0 & 0 & 0 & | & 3 \end{bmatrix}$$
The last row gives $0 \cdot u + 0 \cdot v + 0 \cdot w = 3$
or $0 = 3$. Thus, no solution

9. The augmented matrix is:

$$\begin{bmatrix} 1 & 2 & -3 & -1 & | & 2 \\ 2 & 4 & 1 & -1 & | & 1 \\ 3 & 6 & 2 & 1 & | & -7 \\ 1 & 2 & 1 & 1 & | & 6 \end{bmatrix} \xrightarrow[\substack{R_2-2R_1 \\ R_3-3R_1 \\ R_4-R_1}]{} \begin{bmatrix} 1 & 2 & -3 & -1 & | & 2 \\ 0 & 0 & 7 & 1 & | & -3 \\ 0 & 0 & 11 & 4 & | & -13 \\ 0 & 0 & 4 & 2 & | & 4 \end{bmatrix} \xrightarrow{1/11(R_3)}$$

$$\begin{bmatrix} 1 & 2 & -3 & -1 & | & 2 \\ 0 & 0 & 7 & -1 & | & -3 \\ 0 & 0 & 1 & 4/11 & | & -13/11 \\ 0 & 0 & 4 & 2 & | & 4 \end{bmatrix} \xrightarrow[\substack{R_1+3R_3 \\ R_2-7R_3 \\ R_4-4R_3}]{} \begin{bmatrix} 1 & 2 & 0 & 1/11 & | & -17/11 \\ 0 & 0 & 0 & -15/11 & | & 58/11 \\ 0 & 0 & 1 & 4/11 & | & -13/11 \\ 0 & 0 & 0 & 6/11 & | & 96/11 \end{bmatrix}$$

$$\xrightarrow[\substack{(11/6)R_4}]{(-11/15)R_2} \begin{bmatrix} 1 & 2 & 0 & 1/11 & | & -17/11 \\ 0 & 0 & 0 & 1 & | & -58/15 \\ 0 & 0 & 1 & 4/11 & | & -13/11 \\ 0 & 0 & 0 & 1 & | & 96/6 \end{bmatrix} \xrightarrow{R_4-R_2} \begin{bmatrix} 1 & 2 & 0 & 1/11 & | & -17/11 \\ 0 & 0 & 0 & 1 & | & -58/15 \\ 0 & 0 & 0 & 4/11 & | & -13/11 \\ 0 & 0 & 0 & 0 & | & 298/15 \end{bmatrix}$$

The last row implies: $0x + 0y + 0z + 0t = 298/15$ or $0 = 298/15$, which is not true. Thus, __no solution__.

13. The augmented matrix is:

$$\begin{bmatrix} 1 & 1 & -2 & | & -3 \\ 2 & 3 & 1 & | & 10 \\ -1 & 2 & 3 & | & 9 \\ 3 & 1 & -1 & | & 4 \\ 1 & -2 & -1 & | & 2 \end{bmatrix} \xrightarrow[\substack{R_2-2R_1 \\ R_3+R_1 \\ R_4-3R_1 \\ R_5-R_1}]{} \begin{bmatrix} 1 & 1 & -2 & | & -3 \\ 0 & 1 & 5 & | & 16 \\ 0 & 3 & 1 & | & 6 \\ 0 & -2 & 5 & | & 13 \\ 0 & -3 & 1 & | & 5 \end{bmatrix} \xrightarrow[\substack{R_1-R_2 \\ R_3-3R_2 \\ R_4+2R_2 \\ R_5+3R_2}]{}$$

$$\begin{bmatrix} 1 & 0 & -7 & | & -19 \\ 0 & 1 & 5 & | & 16 \\ 0 & 0 & -14 & | & -42 \\ 0 & 0 & 15 & | & 45 \\ 0 & 0 & 16 & | & 53 \end{bmatrix} \xrightarrow[\substack{(1/15)R_4 \\ (1/16)R_5}]{(-1/14)R_3} \begin{bmatrix} 1 & 0 & -7 & | & -19 \\ 0 & 1 & 5 & | & 16 \\ 0 & 0 & 1 & | & 3 \\ 0 & 0 & 1 & | & 3 \\ 0 & 0 & 1 & | & 53/16 \end{bmatrix} \xrightarrow[\substack{R_4-R_3}]{R_5-R_3}$$

$$\begin{bmatrix} 1 & 0 & -7 & | & -19 \\ 0 & 1 & 5 & | & 16 \\ 0 & 0 & 1 & | & 3 \\ 0 & 0 & 0 & | & 0 \\ 0 & 0 & 0 & | & 5/16 \end{bmatrix}$$

The last row gives the equations: $0x + -y + 0z = 5/16$ or $0 = 5/16$ which is not true. Thus, __no solution__.

17. The augmented matrix is:

$$\begin{bmatrix} 1 & 1 & -1 & | & 2 \\ 2 & -3 & 4 & | & -3 \end{bmatrix} \xrightarrow{R_2-2R_1} \begin{bmatrix} 1 & 1 & -1 & | & 2 \\ 0 & -5 & 6 & | & -7 \end{bmatrix} \xrightarrow{(-1/5)R_2} \begin{bmatrix} 1 & 1 & -1 & | & 2 \\ 0 & 1 & -6/5 & | & 7/5 \end{bmatrix}$$

$$\xrightarrow{R_1-R_2} \begin{bmatrix} 1 & 0 & 1/5 & | & 3/5 \\ 0 & 1 & -6/5 & | & 7/5 \end{bmatrix}$$

This gives the system of equations: $x + z/5 = 3/5$ and $y - 6z/5 = 7/5$.

or $x = (3-z)/5$, $y = (7+6z)/5$.

21. Let the company make x, y and z houses of the first, second and third type. Then $3x + 2y + 4z = 100$, $2x+3y+2z = 80$, and $5x+5y+6z = 200$. Adding the first two equations, we have $5x + 5y + 6z = 180$. Subtracting this from the third equation gives $0 = 20$, which is not true. Thus, <u>no solution</u>.

REVIEW EXERCISES ON CHAPTER - 9

1. See answers in the text book.

5. $\begin{bmatrix} 1 & 0 & -1 \\ 2 & 1 & 0 \end{bmatrix}\begin{bmatrix} 2 & -1 \\ 1 & 3 \\ -3 & 2 \end{bmatrix} + 2\begin{bmatrix} 1 & 2 \\ 3 & 4 \end{bmatrix} = \begin{bmatrix} 5 & -3 \\ 5 & 1 \end{bmatrix} + \begin{bmatrix} 2 & 4 \\ 6 & 8 \end{bmatrix} = \begin{bmatrix} 7 & 1 \\ 11 & 9 \end{bmatrix}$

9. The given system is: $3x+2y = 7$, $-x+y = 1$. The augmented matrix is:

$\begin{bmatrix} 3 & 2 & | & 7 \\ -1 & 1 & | & 1 \end{bmatrix} \xrightarrow{R_1 \leftrightarrow R_2} \begin{bmatrix} -1 & 1 & | & 1 \\ 3 & 2 & | & 7 \end{bmatrix} \xrightarrow{(-1)R_1} \begin{bmatrix} 1 & -1 & | & -1 \\ 3 & 2 & | & 7 \end{bmatrix} \xrightarrow{R_2 - 3R_1}$

$\begin{bmatrix} 1 & -1 & | & -1 \\ 0 & 5 & | & 10 \end{bmatrix} \xrightarrow{(1/5)R_2} \begin{bmatrix} 1 & -1 & | & -1 \\ 0 & 1 & | & 2 \end{bmatrix} \xrightarrow{R_1 + R_2} \begin{bmatrix} 1 & 0 & | & 1 \\ 0 & 1 & | & 2 \end{bmatrix}$

Thus, $x=1$, $y=2$.

13. The augmented matrix is:

$\begin{bmatrix} 2 & -1 & | & -4 \\ 1 & 3 & | & 5 \end{bmatrix} \xrightarrow{R_1 \leftrightarrow R_2} \begin{bmatrix} 1 & 3 & | & 5 \\ 2 & -1 & | & -4 \end{bmatrix} \xrightarrow{R_2 - 2R_1} \begin{bmatrix} 1 & 3 & | & 5 \\ 0 & -7 & | & -14 \end{bmatrix} \xrightarrow{(-1/7)R_2}$

$\begin{bmatrix} 1 & 3 & | & 5 \\ 0 & 1 & | & 2 \end{bmatrix} \xrightarrow{R_1 - 3R_2} \begin{bmatrix} 1 & 0 & | & -1 \\ 0 & 1 & | & 2 \end{bmatrix}$ Thus, $x = -1$, $y = 2$.

17. <u>X</u> must be 2×2. Let $\underline{X} = \begin{bmatrix} a & b \\ c & d \end{bmatrix}$ Then,

$\begin{bmatrix} 2 & -1 \\ 3 & 1 \end{bmatrix} = \begin{bmatrix} 2 & 1 \\ 3 & 4 \end{bmatrix} \underline{X} = \begin{bmatrix} 2 & 1 \\ 3 & 4 \end{bmatrix}\begin{bmatrix} a & b \\ c & d \end{bmatrix} = \begin{bmatrix} 2a+c & 2b+d \\ 3a+4c & 3b+4d \end{bmatrix}$

gives $2 = 2a+c$ and $-1 = 2b + d$
        $3 = 3a + 4c$ $1 = 3b + 4d$.
Solving, we get $a=1$, $c=0$, $b = -1$, $d=1$.   Thus,

$\underline{X} = \begin{bmatrix} a & b \\ c & d \end{bmatrix} = \begin{bmatrix} 1 & -1 \\ 0 & 1 \end{bmatrix}$.

21. There are many answers. Let $\underline{A} = \begin{bmatrix} a & b \\ c & d \end{bmatrix}$ where a, b, c, d are arbitraty. Then,

$$\underline{B} = 2\underline{I} - \underline{A} = 2\begin{bmatrix} 1 & 0 \\ 0 & 1 \end{bmatrix} - \begin{bmatrix} a & b \\ c & d \end{bmatrix} = \begin{bmatrix} 2 & 0 \\ 0 & 2 \end{bmatrix} - \begin{bmatrix} a & b \\ c & d \end{bmatrix} = \begin{bmatrix} 2-a & -b \\ -c & 2-d \end{bmatrix}$$

25. (a) $\begin{bmatrix} 13 & 27 & 15 \\ 12 & 14 & 24 \end{bmatrix} + \begin{bmatrix} 20 & 32 & 18 \\ 35 & 24 & 30 \end{bmatrix} = \begin{bmatrix} 33 & 59 & 33 \\ 47 & 38 & 54 \end{bmatrix}$

(b) $(1.20)\begin{bmatrix} 13 & 27 & 15 \\ 12 & 14 & 24 \end{bmatrix} + \begin{bmatrix} 20 & 32 & 18 \\ 35 & 24 & 30 \end{bmatrix} = \begin{bmatrix} 35.6 & 61.4 & 36 \\ 49.4 & 40.8 & 58.8 \end{bmatrix}$

29. $\underline{P}\,\underline{A} = \begin{bmatrix} 5 & 6 & 1.5 \end{bmatrix}\begin{bmatrix} 15 & 10 & 16 & 12 \\ 6 & 4 & 2 & 3 \\ 2 & 7 & 0 & 4 \end{bmatrix} = \begin{bmatrix} 114 & 84.5 & 92 & 84 \end{bmatrix}$;

elements are the earnings in weeks I - IV.

REVIEW TEST ON CHAPTER - 9

FILL IN THE BLANKS:

1. A matrix $\underline{A}$ is said to be of size p × q if it has ___*q*___ columns and ___*p*___ rows.

2. If $\begin{bmatrix} 3 & x & 2 \\ u & 1 & v \end{bmatrix} = \begin{vmatrix} t & 4 & y \\ 3 & 1 & 2 \end{vmatrix}$, then x = __*4*__, y = __*2*__, u = __*3*__, v = __*2*__ and t = __*3*__.

3. If $\underline{A} = \begin{bmatrix} 1 & 2 \\ 0 & 3 \end{bmatrix}$ and $\underline{B} = \begin{bmatrix} 2 & -1 \\ 3 & 0 \end{bmatrix}$, then 2A - B = _____. $\begin{bmatrix} 0 & 5 \\ -3 & 6 \end{bmatrix}$

4. If the product $\underline{A}\,\underline{B}$ is defined, then the number of rows in matrix *B* is equal to the number of columns in matrix __*A*__.

5. If $\underline{A}$ is of size m × n and $\underline{B}$ is of size p × q and $\underline{A}\,\underline{B}$ is defined, Then __*n=p*__ and $\underline{A}\,\underline{B}$ is of size __*m×q*__.

6. If $\underline{A}$ is of size m×n and the product $\underline{A}\,\underline{B}$ and $\underline{B}\,\underline{A}$ are both defined, then $\underline{B}$ must be of size __*n×m*__.

7. If $\underline{A}$ and $\underline{B}$ are two non-square matrices such that $\underline{A}\,\underline{B}$ and $\underline{B}\,\underline{A}$ are both defined, then $\underline{A}\,\underline{B}$ __*≠*__ $\underline{B}\,\underline{A}$. (= , ≠)

8. If $\underline{A}$ is of size n × n and $\underline{A}\,\underline{B}$ and $\underline{B}\,\underline{A}$ are both defined, then $\underline{B}$ must be of size __*n×n*__.

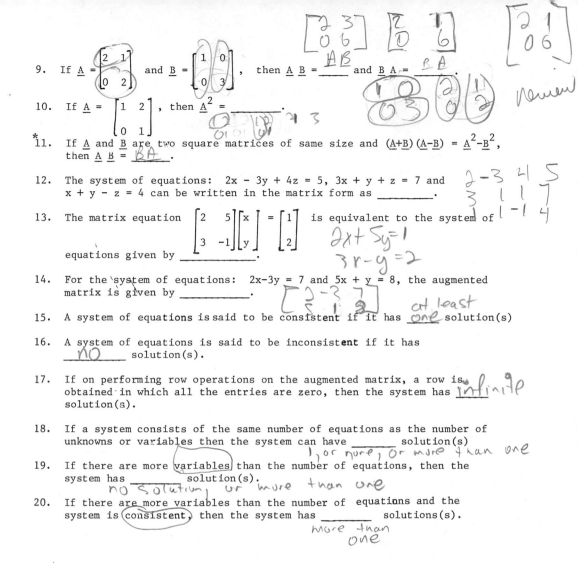

9. If $\underline{A} = \begin{bmatrix} 2 & 1 \\ 0 & 2 \end{bmatrix}$ and $\underline{B} = \begin{bmatrix} 1 & 0 \\ 0 & 3 \end{bmatrix}$, then $\underline{A}\,\underline{B} = \underline{\hspace{1cm}}$ and $\underline{B}\,\underline{A} = \underline{\hspace{1cm}}$.

$\begin{bmatrix} 2 & 3 \\ 0 & 6 \end{bmatrix} \begin{bmatrix} 2 & 1 \\ 0 & 6 \end{bmatrix}$ AB BA $\begin{bmatrix} 2 & 1 \\ 0 & 6 \end{bmatrix}$ review

10. If $\underline{A} = \begin{bmatrix} 1 & 2 \\ 0 & 1 \end{bmatrix}$, then $\underline{A}^2 = \underline{\hspace{1cm}}$.

$\begin{bmatrix} 1 & 2 \\ 0 & 1 \end{bmatrix} \begin{bmatrix} 1 & 2 \\ 0 & 1 \end{bmatrix}$ $\to 3$ $\begin{bmatrix} 1 & 2 \\ 0 & 1 \end{bmatrix}$

*11. If $\underline{A}$ and $\underline{B}$ are two square matrices of same size and $(\underline{A}+\underline{B})(\underline{A}-\underline{B}) = \underline{A}^2-\underline{B}^2$, then $\underline{A}\,\underline{B} = \underline{BA}$.

12. The system of equations: $2x - 3y + 4z = 5$, $3x + y + z = 7$ and $x + y - z = 4$ can be written in the matrix form as $\underline{\hspace{1cm}}$.

$\begin{bmatrix} 2 & -3 & 4 & 5 \\ 3 & 1 & 1 & 7 \\ 1 & -1 & 4 \end{bmatrix}$

13. The matrix equation $\begin{bmatrix} 2 & 5 \\ 3 & -1 \end{bmatrix}\begin{bmatrix} x \\ y \end{bmatrix} = \begin{bmatrix} 1 \\ 2 \end{bmatrix}$ is equivalent to the system of equations given by $\underline{\hspace{1cm}}$.

$2x + 5y = 1$
$3x - y = 2$

14. For the system of equations: $2x-3y = 7$ and $5x + y = 8$, the augmented matrix is given by $\underline{\hspace{1cm}}$.

$\begin{bmatrix} 2 & -3 & 7 \\ 5 & 1 & 8 \end{bmatrix}$

15. A system of equations is said to be consistent if it has $\underline{\text{one}}$ solution(s).   at least

16. A system of equations is said to be inconsistent if it has $\underline{\text{no}}$ solution(s).

17. If on performing row operations on the augmented matrix, a row is obtained in which all the entries are zero, then the system has $\underline{\text{infinite}}$ solution(s).

18. If a system consists of the same number of equations as the number of unknowns or variables then the system can have $\underline{\hspace{1cm}}$ solution(s)
1, or more, or more than one

19. If there are more variables than the number of equations, then the system has $\underline{\hspace{1cm}}$ solution(s).
no solution, or more than one

20. If there are more variables than the number of equations and the system is consistent, then the system has $\underline{\hspace{1cm}}$ solutions(s).
more than one

SEE ANSWERS AT THE END THIS BOOK.

CHAPTER - 10

YOU SHOULD BE FAMILIAR WITH THE FOLLOWING TERMS:

The inverse of a matrix ; invertible (non-singular) matrix, singular matrix.

Input-output model, input-output matrix ; output matrix, demand matrix.

Random process (Stochastic process) ; Markov process.

Transition probabilities ; transition matrix.

State ; state matrix (or state vector).

Steady state matrix. Regular transition matrix.

Determinant (of order n).

Minor, cofactor ; expansion of a determinant by any row or column.

Cramer's rule ; determinant of coefficients.

Transpose of a matrix.

Co-factor matrix ; adjoint of a matrix.

OBJECTIVES

AFTER READING THIS CHAPTER YOU SHOULD BE ABLE TO DO THE FOLLOWING:

1. Use the method of row reduction to determine the inverse of a square matrix (if it exists) or to ascertain whether the matrix is singular or non-singular.

2. Use the inverse of the coefficient matrix to solve a system of linear algebraic equations (where the number of equations equals the number of unknowns).

3. Compute an input-output matrix from an input-output table. Use this matrix to calculate new outputs for the different sectors if there is a change in final demands.

4. For a Markov process:

    (a) Compute the transition matrix from given empirical statements.

    (b) Compute future state matrices given the current state or state matrix, and interpret the results as probability statements.

    (c) Compute the steady-state matrix and interpret its elements.

5. Calculate determinants of orders 2, 3 and 4 using expansion by any row or column.

6. Apply Cramer's rule to determine whether a system of n linear equations in n unknowns has a unique solution, no solution or an infinite number of solutions, and to determine the solution if it is unique.

7. Use co-factors and determinants to calculate the inverse of a matrix.

SOLUTIONS TO ALTERNATE ODD PROBLEMS

EXERCISES - 10.1

1. $\underline{A} \mid \underline{I} = \begin{bmatrix} 2 & 5 & 1 & 0 \\ 3 & 4 & 0 & 1 \end{bmatrix} \xrightarrow{(1/2)R_1} \begin{bmatrix} 1 & 5/2 & 1/2 & 0 \\ 3 & 4 & 0 & 1 \end{bmatrix} \xrightarrow{R_2 - 3R_1}$

$\begin{bmatrix} 1 & 5/2 & 1/2 & 0 \\ 0 & -7/2 & -3/2 & 1 \end{bmatrix} \xrightarrow{(-2/7)R_2} \begin{bmatrix} 1 & 5/2 & 1/2 & 0 \\ 0 & 1 & 3/7 & -2/7 \end{bmatrix}$

$\xrightarrow{R_1 - (5/2)R_2} \begin{bmatrix} 1 & 0 & -4/7 & 5/7 \\ 0 & 1 & 3/7 & -2/7 \end{bmatrix} = \underline{I} \mid \underline{A}^{-1}$

Thus, $\underline{A}^{-1} = \begin{bmatrix} -4/7 & 5/7 \\ 3/7 & -2/7 \end{bmatrix}$

5. $\underline{A} \quad I = \begin{bmatrix} 2 & 3 & 4 & 1 & 0 & 0 \\ 1 & 2 & 0 & 0 & 1 & 0 \\ 4 & 5 & 6 & 0 & 0 & 1 \end{bmatrix} \xrightarrow{R_1 \leftrightarrow R_2} \begin{bmatrix} 1 & 2 & 0 & 0 & 1 & 0 \\ 2 & 3 & 4 & 1 & 0 & 0 \\ 4 & 5 & 6 & 0 & 0 & 1 \end{bmatrix}$

$\begin{matrix} R_2 - 2R_1 \\ \overline{} \\ R_3 - 4R_1 \end{matrix} \begin{bmatrix} 1 & 2 & 0 & 0 & 1 & 0 \\ 0 & -1 & 4 & 1 & -2 & 0 \\ 0 & -3 & 6 & 0 & -4 & 1 \end{bmatrix} \xrightarrow{(-1)R_2} \begin{bmatrix} 1 & 2 & 0 & 0 & 1 & 0 \\ 0 & 1 & -4 & -1 & 2 & 0 \\ 0 & -3 & 6 & 0 & -4 & 1 \end{bmatrix}$

$\begin{matrix} R_1 - 2R_2 \\ \overline{} \\ R_3 + 3R_2 \end{matrix} \begin{bmatrix} 1 & 0 & 8 & 2 & -3 & 0 \\ 0 & 1 & -4 & -1 & 2 & 0 \\ 0 & 0 & -6 & -3 & 2 & 1 \end{bmatrix} \xrightarrow{(-1/6)R_3} \begin{bmatrix} 1 & 0 & 8 & 2 & -3 & 0 \\ 0 & 1 & -4 & -1 & 2 & 0 \\ 0 & 0 & 1 & \frac{1}{2} & \frac{-1}{3} & \frac{-1}{6} \end{bmatrix}$

$\begin{matrix} R_1 - 8R_3 \\ \overline{} \\ R_2 + 4R_3 \end{matrix} \begin{bmatrix} 1 & 0 & 0 & -2 & -1/3 & 4/3 \\ 0 & 1 & 0 & 1 & 2/3 & -2/3 \\ 0 & 0 & 1 & 1/2 & -1/3 & -1/6 \end{bmatrix} = \underline{I} \mid \underline{A}^{-1}.$

Thus, $\underline{A}^{-1} = \begin{bmatrix} -2 & -1/3 & 4/3 \\ 1 & 2/3 & -2/3 \\ 1/2 & -1/3 & -1/6 \end{bmatrix} = (1/6) \begin{bmatrix} -12 & -2 & 8 \\ 6 & 4 & -4 \\ 3 & -2 & -1 \end{bmatrix}$

13. $\underline{A} \mid \underline{I} = \begin{bmatrix} -1 & 2 & -3 & 1 & 0 & 0 \\ 2 & -1 & 1 & 0 & 1 & 0 \\ 3 & 1 & 2 & 0 & 0 & 1 \end{bmatrix} \xrightarrow{(-1)R_1} \begin{bmatrix} 1 & -2 & 3 & -1 & 0 & 0 \\ 2 & -1 & 1 & 0 & 1 & 0 \\ 3 & 1 & 2 & 0 & 0 & 1 \end{bmatrix}$

$\xrightarrow[\overrightarrow{R_3-3R}]{R_2-2R_1} \begin{bmatrix} 1 & -2 & 3 & -1 & 0 & 0 \\ 0 & 3 & -5 & 2 & 1 & 0 \\ 0 & 7 & -7 & 3 & 0 & 1 \end{bmatrix} \xrightarrow{(1/3)R_2} \begin{bmatrix} 1 & -2 & 3 & -1 & 0 & 0 \\ 0 & 1 & -5/3 & 2/3 & 1/3 & 0 \\ 0 & 7 & -7 & 3 & 0 & 1 \end{bmatrix}$

$\xrightarrow[\overrightarrow{R_3-7R_2}]{R_1+2R_2} \begin{bmatrix} 1 & 0 & -1/3 & 1/3 & 2/3 & 0 \\ 0 & 1 & -5/3 & 2/3 & 1/3 & 0 \\ 0 & 0 & 14/3 & -5/3 & -7/3 & 1 \end{bmatrix} \xrightarrow{(3/14)R_3}$

$\begin{bmatrix} 1 & 0 & -1/3 & 1/3 & 2/3 & 0 \\ 0 & 1 & -5/3 & 2/3 & 1/3 & 0 \\ 0 & 0 & 1 & -5/14 & -1/2 & 3/14 \end{bmatrix}$

$\xrightarrow[\overrightarrow{R_2+(5/3)R_3}]{R_1+(1/3)R_3} \begin{bmatrix} 1 & 0 & 0 & 3/14 & 1/2 & 1/14 \\ 0 & 1 & 0 & 1/14 & -1/2 & 5/14 \\ 0 & 0 & 1 & -5/14 & -1/2 & 3/14 \end{bmatrix} = \underline{I} \mid \underline{A}^{-1}$

Thus, $\underline{A}^{-1} = \begin{bmatrix} 3/14 & 1/2 & 1/14 \\ 1/14 & -1/2 & 5/14 \\ -5/14 & -1/2 & 3/14 \end{bmatrix} = (1/14) \begin{bmatrix} 3 & 7 & 1 \\ 1 & -7 & 5 \\ -5 & -7 & 3 \end{bmatrix}$

17. $\underline{A} \mid \underline{I} = \begin{bmatrix} 2 & -3 & 1 & 0 \\ 3 & 4 & 0 & 1 \end{bmatrix} \xrightarrow{(1/2)R_1} \begin{bmatrix} 1 & -3/2 & 1/2 & 0 \\ 3 & 4 & 0 & 1 \end{bmatrix}$

$\xrightarrow{R_2 - 3R_1} \begin{bmatrix} 1 & -3/2 & 1/2 & 0 \\ 0 & 17/2 & -3/2 & 1 \end{bmatrix} \xrightarrow{(2/17)R_2} \begin{bmatrix} 1 & -3/2 & 1/2 & 0 \\ 0 & 1 & -3/17 & 2/17 \end{bmatrix}$

$\xrightarrow{R_1+(3/2)R_2} \begin{bmatrix} 1 & 0 & 4/17 & 3/17 \\ 0 & 1 & -3/17 & 2/17 \end{bmatrix}, \quad \underline{A}^{-1} = \begin{bmatrix} 4/17 & 3/17 \\ -3/17 & 2/17 \end{bmatrix}$

Thus, $\underline{X} = \begin{bmatrix} x \\ y \end{bmatrix} = \underline{A}^{-1}\underline{B} = \begin{bmatrix} 4/17 & 3/17 \\ -3/17 & 2/17 \end{bmatrix} \begin{bmatrix} 1 \\ 10 \end{bmatrix} = \begin{bmatrix} 2 \\ 1 \end{bmatrix}$ or $x=2$, $y=1$

21. $\underline{A} \mid \underline{I} = \begin{bmatrix} 2 & -1 & 3 & | & 1 & 0 & 0 \\ 1 & 1 & 1 & | & 0 & 1 & 0 \\ 3 & 2 & -1 & | & 0 & 0 & 1 \end{bmatrix} \begin{array}{c} R_1 \leftrightarrow R_2 \end{array} \begin{bmatrix} 1 & 1 & 1 & | & 0 & 1 & 0 \\ 2 & -1 & 3 & | & 1 & 0 & 0 \\ 3 & 2 & -1 & | & 0 & 0 & 1 \end{bmatrix}$

$\begin{array}{c} R_2 - 2R_1 \\ \xrightarrow{\hspace{1cm}} \\ R_3 - 3R_1 \end{array} \begin{bmatrix} 1 & 1 & 1 & | & 0 & 1 & 0 \\ 0 & -3 & 1 & | & 1 & -2 & 0 \\ 0 & -1 & -4 & | & 0 & -3 & 1 \end{bmatrix} \xrightarrow{(-1/3)R_2} \begin{bmatrix} 1 & 1 & 1 & | & 0 & 1 & 0 \\ 0 & 1 & -1/3 & | & -1/3 & 2/3 & 0 \\ 0 & -1 & -4 & | & 0 & -3 & 1 \end{bmatrix}$

$\begin{array}{c} R_1 - R_2 \\ \xrightarrow{\hspace{1cm}} \\ R_3 + R_2 \end{array} \begin{bmatrix} 1 & 0 & 4/3 & | & 1/3 & 1/3 & 0 \\ 0 & 1 & -1/3 & | & -1/3 & 2/3 & 0 \\ 0 & 0 & -13/3 & | & -1/3 & -7/3 & 1 \end{bmatrix}$

$\xrightarrow{(-3/13)R_3} \begin{bmatrix} 1 & 0 & 4/3 & | & 1/3 & 1/3 & 0 \\ 0 & 1 & -1/3 & | & -1/3 & 2/3 & 0 \\ 0 & 0 & 1 & | & 1/13 & 7/13 & -3/13 \end{bmatrix}$

$\begin{array}{c} R_1 - (4/3)R_3 \\ \xrightarrow{\hspace{1cm}} \\ R_2 + (1/3)R_3 \end{array} \begin{bmatrix} 1 & 0 & 0 & | & 3/13 & -5/13 & 4/13 \\ 0 & 1 & 0 & | & -4/13 & 11/13 & -1/13 \\ 0 & 0 & 1 & | & 1/13 & 7/13 & -3/13 \end{bmatrix}$

Thus, $\underline{A}^{-1} = (1/13) \begin{bmatrix} 3 & -5 & 4 \\ -4 & 11 & -1 \\ 1 & 7 & -3 \end{bmatrix}$

$\underline{X} = \begin{bmatrix} x \\ y \\ z \end{bmatrix} = \underline{A}^{-1}\underline{B} = (1/13) \begin{bmatrix} 3 & -5 & 4 \\ -4 & 11 & -1 \\ 1 & 7 & -3 \end{bmatrix} \begin{bmatrix} -3 \\ 2 \\ 8 \end{bmatrix} = \begin{bmatrix} 1 \\ 2 \\ -1 \end{bmatrix} \begin{array}{l} x = 1 \\ \text{or } y = 2 \\ z = -1 \end{array}$

25. Let x hundred pounds of ore P and y hundred pounds of ore Q be required. Then we have:

$\begin{array}{l} 3x + 4y = 72 \\ 5x + 2.5y = 95 \end{array} \quad \text{or} \quad \begin{array}{l} 3x + 4y = 72 \\ 2x + y = 38 \end{array} \quad \text{or} \quad \begin{bmatrix} 3 & 4 \\ 2 & 1 \end{bmatrix} \begin{bmatrix} x \\ y \end{bmatrix} = \begin{bmatrix} 72 \\ 38 \end{bmatrix} \quad \text{gives}$

$\begin{bmatrix} x \\ y \end{bmatrix} = \begin{bmatrix} 3 & 4 \\ 2 & 1 \end{bmatrix}^{-1} \begin{bmatrix} 72 \\ 38 \end{bmatrix} = (-1/5) \begin{bmatrix} 1 & -4 \\ -2 & 3 \end{bmatrix} \begin{bmatrix} 72 \\ 38 \end{bmatrix} = \begin{bmatrix} 16 \\ 6 \end{bmatrix} \quad \text{or} \quad \begin{array}{l} x = 16 \\ y = 6 \end{array}$

i.e. 1600 pounds of ore P and 600 pounds or ore Q.

29. $\underline{A} = \begin{bmatrix} 1 & 3 \\ 2 & 4 \end{bmatrix}$ $\underline{B} = \begin{bmatrix} 2 & -1 \\ -3 & 1 \end{bmatrix}$ gives $\underline{A}^{-1} = \begin{bmatrix} -2 & 3/2 \\ 1 & -1/2 \end{bmatrix}$, $\underline{B}^{-1} = \begin{bmatrix} -1 & -1 \\ -3 & -2 \end{bmatrix}$

$\underline{AB} = \begin{bmatrix} 1 & 3 \\ 2 & 4 \end{bmatrix}\begin{bmatrix} 2 & -1 \\ -3 & 1 \end{bmatrix} = \begin{bmatrix} -7 & 2 \\ -8 & 2 \end{bmatrix}$ gives $(\underline{A}\ \underline{B})^{-1} = \begin{bmatrix} 1 & -1 \\ 4 & -7/2 \end{bmatrix}$

$\underline{B}^{-1}\underline{A}^{-1} = \begin{bmatrix} -1 & -1 \\ -3 & -2 \end{bmatrix}\begin{bmatrix} -2 & 3/2 \\ 1 & -1/2 \end{bmatrix} = \begin{bmatrix} 1 & -1 \\ 4 & -7/2 \end{bmatrix} = (\underline{A}\ \underline{B})^{-1}$

33. If $\underline{B}$ and $\underline{C}$ are both inverses of $\underline{A}$, then by definition,

$\underline{A}\ \underline{B} = \underline{B}\ \underline{A} = \underline{I}$ and $\underline{A}\ \underline{C} = \underline{C}\ \underline{A} = \underline{I}$

Now $\underline{B}\ \underline{A}\ \underline{C} = \underline{B}(\underline{A}\ \underline{C}) = \underline{B}\ \underline{I} = \underline{B}$

and $\underline{B}\ \underline{A}\ \underline{C} = (\underline{B}\ \underline{A})\underline{C} = \underline{I}\ \underline{C} = \underline{C}$. Thus $\underline{B} = \underline{C}$.

EXERCISES - 10.2

1. (a) $\underline{A} = \begin{bmatrix} 20/100 & 56/80 \\ 50/100 & 8/80 \end{bmatrix} = \begin{bmatrix} 0.2 & 0.7 \\ 0.5 & 0.1 \end{bmatrix}$

(b) $\underline{I} - \underline{A} = \begin{bmatrix} 0.8 & -0.7 \\ -0.5 & 0.9 \end{bmatrix}$ gives $(\underline{I} - \underline{A})^{-1} = (1/37)\begin{bmatrix} 90 & 70 \\ 50 & 80 \end{bmatrix}$

$\underline{X} = (\underline{I} - \underline{A})^{-1}\underline{D} = (1/37)\begin{bmatrix} 90 & 70 \\ 50 & 80 \end{bmatrix}\begin{bmatrix} 74 \\ 37 \end{bmatrix} = \begin{bmatrix} 250 \\ 180 \end{bmatrix}$

i.e. 250 units of industry I and 180 units of industry II.

(c) New primary inputs for the two industries are $(30/100)(250)$

and $(16/80)(180)$ or 75 and 36 units.

5. Let demand for industry P increase by x units, so that the demand for industry Q increases by 2x units. Thus, the new demand vector is

$\underline{D} = \begin{bmatrix} 65+x \\ 40+2x \end{bmatrix}$ From #3 above, $(\underline{I} - \underline{A})^{-1} = (5/18)\begin{bmatrix} 8 & 5 \\ 4 & 7 \end{bmatrix}$

Thus, $\underline{X} = (\underline{I} - \underline{A})^{-1}\underline{D} = (5/18)\begin{bmatrix} 8 & 5 \\ 4 & 7 \end{bmatrix}\begin{bmatrix} 65+x \\ 40+2x \end{bmatrix} = \begin{bmatrix} 200 + 5x \\ 150 + 5x \end{bmatrix}$

The new labor inputs for the two industries will be

$(60/200)(200 + 5x) = 60 + 1.5x$ and $(45/150)(150 + 5x) = 45 + 1.5x$

But we are given that the total of new labor requirements will be

150 units, i.e. $(60 + 1.5x) + (45 + 1.5x) = 150$ or $x = 15$.

Thus, the new demand vector is:

$$\underline{D} = \begin{bmatrix} 65+x \\ 40+2x \end{bmatrix} = \begin{bmatrix} 65+15 \\ 40+30 \end{bmatrix} = \begin{bmatrix} 80 \\ 70 \end{bmatrix}$$

EXERCISES - 10.3

1. Yes.   5. No (not a square matrix).

9.
$$\underline{P} = \begin{bmatrix} 1 & 0 \\ 0 & 1 \end{bmatrix} = \underline{I} \quad \text{gives} \quad \underline{P}^n = \underline{I} = \begin{bmatrix} 1 & 0 \\ 0 & 1 \end{bmatrix} \quad \begin{array}{l} \text{for all positive} \\ \text{integers} \quad n. \end{array}$$

Since $\underline{P}^n$ has zero elements, $\underline{P}$ is not regular.

13. Yes.

17. (a) $1/4 = P_{21}$ = probability of transition from state 2 to state 1

(b)

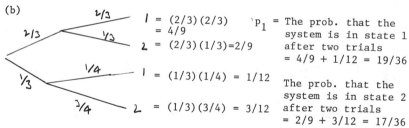

P_1 = The prob. that the system is in state 1 after two trials = $4/9 + 1/12 = 19/36$

The prob. that the system is in state 2 after two trials = $2/9 + 3/12 = 17/36$

Thus, the state matrix is:

$$\begin{bmatrix} 19/36 & 17/36 \end{bmatrix}$$

21. (a) $\underline{A}_0 = \begin{bmatrix} 1 & 0 & 0 \end{bmatrix}$; $\underline{A}_1 = \underline{A}_0\underline{P} = \begin{bmatrix} 1/2 & 1/3 & 1/6 \end{bmatrix}$,

$\underline{A}_2 = \underline{A}_1\underline{P} = \begin{bmatrix} \cdots , & \cdots , & 3/20 \end{bmatrix}$

Thus, the prob. that party Z will win after 2 elections = 3/20.

(b) $\underline{A}_0 = \begin{bmatrix} 0 & 1 & 0 \end{bmatrix}$; $\underline{A}_1 = \begin{bmatrix} 1/4 & 3/4 & 0 \end{bmatrix}$,

$\underline{A}_2 = \underline{A}_1\underline{P} = \begin{bmatrix} 5/16 & \cdots , & \cdots \end{bmatrix}$. Ans. 5/16.

(c) $\underline{A}_0 = \begin{bmatrix} 0 & 0 & 1 \end{bmatrix}$, $\underline{A}_1 = \begin{bmatrix} 1/5 & 2/5 & 2/5 \end{bmatrix}$

$\underline{A}_2 = \begin{bmatrix} \cdots & \cdots & 29/150 \end{bmatrix}$. Ans. = 29/150.

(d)   Let $\underline{B} = \begin{bmatrix} p_1 & p_2 & p_3 \end{bmatrix}$ Then $\underline{B}\,\underline{P} = \underline{B}$ gives

$p_1/2 + p_2/4 + p_3/5 = p_1$, $p_1/3 + 3p_2/4 + 2p_3/5 = p_2$,

$p_1/6 + 2p_3/5 = p_3$

Also $p_1 + p_2 + p_3 = 1$.   The solution is $p_1 = 18/55$

$p_2 = 32/55$, $p_3 = 5/55$

Thus, $\underline{B} = \begin{bmatrix} 18/55 & 32/55 & 5/55 \end{bmatrix}$. This means that the party X will

be in power 18/55 of the time, party Y 32/55 of time and party Z

5/55.

25. $\underline{A}_0 = \begin{bmatrix} 0.3 & 0.4 & 0.3 \end{bmatrix}$

(a) $\underline{A}_1 = \underline{A}_0\underline{P} = \begin{bmatrix} 0.35 & 0.38 & 0.27 \end{bmatrix}$

(b) $\underline{A}_2 = \underline{A}_1\underline{P} = \begin{bmatrix} 0.383 & 0.366 & 0.251 \end{bmatrix}$

(c)   Let $\underline{B} = \begin{bmatrix} p_1 & p_2 & p_2 \end{bmatrix}$.   The equation $\underline{B}\,\underline{P} = \underline{B}$ becomes

$0.8p_1 + 0.2p_2 + 0.1p_3 = p_1$, $0.1p_1 + 0.8p_2 + 0.1p_3 = p_2$

$0.1p_1 + 0.8p_3 = p_3$ with the solution $p_1 = 4/9$, $p_2 = 1/3$, $p_3 = 2/9$

(since $p_1 + p_2 + p_3 = 1$).

EXERCISES - 10.4

1. $\begin{vmatrix} a & c \\ \ell & n \end{vmatrix} = an - \ell c$ 5. $\begin{vmatrix} 3 & -1 \\ 4 & 7 \end{vmatrix} = 3(7) - (-1)(4) = 25$.

9. $a(3) - b(-2) = 3a + 2b$.   13. $59(0) - 3(64) = -192$.

17.   Expanding by the third row, we have: $\Delta = \begin{vmatrix} 1 & 4 \\ 5 & -1 \end{vmatrix} = -1 - 20 = -21$.

21.   Expanding by the first row, $\Delta = 2\begin{vmatrix} 6 & 7 \\ 9 & 10 \end{vmatrix} - 3\begin{vmatrix} 5 & 7 \\ 8 & 10 \end{vmatrix} + 4\begin{vmatrix} 5 & 6 \\ 8 & 9 \end{vmatrix}$

$= 2(60-63) - 3(50-56) + 4(45-48) = 0$

25.   Expanding by the first column, $\Delta = a\begin{vmatrix} d & e \\ 0 & f \end{vmatrix} = adf$.

29. $\begin{vmatrix} x & 3 \\ 2 & 5 \end{vmatrix} = 9$ gives $5x-6 = 9$ or $x=3$.

33. $\Delta = \begin{vmatrix} 3 & 2 \\ 2 & -1 \end{vmatrix} = -7, \quad \Delta_1 = \begin{vmatrix} 1 & 2 \\ 3 & -1 \end{vmatrix} = -7 , \quad \Delta_2 = \begin{vmatrix} 3 & 1 \\ 2 & 3 \end{vmatrix} = 7 ,$ gives

$x = \Delta_1/\Delta = 1$, $y = \Delta_2/\Delta = -1$.

37. $\Delta = -19/60, \quad \Delta_1 = -19/10$, $\Delta_2 = -19/6$ gives $x = \Delta_1/\Delta = 6$, $y = \Delta_2/\Delta = 10$.

41. $\Delta = -17, \quad \Delta_1 = -17$, $\Delta_2 = 17$, $\Delta_3 = 17$ gives

$x = \Delta_1/\Delta = 1$, $y = \Delta_2/\Delta = -1$ and $z = \Delta_3/\Delta = -1$.

45. $\Delta = 4, \Delta_1 = 12, \Delta_2 = 4, \Delta_3 = 8$ gives

$x = \Delta_1/\Delta = 3$, $y = \Delta_2/\Delta = 1$, $z = \Delta_3/\Delta = 2$.

49. $\Delta = 2, \Delta_1 = -2, \quad \Delta_2 = 4$, $\Delta_3 = 2$ gives $x = -1$, $y = 2$, $z = 1$.

EXERCISES - 10.5

1. $\begin{bmatrix} 2 & 3 \\ 3 & -7 \end{bmatrix}$ 5. $\begin{bmatrix} 1 & 0 \\ 0 & 1 \end{bmatrix}$

9. $|\underline{A}| = -1/2$ gives $\underline{A}^{-1} = (1/|\underline{A}|)$ adj. $\underline{A} = (-2) \begin{bmatrix} -1 & -3/2 \\ -2 & -5/2 \end{bmatrix} = \begin{bmatrix} 2 & 3 \\ 4 & 5 \end{bmatrix}$

13. $|\underline{A}| = -9$ gives $\underline{A}^{-1} = (1/|\underline{A}|)$ adj. $\underline{A} = (-1/9) \begin{bmatrix} -1 & 2 & -4 \\ 2 & -4 & -1 \\ -4 & -1 & 2 \end{bmatrix}$

$$= (1/9) \begin{bmatrix} 1 & -2 & 4 \\ -2 & 4 & 1 \\ 4 & 1 & -2 \end{bmatrix}$$

17. (a)

$\underline{A} = \begin{bmatrix} 20/100 & 40/200 & 30/300 \\ 30/100 & 20/200 & 90/300 \\ 40/100 & 100/200 & 60/300 \end{bmatrix} = \begin{bmatrix} 0.2 & 0.2 & 0.1 \\ 0.3 & 0.1 & 0.3 \\ 0.4 & 0.5 & 0.2 \end{bmatrix}$

(b)

$\underline{I} - \underline{A} = \begin{bmatrix} 0.8 & -0.2 & -0.1 \\ -0.3 & 0.9 & -0.3 \\ -0.4 & -0.5 & 0.8 \end{bmatrix}$ gives $(\underline{I}-\underline{A})^{-1} = (1/0.333) \begin{bmatrix} 0.57 & 0.21 & 0.15 \\ 0.36 & 0.60 & 0.27 \\ 0.51 & 0.48 & 0.66 \end{bmatrix}$

$$\underline{X} = (\underline{I} - \underline{A})^{-1} \underline{D} = (1/0.333) \begin{vmatrix} 0.57 & 0.21 & 0.15 \\ 0.36 & 0.60 & 0.27 \\ 0.51 & 0.48 & 0.66 \end{vmatrix} \begin{vmatrix} 150 \\ 280 \\ 420 \end{vmatrix} = \begin{vmatrix} 623 \\ 1007 \\ 1466 \end{vmatrix}$$

i.e.   623, 1007 and 1466 units for industries I, II and III

(c)   The new primary input requirements for the three industries will be $(10/100)(623) = 62.3$, $(40/200)(1007) = 201.4$ and $(120/300)(1466) = 586.4$ units respectively.

REVIEW EXERCISES ON CHAPTER - 10

1.   See answers in the text.

5. $|\underline{A}| = a^2 + b^2$ gives $\underline{A}^{-1} = (1/|\underline{A}|)$ adj. $\underline{A} = (a^2 + b^2)^{-1} \begin{bmatrix} a & -b \\ b & a \end{bmatrix}$

9. $|\underline{A}| = 3$ gives $\underline{A}^{-1} = (1/|\underline{A}|)$ adj. $\underline{A} = (1/3) \begin{bmatrix} -2 & 1 & 1 \\ -8 & 7 & -2 \\ 7 & -5 & 1 \end{bmatrix}$

13.   Not invertible, because $\underline{A}$ is not a square matrix.

17. $|\underline{A}| = \begin{vmatrix} 1 & 1 & 1 \\ 2 & -1 & 3 \\ 3 & 2 & -1 \end{vmatrix} = 13$; $\underline{A}^{-1} = (1/|\underline{A}|)$ adj. $\underline{A} = (1/13) \begin{bmatrix} -5 & 3 & 4 \\ 11 & -4 & -1 \\ 7 & 1 & -3 \end{bmatrix}$

Thus, $\underline{X} = \begin{bmatrix} x \\ y \\ z \end{bmatrix} = \underline{A}^{-1}\underline{B} = (1/13) \begin{bmatrix} -5 & 3 & 4 \\ 11 & -4 & -1 \\ 7 & 1 & -3 \end{bmatrix} \begin{bmatrix} 1 \\ -2 \\ 6 \end{bmatrix} = \begin{bmatrix} 1 \\ 1 \\ -1 \end{bmatrix}$

21. $\Delta = -4$, $\Delta_1 = -4$, $\Delta_2 = -8$, $\Delta_3 = -12$ gives $x = \Delta_1/\Delta = 1$, $y = 2$, $z = 3$.

25. $a^2 - 16 = (a-4)(a+4)$ 29.   Expanding by second column,

$\Delta = -(x^2 - 1) - 1(1-x) = x - x^2 = x(1-x)$.

33. $\begin{bmatrix} 1 & 0 & 0 & 0 \\ 0 & 1 & 0 & 0 \\ 0 & 0 & 1 & 0 \\ 0 & 0 & 0 & 1 \end{bmatrix}$ 37. $\begin{matrix} & \text{Tom} & \text{Dick} \\ \begin{bmatrix} 0.8 & 0.2 \\ 0.4 & 0.6 \end{bmatrix} & \begin{matrix} \text{Tom} \\ \text{Dick} \end{matrix} \end{matrix}$

REVIEW TEST ON CHAPTER - 10

FILL IN THE BLANKS:

1. If B is an inverse of A, then by definition, $AB = BA = I$

2. If A is singular, then A^{-1} ~~does not exist~~ (exist or not)

3. If the matrix B is non-singular, then B^{-1} exists (exist or not)

4. If A is of size m×n and A^{-1} exists, then $n = m$

5. If A is of size 3×3 and A^{-1} exist, then A^{-1} is of size 3×3

6. If A X = B is the matrix equation, then X = $A^{-1}B$ provided A^{-1} exists

7. If A C = A, then C = I , provided A^{-1} exists

8. If A^{-1} = B, then B^{-1} = A

9. If B is a zero matrix of size 3×3, then B^{-1} = does not exist

10. If A is an identity matrix, then A^{-1} = A

11. In the input-output analysis of the interaction of various sectors of

    an economy, if X, A and D denote the output matrix, input-output

    matrix and the demand vector respectively, then the input-output

    equation is given by _____ and its solution is given by

    X = _____

12. If P = P_{ij} is a given transition matrix, the p_{ij} denotes the

    _____ that the Markov system or process will end up in state

    _____ after any trial given that it is in state ____ before the trial.

13. In any transition matrix, the sum of elements in any _____ (row

    or column) is always equal to 1.

14. If P = P_{ij} is a transition matrix, then p_{ij} _____ for all values

    of i, j.

15. Given the transition matrix $P = \begin{bmatrix} 0.2 & 0.5 & 0.3 \\ 0.4 & 0.1 & 0.5 \\ 0.6 & 0.2 & 0.2 \end{bmatrix}$

    the probability that at the next trial, the system will

(a)   change from state 1 to state 3 is _____

(b)   change from state 3 to state 2 is _____

(c)   not change, given that it was in state 3 before the trial is _____

16.   The row matrix $\begin{bmatrix} 1/4 & 1/8 & 3/4 & -1/4 \end{bmatrix}$ _____ (is or is not) a state matrix.

17.   The transition matrix $\underline{P} = \begin{bmatrix} 0 & 1 \\ 1 & 0 \end{bmatrix}$ _____ (is or is not) regular.

18.   If $\Delta = \begin{vmatrix} 1 & 2 & -3 \\ -4 & 4 & 6 \\ 7 & -8 & 9 \end{vmatrix}$, then   (a)   the cofactor of the element

(a)   the cofactor of the element 2 is _____

(b)   the cofactor of the element 9 is _____

(c)   the cofactor of the element -4 is _____

19.   If $\begin{vmatrix} x-1 & 2 & 3 \\ 0 & x-3 & 4 \\ 0 & 0 & x+2 \end{vmatrix} = 0$,   then x = __1, 3 -2__

20.   If $\underline{A}$ denotes the coefficient matrix of a system of equations, then that system has a unique solution if |A| ≠ 0

21.   If $\underline{A} = \begin{bmatrix} 3 & 7 & 2 \\ 1 & -3 & 4 \end{bmatrix}$,   then $\underline{A}^T$ = _____

22.   If $\underline{A} = \begin{bmatrix} 2 & -1 \\ 3 & 4 \end{bmatrix}$, then the cofactor matrix of $\underline{A}$ is _____

and the adj. $\underline{A}$ = _____

23.   If $\underline{A}$ is an invertible matrix, then $\underline{A}^{-1}$ can be found by determinants and is given by $\underline{A}^{-1}$ = _____

24.   A square matrix $\underline{B}$ is invertible only if $|\underline{B}|$ ≠ 0

25.   If $\underline{A} = \begin{bmatrix} 1 & 2 \\ 3 & 7 \end{bmatrix}$, then the cofactor matrix of $\underline{A}$ is

adj. $\underline{A}$ = _____ A = _____ and therefore $\underline{A}^{-1}$ = _____.

86

CHAPTER - 11

YOU SHOULD BE FAMILIAR WITH THE FOLLWING TERMS:

Linear inequality ; graph of a linear inequality or set of inequalities.

Linear programming problem ; constraints , objective function.

Feasible solution ; feasible region.

Indifference curve (constant-profit line) ; optimum solution.

Slack variable ; standard form of a linear programming problem.

Basic feasible solution (BFS) ; vertex of the feasible region.

Pivoting ; departing variable, entering variable ; basis, basic variables.

Simplex tableau ; simplex method.

OBJECTIVES

AFTER READING THIS CHAPTER YOU SHOULD BE ABLE TO DO THE FOLLOWING:

1. Graph the set of points that satisfy a given set of linear inequalities in two variables.

2. Express appropriate word problems in terms of linear inequalities.

3. Solve linear programming problems involving two variables using the graphical method.

4. Construct the simplex tableau for a given linear programming problem. At each stage of the simplex method

   (a) decide the entering variable

   (b) decide the departing variable

   (c) carry out row operations to complete the pivoting

   (d) and decide if and when the optimum solution is achieved.

SOLUTIONS TO ALTERNATE ODD PROBLEMS

EXERCISES 11.1

1. Since $x+y > 1$ or $y > 1-x$, the **graph** is the region strictly above the line $y = 1-x$. (For figure, see answer in your text book).

5. $2x+3 > 0$ or $x > -3/2$ i.e. the region is the set of all points (x,y) which are to the right of the vertical line $x = -3/2$. (For fig. see answer in your text book).

9, 13, 17 For graphs, see answers in your text book.

21.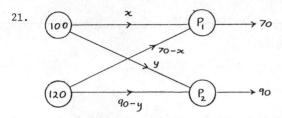

The inequalities satisfied by x, y are $0 \le x \le 70$, $0 \le y \le 90$, $40 \le x+y \le 100$

Total delivery cost (in dollars) is ≤ 2700 or

$15x + 10y + 10(70-x) + 20(90-y) \le 2700$ or $x - 2y \le 40$.

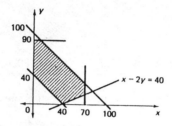

25. Refer to #24 above. The inequalities satisfied in Exercises 24 are: $x \ge 0$, $y \ge 0$. Time required on first machine is $x + 3y \le 100$ and on the second machine is $2x+2y \le 100$. or $x+y \le 50$. Total profit ≥ 1100 gives $20x + 30y \ge 1100$ or $2x + 3y \ge 110$. Thus, the set of inequalities to be satisfied are: $x \ge 0$, $y \ge 0$, $x+3y \le 100$, $x+y \le 50$ and $2x+3y \ge 110$. The graph is as shown.

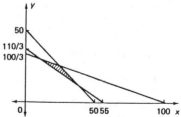

29. Let x beakers of the first size
and y of the second size be stored.
Then $x \geq 300$, $y \geq 400$
$x + y \leq 1200$.

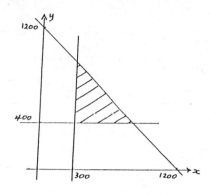

EXERCISES 11.2

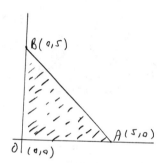

1. The vertices on the feasible region
shown shaded in the figure are
(0,0), A(5,0) and B(0,5).

At (0,0), $Z = 3x+5y = 0$

At A(5,0) $Z = 3(5) + 0 = 15$

At B(0,5), $Z = 3(0) + 5(5) = 25$.

Thus, Z is max. at (0,5).

5. The vertices are (0, 5/2) , (0,0), (7/3, 0), (1,2) and (2,1).

$Z_{max.} = 35/3$ at (7/3 , 0).

9. The vertices are (4,1) (1,4) and (4,4). $Z_{min.} = 8$ at (4,1)

13. Let x gallons of regular and y gallons of super blend be produced.
Then we want to maximize the profits $Z = 5x + 6y$ subject to
$x, y \geq 0$, $x/2 + 2y/3 \leq 3000$ and $x/2 + y/3 \leq 2000$. $Z_{max.} = \$28,000$
when $x = 2000$, $y = 3000$.

17. If x units of A and y units of B are produced, then we want to maximize
the profit $Z = 250x + 300y$ subject to $x, y \geq 0$, $2x + 5y \leq 200$,
$4x + y \leq 240$ and $3x + 2y \leq 190$. $Z_{max.} = \$18,500$ at x=50, y=20.

21. If x acres of the first crop and y acres of the second crop are planted, then we want to maximize the total profits $Z = 100x + 300y$, subject to x, $y \geq 0$, $x+y \leq 100$, $20x + 40y \leq 3000$ and $5x + 20y \leq 1350$.

$Z_{max.} = \$21,000$ when $x = 30$ acres of crop I and $y = 60$ acres of crop II are planted.

25.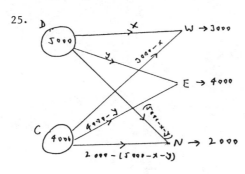

The set of inequalities are:

x, $y \geq 0$, $3000 - x \geq 0$, $4000-y \geq 0$

$5000 - x - y \geq 0$, $2000-(5000-x-y) \geq 0$

These simplify to

$0 \leq x \leq 3000$, $0 \leq y \leq 4000$

and $3000 \leq x+y \leq 5000$.   ... (i)

If T = total shipping cost = $45x + 15y + 25(5000 - x-y) + 60(3000-x)$

$$+ 10(4000-y) + 50\{2000-(5000-x-y)\}$$

$$= 10x + 30y + 195,000$$

T is minimum subject to restraints in (i) if $x = 3000$, $y = 0$.

$T_{min.} = \$225,000$.

EXERCISES 11.3

1. $x + y + t = 5$; $t \begin{bmatrix} x & y & t \\ 1 & 1 & 1 & | & 5 \end{bmatrix}$

5. $3x + y + t = 7$

$x + y + u = 3$

$x + 2y + v = 5$

$\begin{array}{c} t \\ u \\ v \end{array} \begin{bmatrix} x & y & t & u & v \\ 3 & 1 & 1 & 0 & 0 & | & 7 \\ 1 & 1 & 0 & 1 & 0 & | & 3 \\ 1 & 2 & 0 & 0 & 1 & | & 5 \end{bmatrix}$

9. (Refer to #15 in exercises 11.2) If x units of A and y units of B are produced, then we want to maximize $Z = 70x + 50y$ subject to $x \geq 0$, $y \geq 0$, $2x+4y \leq 100$ and $5x+3y \leq 110$. Introducing slack variables, we have:

$$2x + 4y + t = 100$$

$$5x + 3y + u = 110$$

$$\begin{array}{c} \\ t \\ u \end{array} \begin{array}{cccc} x & y & t & u \\ \left[\begin{array}{cccc|c} 2 & 4 & 1 & 0 & 100 \\ 5 & 3 & 0 & 1 & 110 \end{array} \right] \end{array}$$

13. $2x + y + z + t = 5$

$x + 2y + z + u = 4$

$$\begin{array}{c} \\ t \\ u \end{array} \begin{array}{ccccc} x & y & z & t & u \\ \left[\begin{array}{ccccc|c} 2 & 1 & 1 & 1 & 0 & 5 \\ 1 & 2 & 1 & 0 & 1 & 4 \end{array} \right] \end{array}$$

17.

$$\begin{array}{c} \rightarrow t \\ u \end{array} \begin{array}{ccccc} x & y & z & t & u \\ \left[\begin{array}{ccccc|c} 1 & 2 & 1 & 1 & 0 & 5 \\ 3 & 2 & 4 & 0 & 1 & 16 \end{array} \right] \end{array}$$ Apply $(1/2)R_1$ and then $R_2 - 2R_1$

to obtain:

$$\begin{array}{c} y \\ \rightarrow u \end{array} \begin{array}{ccccc} x & y & z & t & u \\ \left[\begin{array}{ccccc|c} 1/2 & 1 & 1/2 & 1/2 & 0 & 5/2 \\ 2 & 0 & 3 & -1 & 1 & 11 \end{array} \right] \end{array}$$ Apply $(1/2)R_2$ and then $R_1 - (1/2)R_2$

to obtain:

$$\begin{array}{c} y \\ x \end{array} \begin{array}{ccccc} x & y & z & t & u \\ \left[\begin{array}{ccccc|c} 0 & 1 & 1/4 & 3/4 & -1/4 & -1/4 \\ 1 & 0 & 3/2 & -1/2 & 1/2 & 11/2 \end{array} \right] \end{array}$$ The second solution is not

feasible, because when

z, t, u = 0, we have $y = -1/4 < 0 \cdot$ See graph in your text book (Answers).

21. p is the departing variable and x the entering variable. Apply

$(1/3)R_1$ and then $R_2 - R_1$, $R_3 - R_1$ to obtain:

$$\begin{array}{c} \rightarrow x \\ q \\ r \end{array} \begin{array}{ccccc} x & y & p & q & r \\ \left[\begin{array}{ccccc|c} 1 & 2/3 & 1/3 & 0 & 0 & 5/3 \\ 0 & 4/3 & -1/3 & 1 & 0 & 4/3 \\ 0 & 13/3 & -1/3 & 0 & 1 & 13/3 \end{array} \right] \end{array}$$ Apply $(3/4)R_2$ and then

$R_1 - (2/3)R_2$, $R_3 - (13/3)R_2$ to

obtain,

$$\begin{array}{c} x \\ y \\ \rightarrow r \end{array} \begin{array}{ccccc} x & y & p & q & r \\ \left[\begin{array}{ccccc|c} 1 & 0 & 1/2 & -1/2 & 0 & 1 \\ 0 & 1 & -1/4 & 3/4 & 0 & 1 \\ 0 & 0 & 3/4 & -13/4 & 1 & 0 \end{array} \right] \end{array}$$ Apply $(-4/13)R_3$ and then

$R_1 + (1/2)R_3$, $R_2 - (3/4)R_3$

to obtain:

$$\begin{array}{c} x \\ y \\ q \end{array} \begin{array}{ccccc} x & y & p & q & r \\ \left[\begin{array}{ccccc|c} 1 & 0 & 5/13 & 0 & -2/13 & 1 \\ 0 & 1 & -1/13 & 0 & 3/13 & 1 \\ 0 & 0 & -3/13 & 1 & -4/13 & 0 \end{array} \right] \end{array}$$ See graph in your text book

(Answers).

EXERCISES 11.4

1. $\rightarrow$ t $\begin{bmatrix} \overset{x}{1} & \overset{y}{1} & \overset{t}{1} & 5 \\ \underset{\uparrow}{3} & 2 & 0 & Z \end{bmatrix}$ $\implies$ x $\begin{bmatrix} \overset{x}{1} & \overset{y}{1} & \overset{t}{1} & 5 \\ 0 & -1 & -3 & Z - 15 \end{bmatrix}$

$Z_{max.} = 15$ at x=5, y=0.

5. $\rightarrow$ t $\begin{bmatrix} \overset{x}{3} & \overset{y}{1} & \overset{t}{1} & \overset{u}{0} & \overset{v}{0} & 7 \\ 1 & 1 & 0 & 1 & 0 & 3 \\ 1 & 2 & 0 & 0 & 1 & 5 \\ \underset{\uparrow}{5} & 1 & 0 & 0 & 0 & Z \end{bmatrix}$ $\Rightarrow$

x $\begin{bmatrix} \overset{x}{1} & \overset{y}{1/3} & \overset{t}{1/3} & \overset{u}{0} & \overset{v}{0} & 7/3 \\ 0 & 2/3 & -1/3 & 1 & 0 & 2/3 \\ 0 & 5/3 & -1/3 & 0 & 1 & 8/3 \\ 0 & -2/3 & -5/3 & 0 & 0 & Z-35/3 \end{bmatrix}$

(rows labelled x, u, v)

Thus, $Z_{max.} = 35/3$ at x = 7/3, y = 0.

9. (Refer to #15 in Exercises 11.2). We want to maximize Z = 70x + 50y

subject to $x+2y \le 50$, $5x+3y \le 110$ and $x,y \ge 0$.

t $\begin{bmatrix} \overset{x}{1} & \overset{y}{2} & \overset{t}{1} & \overset{u}{0} & 50 \\ 5 & 3 & 0 & 1 & 110 \\ \underset{\uparrow}{70} & 50 & 0 & 0 & Z \end{bmatrix}$ $\Rightarrow$

$\begin{matrix} t \\ x \end{matrix}$ $\begin{bmatrix} \overset{x}{0} & \overset{y}{7/5} & \overset{t}{1} & \overset{u}{-1/5} & 28 \\ 1 & 3/5 & 0 & 1/5 & 22 \\ 0 & \underset{\uparrow}{8} & 0 & -14 & Z - 1540 \end{bmatrix}$ $\Rightarrow$

y $\begin{bmatrix} \overset{x}{0} & \overset{y}{1} & \overset{t}{5/7} & \overset{u}{-1/7} & 20 \\ 1 & 0 & -3/7 & 2/7 & 10 \\ 0 & 0 & -40/7 & -90/7 & Z - 1700 \end{bmatrix}$ (rows y, x)

Answer: $Z_{max.} = 1700$ at x=10, y=20.

13. (Refer to #21 of Exercises 11.2). We want to maximize Z = 100x + 300y

subject to x, y $\ge$ 0 $x+y \le 100$, $x + 2y \le 150$ and $x+4y \le 270$.

t $\begin{bmatrix} \overset{x}{1} & \overset{y}{1} & \overset{t}{1} & \overset{u}{0} & \overset{v}{0} & 100 \\ 1 & 2 & 0 & 1 & 0 & 150 \\ 1 & 4 & 0 & 0 & 1 & 270 \\ 100 & \underset{\uparrow}{300} & 0 & 0 & 0 & Z \end{bmatrix}$ $\Rightarrow$

t $\begin{bmatrix} \overset{x}{3/4} & \overset{y}{0} & \overset{t}{1} & \overset{u}{0} & \overset{v}{-1/4} & 32.5 \\ 1/2 & 0 & 0 & 1 & -1/2 & 15 \\ 1/4 & 1 & 0 & 0 & 1/4 & 67.5 \\ \underset{\uparrow}{25} & 0 & 0 & 0 & -75 & Z-20250 \end{bmatrix}$ (rows t, u, y)

$$
\Rightarrow
\begin{array}{c}
\begin{array}{c} \\ t \\ x \\ y \\ \\ \end{array}
\begin{array}{cccccc}
x & y & t & u & v & \\
\end{array}
\left[
\begin{array}{ccccc|c}
0 & 0 & 1 & -3/2 & 1/3 & 10 \\
1 & 0 & 0 & 2 & -1 & 30 \\
0 & 1 & 0 & -1/2 & 1/2 & 60 \\
0 & 0 & 0 & -50 & -50 & Z-21000 \\
\end{array}
\right]
\end{array}
\qquad
\begin{array}{l}
Z_{max.} = 21,000 \\
\text{at } x = 30,\ y = 60.
\end{array}
$$

17. If x,y,z lbs. of regular, super and deluxe type nuts are made, then we
     want to maximize the total profit (in cents).

   $Z = 10(x+y+z)$ subject to $x,y,z \geq 0$, $8x+5y+3z \leq 43000$,

   $2x + 3y + 3z \leq 25000$ and $2y + 4z \leq 22000$.

$$
\begin{array}{c}
\begin{array}{cccccc}
x & y & z & t & u & v \\
\end{array} \\
\begin{array}{c} t \\ u \\ \to v \\ \\ \end{array}
\left[
\begin{array}{cccccc|c}
8 & 5 & 3 & 1 & 0 & 0 & 43000 \\
2 & 3 & 3 & 0 & 1 & 0 & 25000 \\
0 & 1 & 2 & 0 & 0 & 1 & 11000 \\
10 & 10 & 10 & 0 & 0 & 0 & Z \\
\end{array}
\right]
\end{array}
\begin{array}{c}
\to t \\
\Rightarrow
\end{array}
\begin{array}{c}
\begin{array}{cccccc}
x & y & z & t & u & v \\
\end{array} \\
\begin{array}{c} t \\ u \\ z \\ \\ \end{array}
\left[
\begin{array}{cccccc|c}
8 & 7/2 & 0 & 1 & 0 & -3/2 & 26500 \\
2 & 3/2 & 0 & 0 & 1 & -3/2 & 8500 \\
0 & 1/2 & 1 & 0 & 0 & 1/2 & 5500 \\
10 & 5 & 0 & 0 & 0 & -5 & Z-55000 \\
\end{array}
\right]
\end{array}
$$

$$
\to u
\begin{array}{c}
\begin{array}{cccccc}
x & y & z & t & u & v \\
\end{array} \\
\begin{array}{c} x \\ \to u \\ z \\ \\ \end{array}
\left[
\begin{array}{cccccc|c}
1 & 7/16 & 0 & 1/8 & 0 & -3/16 & 3312.5 \\
0 & 5/8 & 0 & -1/4 & 1 & -9/8 & 1875 \\
0 & 1/2 & 1 & 0 & 0 & 1/2 & 5500 \\
0 & 5/8 & 0 & -5/4 & 0 & -25/8 & Z-88125 \\
\end{array}
\right]
\end{array}
\qquad \Longrightarrow
$$

$$
\begin{array}{c}
\begin{array}{cccccc}
x & y & z & t & u & v \\
\end{array} \\
\begin{array}{c} x \\ y \\ z \\ \\ \end{array}
\left[
\begin{array}{cccccc|c}
1 & 0 & 0 & 3/10 & -7/10 & 3/5 & 2000 \\
0 & 1 & 0 & -2/5 & 8/5 & -9/5 & 3000 \\
0 & 0 & 1 & 1/5 & -4/5 & 7/5 & 4000 \\
0 & 0 & 0 & -1 & -1 & -2 & Z-90000 \\
\end{array}
\right]
\end{array}
$$

   Thus, $Z_{max.} = 90,000\mathcal{c} = \$900$ when x = 2000 lbs. of regular,

   y = 3000 lbs. of super and z = 4000 lbs. of deluxe type are made.

21.

	x	y	z	t	u	v	
t	1	2	1	1	0	0	5
u	2	1	2	0	1	0	7
v	2	3	4	0	0	1	13
	1	1	1	0	0	0	Z

$\rightarrow$ u, $\uparrow$

	x	y	z	t	u	v	
t	0	3/2	0	1	-1/2	0	3/2
x	1	1/2	1	0	1/2	0	7/2
v	0	2	2	0	-1	1	6
	0	1/2	0	0	-1/2	0	Z-7/2

$\rightarrow$ t, $\uparrow$

	x	y	z	t	u	v	
y	0	1	0	2/3	-1/3	0	1
x	1	0	1	-1/3	2/3	0	3
v	0	0	2	-4/3	-1/3	1	4
	0	0	0	-1/3	-1/3	0	Z-4

Answer: $Z_{max.}$ = 4 at x=3, y=1, z=0.

$Z_{max.}$ = 4 is also attained at x=1, y=1, z=2.

REVIEW EXERCISES ON CHAPTER-11

1. See answers in the text book.

5. (a) The vertices of the feasible region are (0,0), (7/3, 0), (1,2) and (0, 12/5). $Z_{max.}$ = 19 at (1,2).

    (b)

	x	y	t	u	
t	3	2	1	0	7
u	2	5	0	1	12
	5	7	0	0	Z

$\rightarrow$ u, $\uparrow$

	x	y	t	u	
t	11/5	0	1	-2/5	11/5
y	2/5	1	0	1/5	12/5
	11/5	0	0	-7/5	Z-84/5

$\uparrow$ $\Rightarrow$

	x	y	t	u	
x	1	0	5/11	-2/11	1
y	0	1	-2/5	3/11	2
	0	0	-1	-1	Z - 19

Answer: $Z_{max.}$ = 19 at x=1, y=2.

9. (a) The vertices are (2,0), (5,0), (5,1) and (2,4). $Z_{max.}$ = 15 at (5,0).

    (b) To tackle $x \geq 2$, we set z = x-2. Then, in terms of y and z, we want to maximize Z = 3z - y + 6 subject to $y, z \geq 0$, $z \leq 3$, $y + z \leq 4$.

$$\begin{array}{c}\rightarrow t\\u\\\\\end{array}\begin{bmatrix}\begin{array}{cccc}y&z&t&u\\0&1&1&0\\1&1&0&1\\-1&\underset{\uparrow}{3}&0&0\end{array}&\begin{array}{c}3\\4\\Z-6\end{array}\end{bmatrix}\Rightarrow\begin{array}{c}z\\u\\\\\end{array}\begin{bmatrix}\begin{array}{cccc}y&z&t&u\\0&1&1&0\\1&0&-1&1\\-1&0&-3&0\end{array}&\begin{array}{c}3\\1\\Z-15\end{array}\end{bmatrix}$$

$Z_{max.}$ = 15 at y=0, z = x-2 = 3 or x=5, y=0.

13.
$$\begin{array}{c}t\\\rightarrow u\\v\\\\\end{array}\begin{bmatrix}\begin{array}{cccccc}x&y&z&t&u&v\\1&1&1&1&0&0\\2&1&2&0&1&0\\3&2&1&0&0&1\\1&3&\underset{\uparrow}{4}&0&0&0\end{array}&\begin{array}{c}4\\6\\8\\Z\end{array}\end{bmatrix}\Rightarrow\begin{array}{c}\rightarrow t\\z\\v\\\\\end{array}\begin{bmatrix}\begin{array}{cccccc}x&y&z&t&u&v\\0&1/2&0&1&-1/2&0\\1&1/2&1&0&1/2&0\\2&3/2&0&0&-1/2&1\\-3&\underset{\uparrow}{1}&0&0&-2&0\end{array}&\begin{array}{c}1\\3\\5\\Z-12\end{array}\end{bmatrix}$$

$$\Rightarrow\begin{array}{c}y\\z\\v\\\\\end{array}\begin{bmatrix}\begin{array}{cccccc}x&y&z&t&u&v\\0&1&0&2&-1&0\\1&0&1&-1&1&0\\2&0&0&-3&1&1\\-3&0&0&-1&-1&0\end{array}&\begin{array}{c}2\\2\\2\\Z-14\end{array}\end{bmatrix}\qquad$$

Answer: $Z_{max.}$ = 14 at x=0, y = 2, z = 2.

17. (Refer to # 19-20 of Exercises - 11.1). We want to minimize the total cost   C = 15x + 10y + 10(70-x) + 20(90-y) = 5x - 10y + 2500

subject to x, y, ≥ 0, x ≤ 70, y ≤ 90, x + y ≥ 40 and x+y ≤ 100.
To deal with the inequality x + y $\geq$ 40, we arbitrarily define
y' = y - 40.

In terms of x, y', the problem reduces to:

'To minimize C = 2100 - 5(2y'-x) subject to x, y' $\geq$ 0, x $\leq$ 70,

y' $\leq$ 50 and x+y' $\leq$ 60'. Now C is minimum when Z = 2y' - x is

maximum. The simplex tableau is:

$$\begin{array}{c}t\\\rightarrow u\\v\\\\\end{array}\begin{bmatrix}\begin{array}{ccccc}x&y'&t&u&v\\1&0&1&0&0\\0&1&0&1&0\\1&1&0&0&1\\-1&\underset{\uparrow}{2}&0&0&0\end{array}&\begin{array}{c}70\\50\\60\\Z\end{array}\end{bmatrix}\quad\begin{array}{c}t\\y'\\y\\\\\end{array}\begin{bmatrix}\begin{array}{ccccc}x&y'&t&u&v\\1&0&1&0&0\\0&1&0&1&0\\1&0&0&-1&1\\-1&0&0&-2&0\end{array}&\begin{array}{c}70\\50\\10\\Z-100\end{array}\end{bmatrix}$$

Thus, $Z_{max.}$ = 100 when x=0, y' = y - 40 = 50 or when x=0, y = 90.

Now $C_{min.}$ = 2100 - 5($Z_{max.}$) = 2100 - 5(100) = 1600 dollars.

FILL IN THE BLANKS:

1. The graph of the inequality $3x - 4 > 0$ is the half plane to the

   _____ (left or right) of the line $3x = 4$.

2. The graph of $5 - 2y < 0$ is the half plane _____ (above or below) the

   line $5 - 2y = 0$.

3. The graph of the inequality $y > mx + b$ is the set of points (x, y)

   which lie _____ the line $y = mx + b$

4. The graph of $y \leq mx + b$ is the set of points (x,y) which lie _____

   the line $y = mx + b$.

5. The graph of the inequality $3x - 2y \leq 4$ is the set of points (x,y)

   which lie _____ the line $3x - 2y = 4$.

6. The graph of the inequality $3x - 4y > 2$ is the set of points (x,y)

   which lie _____ the line $3x - 4y = 2$.

7. The graph of the inequality $2x + 3y \leq 3x - 2y + 4$ is the set of points

   (x,y) which lies _____ (on, above, below) the line _____.

8. The graph of the system of inequalities: $2x + y > 4$, $x + 2y < 4$ and

   $2x - 3y < 3$ is the set of points (x,y) which lie above the line(s) given

   by _____ and below the line(s) given by _____.

9. The graph of the system of inequalities $1 \leq x + y \leq 4$, $y - x \geq 0$

   and $x - 2y \leq 1$ is the set of points (x,y) which lie on or above the

   line(s) _____ and on or below the line(s) _____.

10. The inequalities that are to be satisfied by the variables in a linear

    programming problem are called the _____ and the linear function that

    is to be maximized or minimized is called the _____ function.

11. If a linear programming problem involves only two variables, then

    (i) the region in the xy-plane satisfied by the given set of

         inequalities is called the _____ region.

(ii)   If the region in (i) above is polygon (closed or open) then the maxima and minima of the objective function occurs at the _____ of the polygon.

12.   When solving the linear programming problem by simplex method, we first change all the inequalities into _____ by introducing the _____ variables which are _____ 0.

13.   Find the optimum of $Z = x - y$ subject to $x \geq 0$, $y \geq 0$, $x + y \geq 4$ and $x + 2y \leq 10$. When reduced to standard form, this problem becomes: 'Find the optimum of $Z = x - y$ where x, y, u, v are non-negative variables satisfying the equations _____.'

14.   Find the maximum of $Z = 3x + y + 2z$ subject to $x, y, z \geq 0$ and $x + y + z \leq 5$, $2x + y + 3z \leq 7$ and $2x + 3y + 4z \leq 13$.

(a)   Introducing the slack variables t, u, v (all ≥ 0) in this order, these inequalities reduce to equations given by _____.

(b)   The simplex tableau (which consists of entries of the objective function Z in the last row) is _____.

(c)   The elements in the bottom row of the simplex tableau in (b) above are called the _____.

(d)   The starting B.F.S. has the variables _____ equal to zero and the basis for this feasible solution is _____ and for this B.F.S. the objective function is $Z =$ _____

(e)   In using the simplex method, we move from one B.F.S. to another by replacing the variables in the basis one at a time by variables outside the basis. The variable that is removed from the basis is called the _____ variable and the variable that enters the basis is called the _____ variable.

(f)   For this problem (refer to tableau in (b) part above), the departing variable is _____ and the entering variable is _____ giving the new B.F.S. as _____.

(g)   At each stage the _____ variable is the one which has the largest positive indicator.

SEE ANSWERS AT THE END OF THIS BOOK.

CHAPTER - 12

YOU SHOULD BE FAMILIAR WITH THE FOLLOWING IMPORTANT TERMS:

Increment.   Average rate of change.

Instantaneous rate of change.   Limit (limiting value).

Continuous and discontinuous function.

The derivative of a function; differentiable function, differentiation.

Marginal rate: marginal cost, marginal revenue, marginal profit,
                 marginal productivity, marginal yield, marginal tax rate,
                 marginal propensity to save or consume.

One-sided limits; limit from above, limit from below.   Jump discontinuity.

OBJECTIVES

AFTER READING THIS CHAPTER YOU SHOULD BE ABLE TO DO THE FOLLOWING:

1.   Compute the increment in a variable when there is an increment in
     another variable on which it depends.

2.   Compute the average rate of change of a variable when there is an
     increment in another variable on which it depends.

3.   Compute the limiting value of a rational or algebraic function as its
     argument approaches any point (if the limit exists) by using the three
     theorems on limits given in the text.

4.   Calculate the derivatives of power functions, polynomial functions or
     simple rational and algebraic functions by using the definition as a
     limit.

5.   Find the slope and equation of the tangent line to the graph of a
     function.

6.   Apply differentiation to calculate the rate of change of any quantity
     varying with time, in particular to compute the instantaneous velocity
     of a moving object.

7.   Differentiate powers and combinations of powers by using the power
     rule and theorems on differentiation.

8.   Apply differentiation to calculate marginal cost from a cost function,
     marginal revenue from a revenue function or from a demand relation,
     and marginal profit, as well as other marginal rates.

9.   Calculate one-sided limits of rational and algebraic functions.

10. Test simple functions for continuity or differentiability.

EXERCISES - 12.1

1. $\Delta y = f(x+\Delta x) - f(x) = f(3.2) - f(3) = 13.4 - 13 = 0.4$

5. $\Delta p = p(t+\Delta t) - p(t) = p(3) - p(2) = 2050 - 2100 = -50.$

9. $\Delta y/\Delta x = \{f(2.5) - f(2)\}/(0.5) = \{(-14.5) - (-11)\}/0.5 = -7.$

13. $\Delta y/\Delta t = \{f(5+1.24) - f(5)\}/1.24 = (\sqrt{10.24} - \sqrt{9})/1.24 = (3.2-3)/1.24$
        $= 0.1613$

17. (a) $\Delta p/\Delta t = \{p(5) - p(3)\}/(5-3) = (12000-11920)/2 = 40.$

    (b) $\Delta p/\Delta t = \{p(4) - p(3)\}/(4-3) = (12080-11920)/1 = 160.$

    (c) $\Delta p/\Delta t = \{p(7/2) - p(3)\}/(7/2 -3) = (12030 - 11920)/(1/2) = 220.$

    (d) $\Delta p/\Delta t = \{p(13/4) - p(3)\}/(13/4 - 3) = (11982.5 - 11920)/(1/4)$
        $= 250.$

    (e) $\Delta p/\Delta t = \{p(t+\Delta t) - p(t)\}/\Delta t$

$$= \left[\{10,000 + 100(t+\Delta t) - 120(t+\Delta t)^2\} - (10,000+100t-12t^2)\right]/\Delta t$$

$$= 1000 - 240t - 120\Delta t.$$

21. $R(p) = \text{revenue} = px = 100p/(\sqrt{p}+1)$

$\Delta R = R(p+\Delta p) - R(p) = R(6.25) - R(4)$

$\quad = 1000(6.25)/(3.25) - 4000/3 = 452.38.$

$\Delta R/\Delta p = (452.38)/(6.25-4) = 201.06.$

25. $s = f(t) = 100t - 16t^2$

    (a) $\Delta s/\Delta t = \{f(3)-f(2)\}/(3-2) = (156-136)/1 = 20.$

    (b) $\Delta s/\Delta t = \{f(5) - f(3)\}/(5-3) = (100-156)/2 = -28$
        i.e.   the body is descending.

    (c) $\Delta s/\Delta t = \{f(t+ t) - f(t)\}/\Delta t$

$$= \left[\{100(t+\Delta t) - 16(t+\Delta t)^2\} - (100t - 16t^2)\right]/\Delta t$$

$$= 100 - 32t - 16\Delta t.$$

EXERCISES - 12.2

1. $\lim\limits_{x\to 2} (3x^2+7x-1) = 3\cdot 2^2 + 7\cdot 2 - 1 = 12 + 14 - 1 = 25.$

5. $\lim\limits_{x \to 5} \dfrac{x^2-25}{\sqrt{x^2+11}} = \dfrac{25-25}{\sqrt{25+11}} = 0/6 = 0$

9. $\lim\limits_{x \to 3} \dfrac{x^2-5x+6}{x-3} = \lim\limits_{x \to 3} \dfrac{(x-2)(x-3)}{x-3} = \lim\limits_{x \to 3} (x-2) = 3-2 = 1.$

13. $\lim\limits_{x \to -2} \dfrac{x^2+4x+4}{x^2-4} = \lim\limits_{x \to -2} \dfrac{(x+2)(x+2)}{(x+2)(x-2)} = \lim\limits_{x \to -2} \dfrac{x+2}{x-2} = \dfrac{-2+2}{-2-2} = 0$

17. $\lim\limits_{x \to 9} \dfrac{9-x}{\sqrt{x}-3} = \lim\limits_{x \to 9} \dfrac{(3-\sqrt{x})(3+\sqrt{x})}{\sqrt{x}-3} = \lim\limits_{x \to 9} -(\sqrt{x}+3) = (\sqrt{9}+3) = -6.$

$\underline{OR}$ $\lim\limits_{x \to 9} \dfrac{9-x}{\sqrt{x}-3} = \lim\limits_{x \to 9} \dfrac{9-x}{\sqrt{x}-3} \cdot \dfrac{\sqrt{x}+3}{\sqrt{x}+3} = \lim\limits_{x \to 9} \dfrac{(9-x)(\sqrt{x}+3)}{x-9} = \lim\limits_{x \to 9} -(\sqrt{x}+3)$

$= -(\sqrt{9}+3) = -6.$

21. $\lim\limits_{x \to 4} \dfrac{\sqrt{x}-2}{x^3-4^3} = \lim\limits_{x \to 4} \dfrac{\sqrt{x}-2}{(x-4)(x^2+4x+16)}$ $\quad | \ a^3-b^3 = (a-b)(a^2+ab+b^2)$

$= \lim\limits_{x \to 4} \dfrac{\sqrt{x}-2}{(\sqrt{x}-2)(\sqrt{x}+2)(x^2+4x+16)} = \lim\limits_{x \to 4} \dfrac{1}{(\sqrt{x}+2)(x^2+4x+16)}$

$= \dfrac{1}{(2+2)(16+16+16)} = \dfrac{1}{4(48)} = \dfrac{1}{192}$

25. $\lim\limits_{x \to 0} \dfrac{\sqrt{4+x}-2}{x} = \lim\limits_{x \to 0} \dfrac{\sqrt{4+x}-2}{x} \cdot \dfrac{\sqrt{4+x}+2}{\sqrt{4+x}+2}$

$= \lim\limits_{x \to 0} \dfrac{(4+x)-4}{x(\sqrt{4+x}+2)} = \lim\limits_{x \to 0} \dfrac{1}{\sqrt{4+x}+2} = \dfrac{1}{\sqrt{4+0}+2} = 1/4.$

29. $\lim\limits_{x \to 0} \dfrac{\sqrt{1+x}-1}{\sqrt{4+x}-2} = \lim\limits_{x \to 0} \dfrac{\sqrt{1+x}-1}{\sqrt{4+x}-2} \cdot \dfrac{\sqrt{1+x}+1}{\sqrt{1+x}+1} \cdot \dfrac{\sqrt{4+x}+2}{\sqrt{4+x}+2}$

$= \lim\limits_{x \to 0} \dfrac{\{(1+x)-1^2\}(\sqrt{4+x}+2)}{\{(4+x)-2^2\}(\sqrt{1+x}+1)}$

$= \lim\limits_{x \to 0} \dfrac{\sqrt{4+x}+2}{\sqrt{1+x}+1} = \dfrac{\sqrt{4}+2}{\sqrt{1}+1} = \dfrac{4}{2} = 2.$

33. $\lim\limits_{x \to 2} f(x) = \lim\limits_{x \to 2} \dfrac{x^2-4}{x-2} = \lim\limits_{x \to 2} \dfrac{(x-2)(x+2)}{x-2} = \lim\limits_{x \to 2} (x+2) = 4.$

37. $f(x) = 2x^2 + 3x + 1$ gives $f(1) = 6$ and

$f(1+h) = 2(1+h)^2 + 3(1+h) + 1 = 6 + 7h + 2h^2.$ Thus,

$\lim\limits_{h \to 0} \dfrac{f(1+h)-f(1)}{h} = \lim\limits_{h \to 0} \dfrac{(6+7h+2h^2)-6}{h} = \lim\limits_{h \to 0} (7+2h) = 7.$

41. $f(x) = 2x^2 + 5x + 1$ gives

$f(x+h) = 2(x+h)^2 + 5(x+h) + 1 = (2x^2+5x+1) + h(4x+2h+5)$ Thus,

$$\lim_{h\to 0} \frac{f(x+h) - f(x)}{h} = \lim_{h\to 0} \frac{\{2x^2+5x+1 + h(4x+2h+5)\} - (2x^2+5x+1)}{h}$$

$$= \lim_{h\to 0} (4x + 2h + 5) = 4x + 5$$

45.

x	= 1.2	1.1	1.05	1.01	1.005	1.001	→ 1
f(x)	= 1.4747	1.4021	1.3672	1.3400	1.3367	1.334	→ 4/3

$$\lim_{x\to 1} f(x) = \lim_{x\to 1} \frac{x^4-1}{x^3-1} = \lim_{x\to 1} \frac{(x-1)(x+1)(x^2+1)}{(x-1)(x^2+x+1)} = \lim_{x\to 1} \frac{(x+1)(x^2+1)}{x^2+x+1} =$$

$$= \frac{(1+1)(1+1)}{(1+1+1)} = 4/3$$

EXERCISES - 12.3

$$\left[f'(x) = \lim_{h\to 0} \frac{f(x+h) - f(x)}{h} \right].$$

1. $f(x) = 2x - 5$ gives $f(x+h) = 2(x+h) - 5$ Thus,

$$f'(x) = \lim_{h\to 0} \frac{f(x+h) - f(x)}{h} = \lim_{h\to 0} \frac{\{2(x+h) - 5\} - (2x-5)}{h}$$

$$= \lim_{h\to 0} \frac{2h}{h} = \lim_{h\to 0} (2) = 2.$$

5. $f'(x) = \lim_{h\to 0} \dfrac{f(x+h) - f(x)}{h} = \lim_{h\to 0} \dfrac{(x+h)^2 - x^2}{h} = \lim_{h\to 0} (2x+h) = 2x.$

9. $h'(x) = \lim_{h\to 0} \dfrac{h(x+h) - h(x)}{h} = \lim_{h\to 0} \dfrac{\{7 - 3(x+h)^2\} - (7-3x^2)}{h} = -6x$

13. $f(t+h) - f(t) = \dfrac{1}{2(t+h)+3} - \dfrac{1}{2t+3} = \dfrac{-2h}{(2t+3)(2t+3+2h)}$

$$f'(t) = \lim_{h\to 0} \frac{f(t+h) - f(t)}{h} = \lim_{h\to 0} \frac{1}{h} \frac{-2h}{(2t+3)(2t+3+2h)}$$

$$= \lim_{h\to 0} \frac{-2}{(2t+3)(2t+3+2h)} = \frac{-2}{(2t+3)(2t+3+0)} = \frac{-2}{(2t+3)^2}$$

17. (a) $x = f(y) = \sqrt{y}$ gives

$$\frac{dx}{dy} = \lim_{h\to 0} \frac{f(y+h) - f(y)}{h} = \lim_{h\to 0} \frac{\sqrt{y+h} - \sqrt{y}}{h}$$

$$= \lim_{h\to 0} \frac{\sqrt{y+h} - y}{h} \cdot \frac{\sqrt{y+h} + \sqrt{y}}{\sqrt{y+h} + \sqrt{y}} = \lim_{h\to 0} \frac{(y+h) - y}{h(\sqrt{y+h} + \sqrt{y})}$$

$$= \lim_{h \to 0} \frac{1}{\sqrt{y+h} + \sqrt{y}} = \frac{1}{\sqrt{y+0} + \sqrt{y}} = \frac{1}{2\sqrt{y}}$$

(b) $x = f(y) = (y+1)/y^2$ gi-es

$$\frac{dx}{dy} = \lim_{h \to 0} \frac{f(y+h) - f(y)}{h}$$

$$= \lim_{h \to 0} \frac{1}{h} \{ \frac{y+h+1}{(y+h)^2} - \frac{y+1}{y^2} \} = \lim_{h \to 0} \frac{1}{h} \{ \frac{h(-y^2-2y-yh-h)}{y^2(y+h)^2} \}$$

$$= (-y^2-2y)/y^2(y+0)^2 = -(y+2)/y^3$$

21. $F'(t) = \lim_{h \to 0} \frac{F(t+h) - F(t)}{h} = \lim_{h \to 0} \frac{\{(t+h)^2 - 3(t+h)\} - (t^2-3t)}{h}$

$$= \lim_{h \to 0} (2t + h - 3) = 2t - 3. \quad \text{Thus } F'(3) = 2(3) - 3 = 3.$$

25. $y = f(x) = 3x^2 - 4$ gives

$$\lim_{h \to 0} \frac{f(x+h) - f(x)}{h} = \lim_{h \to 0} \frac{\{3(x+h)^2 - 4\} - (3x^2-4)}{h} = 6x.$$

Thus, slope of the tangent line at x=2 is m = f'(2) = 6(2) = 12.
When x=2, y = f(2) = 3(4) - 4 = 8. The equation of the tangent
line through the point (2,8) and slope m = 12 is:

$$y-8 = 12(x-2) \quad \text{or} \quad y = 12x - 16.$$

29. $y = f(x) = (x+1)/x = 1 + 1/x$ gives

$$f'(x) = \lim_{h \to 0} \frac{f(x+h) - f(x)}{h} = \lim_{h \to 0} \frac{\{1 + 1/(x+h)\} - (1 + 1/x)}{h}$$

$$= \lim_{h \to 0} \frac{-1}{x(x+h)} = -1/x^2. \quad \text{Thus slope at x=1 is}$$

m = f'(1) = -1/1 = -1. When x=1, y = f(1) = 1 + 1/1 = 2.
Equation of tangent line through (1,2) with slope m = -1 is:
$$y-2 = -1(x-1) \quad \text{or} \quad y = -x+3.$$

33. $S(t) = 10,000 + 2000t - 200t^2$ gives

$$S'(t) = \lim_{h \to 0} \frac{S(t+h) - S(t)}{h}$$

$$= \lim_{h \to 0} \frac{1}{h} \{10,000 + 2000(t+h) - 200(t+h)^2 - (10,000 + 2000t - 200t^2)\}$$

$$= 200 - 400t. \quad \text{Thus}$$
(a) S'(0) = 2000   (b) S'(4) = 2000 - 1600 = 400   (c) S'(8) = -1200.

EXERCISES - 12.4

1. $y = x^5$ gives $y' = 5x^{5-1} = 5x^4$.

5. $y = 1/5u^5 = (1/5)u^{-5}$ gives $dy/du = (1/5)(-5u^{-6}) = -u^{-6}$.

9. $y = 4x^3 - 3x^2 + 7$ gives $y' = 4(3x^2) - 3(2x^1) + 0 = 12x^2 - 6x$.

13. $y = 3u^2 + 3/u^2 = 3u^2 + 3u^{-2}$ gives $dy/du = 3(2u) + 3(-2u^{-3}) = 6u - 6/u^3$

17. $y = 2\sqrt{x} + 2/\sqrt{x} = 2x^{1/2} + 2x^{-1/2}$ gives $y' = 2(1/2)x^{-1/2} + 2(-1/2)x^{-3/2}$
$$= x^{-1/2} - x^{-3/2}$$

21. $y = 2x^{3/2} + 4x^{5/4}$ gives $y' = 2(3/2)x^{1/2} + 4(5/4)x^{1/4} = 3x^{1/2} + 5x^{1/4}$.

25. $y = (x-7)(2x-9) = 2x^2 - 23x + 63$ gives $dy/dx = 4x - 23$.

29. $y = (t+1)(3t-1)^2 = 9t^3 + 3t^2 - 5t + 1$ gives $dy/dt = 27t^2 + 6t - 5$.

33. $y = (\frac{x+1}{x})^3 = (1 + 1/x)^3 = 1 + 3/x + 3/x^2 + 1/x^3 = 1 + 3x^{-1} + 3x^{-2} + x^{-3}$

gives $y' = 0 + 3(-1x^{-2}) + 3(-2x^{-3}) + (-3x^{-4}) = -3x^{-2} - 6x^{-3} - 3x^{-4}$.

37. $y = (x+1)^2/x = (x^2+2x+1)/x = x + 2 + x^{-1}$ gives $y' = 1+0-1x^{-2} = 1 - 1/x^2$.

41. $y = x^{1.6}/x^{2.3} = x^{1.6-2.3} = x^{-0.7}$ gives $y' = -0.7\,x^{-1.7}$

45. $y = (16t)^{3/4} - (16t)^{-3/4} = (16)^{3/4}t^{3/4} - (16)^{-3/4}t^{-3/4} = 8t^{3/4} - (1/8)t^{-3/4}$

gives $dy/dt = 8(3/4)t^{-1/4} - (1/8)(-3/4)t^{-7/4} = 6t^{-1/4} + (3/32)t^{-7/4}$

49. $y = u^3 - 5u^2 + (7/3)u^{-2} + 6$ gives $dy/du = 3u^2 - 10u + (7/3)(-2u^{-3}) + 0$

53. $f(x) = x^2 - 3x + 4$ gives $f'(x) = 2x - 3$. At x=1, $f'(1) = 2-3 = -1$,

Equation of tangent line through (1,2) with slope $m = f'(1) = -1$ is:
$$y - 2 = -1(x-1) \quad \text{or} \quad y = -x + 3.$$

57. $y = x^2 - 3x + 7$ gives the slope of tangent line, $y' = 2x - 3$.

The line $x - y + 4 = 0$ or $y = x+4$ has a slope of 1. The tangent line

is parallel if $2x - 3 = 1$ or $x = 2$. When x=2, $y = 2^2 - 3(2) + 7 = 5$. Thus,

the point is (2,5).

61. $I = 5 + 0.1x + 0.01x^2$ (billion) gives $dI/dx = 0.1 + 0.02x$.

(a) 1950 is x=0 : $dI/dx = 0.01$

(b) 1960 is x=10 : $dI/dx = 0.1 + 0.02(10) = 0.3$

(c) 1970 is x=20 ; $dI/dx = 0.1 + 0.02(20) = 0.5$.

65. $y = k\sqrt{cat} = k\sqrt{ca}\ t^{1/2}$ gives $dy/dt = k\sqrt{ca}(1/2)t^{-1/2} = (k\sqrt{ca}/2)t^{-1/2}$.

69. $b(t) = c_2 t^{1/4} = 15t^{1/4}$ and $a(t) = b(t) + c_1 t^{3/4} = 15t^{1/4} + 0.2t^{3/4}$

$A(t) = \pi ab = \pi(15t^{1/4} + 0.2t^{3/2})(15t^{1/4}) = \pi(225t^{1/2} + 3t)$

$A'(t) = \pi\{225(1/2)t^{-1/2} + 3\} = \pi(112.5/\sqrt{t} + 3)$

$A(15) = \pi\{225\sqrt{15} + 3(15)\} = 2879 m^2$

$A'(15) = \pi(112.5/\sqrt{15} + 3) = 100.7\ m^2/min.$

$A(30) = \pi(225\sqrt{30} + 90) = 4154\ m^2$

$A'(30) = \pi(112.5/\sqrt{30} + 3) = 74.0 m^2/min.$

EXERCISES - 12.5

1. marg. cost = $C'(x) = d/dx(100 + 2x) = 2$.

5. marg. rev. = $R'(x) = d/dx(x - 0.01x^2) = 1 - 0.02x$.

9. $x + 4p = 100$ gives $p = 25 - x/4$. Thus revenue is

$R(x) = p \cdot x = x(25-x/4) = 25x - (1/4)x^2$. $R'(x) = 25 - x/2$.

13. Profit = $P(x)$ = rev. - cost = $R(x) - C(x) = (25x - x^2/4) - (100 + 5x)$

or $P(x) = 20x - x^2/4 - 100$. Thus, $P'(x) = 20 - x/2$.

17. Form Ex. 13, $P'(x) = 20 - x/2 = 0$ when x=40. Then

$P(40) = 20(40) - 40^2/4 - 100 = 300$. When the profit P is maximum

x=40. Then the demand relation (refer to #9) $x + 4p = 100$ gives

$40 + 4p = 100$ or $p = 15$.

21. marg. cost = $C'(x) = 2ax + b$; Aver. cost = $\overline{C}(x) = C(x)/x = ax+b+c/x$
$C'(x) = \overline{C}(x)$ gives $2ax + b = ax+b+c/x$ or $ax^2 = c$ or $x = \sqrt{c/a}$
$d/dx(\overline{C}(x)) = d/dx(ax + b + cx^{-1}) = a - cx^{-2} = a - c/x^2$.

At $x = c/a$, $\overline{C}'(x) = a - c/(\sqrt{c/a})^2 = a - a = 0$.

EXERCISES - 12.6

1. (a) 1 (b) 2 (c) Since $\lim\limits_{x\to 2^-} f(x) = 1 \neq 2 = \lim\limits_{x\to 2^+} f(x)$,
$\lim\limits_{x\to 2^+} f(x)$ does not exist.

5. $\lim\limits_{x\to 1^+} \sqrt{x-1} = \sqrt{1-1} = 0$

9. As $x \to 1^+$, $x-1 > 0$ and $|x-1| = x-1$.

Thus, $\lim\limits_{x\to 1^+} \dfrac{|x-1|}{x-1} = \lim\limits_{x\to 1} \dfrac{x-1}{x-1} = \lim\limits_{x\to 1} (1) = 1$.

13. $\lim\limits_{x\to 0^-} \dfrac{1}{x^2}$. As $x \to 0$ through negative values, $x^2 \to 0$ through positive

values and $1/x^2$ becomes positively larger and larger. Thus,

$\lim\limits_{x\to 0^-} (1/x^2) = +\infty$.

17. $f(x) = x^2/x$ is not defined at x=0.

Thus, $f(x)$ is not continuous at
x=0. Now $y = f(x) = x^2/x = x$ for
all $x \neq 0$. Thus the graph of $f(x)$
is the st. line y=x with a hole at x=0.

21.
Since $G(x) = \begin{cases} 0 & \text{if } x < 0 \\ 1 & \text{if } x > 0 \end{cases}$

is not defined at x=0, $G(x)$ is
discontinuous at x=0. The graph
is as shown.

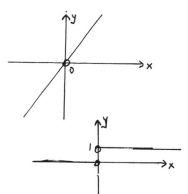

25. (i) We have: $f(3) = 0$ (given)

(ii) $\lim\limits_{x\to 3^-} f(x) = \lim\limits_{x\to 3^-} \dfrac{|x-3|}{x-3} = \lim\limits_{x\to 3} \dfrac{-(x-3)}{x-3} = -1$

and $\lim\limits_{x\to 3^+} f(x) = \lim\limits_{x\to 3^+} \dfrac{|x-3|}{x-3} = \lim\limits_{x\to 3} \dfrac{x-3}{x-3} = 1$

Since $\lim\limits_{x\to 3^-} f(x) \neq \lim\limits_{x\to 3^+} f(x)$, $\lim\limits_{x\to 3} f(x)$ does

not exist. Thus, $f(x)$ is discontinuous
at x=3.

29. Since $f(x) = (x+1)/(x-2)$ is not defined at $x = 2$, $f(x)$ is not
continuous at x=2.

33. $f(x) = \dfrac{x^2+2x+3}{x^2+2x+4} = \dfrac{x^2+2x+3}{(x+1)^2+3}$, Since, the denominator is never zero for
any value of x, $f(x)$ is continuous for all x i.e. no point of
discontinuity.

37. Since $f(x)$ is continuous at x=1,
$\lim\limits_{x\to 1^-} f(x) = \lim\limits_{x\to 1^+} f(x)$ or $h+3 = 3-h$ or $h=0$.

41. $f(x) = \sqrt{x-1}$ is not continuous at x=1, because $\lim\limits_{x\to 1^-} \sqrt{x-1}$ does not
exist. Thus, $f(x)$ is not differentiable at x=1.

45. From #44, we have:
T = 0.1I   if $I \leq 2000$
   = 0.25I - 300   if $2000 < I \leq 6000$
   = 0.4I - 1200   if $I \geq 600$.

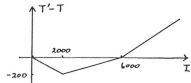

Let T' = new tax. Than,
T' = 0 if I $\leq$ 2000.
T' = 0.3(I - 2000).
   = 0.3I - 600 if 2000 $\leq$ I $\leq$ 6000
T' = 1200 + 0.5(I-6000) = 0.5I - 1800 if I $\geq$ 6000.

$$T'-T = \begin{cases} 0 - 0.1I = -0.1I & \text{if } I \leq 6000 \\ 0.3I - 6000 - (0.25I-300) = 0.05I - 300 & \text{if } 2000 \leq I \leq 6000 \\ 0.5I - 1800 - (0.4I-1200) = 0.1I - 600 & \text{if } I \geq 6000. \end{cases}$$

REVIEW EXERCISES ON CHAPTER - 12

1. See answers in the text book.

5. $\lim\limits_{x \to 5} \dfrac{x^2-25}{x+15} = \dfrac{25-25}{5+15} = 0.$

9. $\lim\limits_{x \to 1} \dfrac{x^2-2x+1}{x^2-1} = \lim\limits_{x \to 1} \dfrac{(x-1)(x-1)}{(x-1)(x+1)} = \lim\limits_{x \to 1} \dfrac{x-1}{x+1} = \dfrac{1-1}{1+1} = 0.$

13. $\lim\limits_{x \to 3} \dfrac{\sqrt{x+1} - 2}{\sqrt{x+6} + 3} = \dfrac{\sqrt{3+1} - 2}{\sqrt{3+6} + 3} = \dfrac{2-2}{3+3} = \dfrac{0}{6} = 0.$

17. $f(x + h) - f(x) = \dfrac{1}{(x+h+1)^2} - \dfrac{1}{(x+1)^2} = \dfrac{(x+1)^2 - (x+1+h)^2}{(x+1)^2(x+h+1)^2}$

$$= \dfrac{-2(h)(x+1) - (h)^2}{(x+1)^2(x+h+1)^2}$$

Thus, $f'(x) = \lim\limits_{h \to 0} \dfrac{f(x+h) - f(x)}{h} = \lim\limits_{h \to 0} \dfrac{1}{h} \left\{ \dfrac{-2h(x+1) - h^2}{(x+1)^2(x+h+1)^2} \right\}$

$$= \lim\limits_{h \to 0} \left\{ \dfrac{-2(x+1) - h}{(x+1)^2(x+h+1)^2} \right\} = \dfrac{-2(x+1)}{(x+1)^2(x+1)^2} = -2/(x+1)^3.$$

21. $y = x^3\sqrt{x} = x^3 \cdot x^{1/2} = x^{3+1/2} = x^{7/2}$ gives $y' = (7/2)x^{5/2}$.

25. $y = x \cdot \sqrt[3]{x} = x^{1/2} \cdot x^{1/3} = x^{1/2+1/3} = x^{5/6}$ gives $y' = (5/6)x^{-1/6}.$

29. $f(y) = (2y^2-1)(y^2+2)/2y^3 = (2y^4+3y^2-2)/2y^3 = y + (3/2)y^{-1} - y^{-3}.$

   gives $f'(y) = 1 + (3/2)(-1y^{-2}) - (-3y^{-4}) = 1 - (3/2)y^{-2} + 3y^{-4}.$

33. $x + 20p = 1000$ gives $p = 50 - 0.05x$. Thus, the revenue,
   $R = px = (50-0.05x)x = 50x - 0.05x^2$ gives $R' = 50 - 0.1x.$

37. $p = 2024 - 2x - x^2$ gives $dp/dx = -2 - 2x$. At $x=30$, we have
   $dp/dx = (-2-2(30)) = -62.$

41. $f(x)$ is not continuous at $x=0$, because $f(0)$ is not defined.

45. Total cost, C(x) is
C(x) = 2x   if   x ≤ 20 ; C(x) = 40 + 1.75(x-20) if 20 ≤ x ≤ 40;
C(x) = 75 + 1.5(x-40)   if   x > 40.
Average cost $\bar{C}(x)$ = C(x)/x is then: $\bar{C}(x)$ = 2 if x ≤ 20;
$\bar{C}(x)$ = 1.75 + 5/x   if   20 < x ≤ 40 ; $\bar{C}(x)$ = 1.5 + 15/x if x > 40.
$\bar{C}$ is continuous for all x but not differentiable at x=20, 40.

REVIEW TEST ON CHAPTER - 12

FILL IN THE BLANKS:

1. If y = f(x) = $\sqrt{x}$, and x changes from 1 to 1.44, then Δy = _____ .

2. If y = f(x) = $1/x^2$, and x changes from 1 to 2, then Δy = _____ .

3. The average rate of change of y=f(x) as x changes to x + Δx is given

   by _____ .

4. The average rate of change of y = f(x) = 3x+2 as x changes from
   2 to 2.01 is given by Δy/Δx = _____ .

5. The average rate of change of y = f(x) = ln x as x changes from 1 to e is
   given by _____ .

6. $\lim\limits_{x \to 2} \{(x^2-4)/(x+2)\}$ _____ $\{\lim\limits_{x \to 2} (x^2-4)\} / \{\lim\limits_{x \to 2} (x+2)\}$ (= , ≠)

7. $\lim\limits_{x \to 3} \{(x^2-9)/(x-3)\}$ _____ $\{\lim\limits_{x \to 3} (x^2-9)\}/\{\lim\limits_{x \to 3} (x-3)\}$ (= , ≠)

8. $\lim\limits_{x \to 2} \dfrac{x^2-1}{x-1}$ = _____ .   9. $\lim\limits_{x \to -1} \dfrac{x^2+1}{x^2-4}$ = _____ .

10. $\lim\limits_{x \to 1} \dfrac{\sqrt{x+3} - 2}{x+1}$ = _____ .   11. $\lim\limits_{x \to 2} \dfrac{x^2+5}{x^2-4}$ = _____ .

12. If f(x) = $|x-3|/(3-x)$, then $\lim\limits_{x \to 3-}$ f(x) = _____

    $\lim\limits_{x \to 3+}$ f(x) = _____ and $\lim\limits_{x \to 3}$ f(x) = _____ .

13. If f(x) = $\begin{cases} 2x - 5 & \text{if } x > 3 \\ x^2+1 & \text{if } x \le 3 \end{cases}$, then

    $\lim\limits_{x \to 1-}$ f(x) = _____ , $\lim\limits_{x \to 5+}$ f(x) = _____ $\lim\limits_{x \to 3-}$ f(x) = ____

    $\lim\limits_{x \to 3+}$ f(x) = _____ and $\lim\limits_{x \to 3}$ f(x) = _____ .

14. If $\lim\limits_{x \to c} f(x)$ exists, then x=c _____ (is or is not necessarily) in the domain of f.

15. If $\lim\limits_{x \to c^-} f(x)$ and $\lim\limits_{x \to c^+} f(x)$ both exist, then $\lim\limits_{x \to c} f(x)$ _____ (exists or not).

16. By definition , f'(x) = _____ .

17. $\frac{d}{dx}(x^{-6})$ = _____ .

18. $\frac{d}{dx}(1/x^5)$ = _____ .

19. $\frac{d}{dt}(1/\sqrt{t})$ = _____ .

20. $\frac{d}{dx}(\frac{x^2+1}{x})$ = _____ .

21. $\frac{d}{dx}(x^3 \ln 2)$ = _____ .

22. $\frac{d}{dx}(x^2 e^5)$ = _____ .

23. By definition, f(x) is continuous at x=c, if _____ .

24. $f(x) = \dfrac{x^2+1}{x^2-x-2}$ is discontinuous at x = _____ .

25. $f(x) = \dfrac{x^2-9}{x^2-x-6}$ is discontinuous at x = _____ .

SEE ANSWERS AT THE END OF THIS BOOK.

CHAPTER - 13

YOU SHOULD BE FAMILIAR WITH THE FOLLOWING TERMS:

Product rule ; quotient rule.

Average cost and marginal average cost.

Chain rule ; "inside" and "outside" parts of a composite function.

Related rates.

Second derivative, third derivative, nth derivative.

Acceleration.

OBJECTIVES

AFTER READING THIS CHAPTER YOU SHOULD BE ABLE TO DO THE FOLLOWING:

1. Use the product rule to calculate the derivative of the product of two functions.

2. Use the quotient rule to calculate the derivative of the ratio of two functions.

3. Recognize the "outside" and "inside" parts of a composite function.

4. Use the chain rule to differentiate composite functions.

5. Use the chain rule to compute the rate of change of one variable given the rate of change of another variable on which it depends – (Related rates.)

6. Calculate the derivatives of exponential and logarithmic functions and more complicated functions involving exponentials and logarithms.

7. Calculate the second and higher derivatives of a function .

SOLUTIONS TO ALTERNATE ODD PROBLEMS

EXERCISES - 13.1

1. $y' = (x+1)(3x^2) + (x^3+3)(1) = 4x^3 + 3x^2 + 3.$

5. $y' = (x^2-5x+1)(2) + (2x+3)(2x-5) = 6x^2-14x-13.$

9. $u = (y+3y^{-1})(y^2-5)$ gives $du/dy = (y+3y^{-1})(2y) + (y^2-5)(1-3y^{-2})$
$$= 3y^2 - 2 + 15y^{-2}.$$

13. $x = 1000 - 2p$ gives $p = 500 - x/2$, so that
$R(x) = px = x(500 - x/2)$. By product rule,
$R'(x) = x(-1/2) + (500 - x/2)(1) = 500 - x$.

17. G.N.P. $= g(t) = PW = (10 + 0.2t + 0.01t^2)(6000 + 500t + 10t^2)$
gives $g'(t) = 6200 + 520t + 21t^2 + 0.4t^3$.

21. $y = \dfrac{u}{u+1}$ gives $dy/du = \dfrac{(u+1) \cdot 1 - u(1)}{(u+1)^2} = 1/(u+1)^2$.

25. $y = \dfrac{t^2 - 7t}{t-5}$ gives $dy/dt = \dfrac{(t-5)(2t-7) - (t^2 - 7t) \cdot 1}{(t-5)^2} = \dfrac{t^2 - 10t + 35}{(t-5)^2}$.

29. $y = 1/(x^2+1)$ gives $dy/dx = \dfrac{(x^2+1) \cdot 0 - 1 \cdot 2x}{(x^2+1)^2} = -2x/(x^2+1)^2$.

33. W = per capita income = (G.N.P.)/(population size) = I/P
$= (10 + 0.4t + 0.01t^2)/(4 + 0.1t + 0.01t^2)$ in thousands of dollars.
$dW/dt = (0.6 - 0.12t - 0.003t^2)(4 + 0.1t + 0.01t^2)^{-2}$.

37. $W = (2t^2 + 3)(t^2 - t + 2)$ $dW/dt = 4t(t^2 - t + 2) + (2t^2 + 3)(2t - 1)$
$= 8t^3 - 6t^2 + 14t - 3$.

EXERCISES - 13.2

1. $y = (3x+5)^7$ gives $y' = 7(3x+5)^6 \cdot \dfrac{d}{dx}(3x+5) = 7(3x+5)^6 \cdot 3$.

5. $f(x) = (x^2+1)^{-4}$ gives $f'(x) = -4(x^2+1)^{-5} \cdot \dfrac{d}{dx}(x^2+1) = -4(x^2+1)^{-5} \cdot 2x$.

9. $x = (t^3+1)^{-1/3}$ gives $dx/dt = (-1/3)(t^3+1)^{-4/3} \cdot (3t^2) = -t^2(t^3+1)^{-4/3}$.

13. $y' = 0.6(x^2+1)^{0.6-1} \cdot (d/dx)(x^2+1) = 0.6(x^2+1)^{-0.4} \cdot (2x) = 1.2x(x^2+1)^{-0.4}$.

17. $f(x) = (x^2+1)^{1/2}/(x^2+1)^{1/3} = (x^2+1)^{1/2-1/3} = (x^2+1)^{1/6}$ gives
$f'(x) = (1/6)(x^2+1)^{-5/6} \cdot (2x) = (x/3)(x^2+1)^{-5/6}$.

21. $f(x) = (x+1)^3 \cdot (2x+1)^4$. Using the product rule, we have:
$f'(x) = (x+1)^3 \{4(2x+1)^3 \cdot 2\} + (2x+1)^4 \{3(x+1)^2 \cdot 1\}$
$= (x+1)^2 (2x+1)^3 \{8(x+1) + 3(2x+1)\}$.

25. $y = \left[(x+1)(x+2) + 3\right]^4 = (x^2+3x+5)^4$ gives
$y' = 4(x^2+3x+5)^3 \cdot (2x+3)$.

29. $\dfrac{dy}{dx} = 3(\dfrac{u^2+1}{u+1})^2 \cdot \dfrac{d}{du}(\dfrac{u^2+1}{u+1}) = 3(\dfrac{u^2+1}{u+1})^2 \cdot \dfrac{(u+1)2u - (u^2+1)\cdot 1}{(u+1)^2}$

$$= 3(u+1)^2(u^2+2u-1)/(u+1)^4.$$

33. $z = x/\sqrt{x^2-1}$. Using the quotient rule, we have:

$$dz/dx = \frac{\sqrt{x^2-1}\cdot 1 - x\{(1/2)(x^2-1)^{-1/2}\cdot 2x\}}{(\sqrt{x^2-1})^2} = \frac{(x^2-1) - x^2}{(x^2-1)^{3/2}}.$$

37. $f'(x) = \{4(2x+1)^3\cdot 2\}(2-3x)^3 + (2x+1)^4\{3(2-3x)^2(-3)\}$. Therefore

$f'(0) = 4(1)^3\cdot 2(2)^3 + (1)^4\cdot 3(2)^2(-3) = 28.$

41. $\overline{C}(x) = \dfrac{C(x)}{x} = \dfrac{\sqrt{x^2 + 100}}{x} = x^{-1}(x^2+100)^{-1/2}$ gives

$\overline{C}'(x) = -100x^{-2}(x^2+100)^{-1/2}.$

45. $\dfrac{dC}{dt} = \dfrac{dC}{dx} \cdot \dfrac{dx}{dt} = (10 - 0.2x + 0.006x^2)\dfrac{dx}{dt}$. Here x=100, dx/dt = 2, so that
$dC/dt = \{10 - 0.2(100) + 0.006(100)^2\}(2) = 100$ per month

49. $A = \pi r^2$. $dA/dt = (dA/dr)(dr/dt) = 2\pi r(dr/dt)$.   Therefore

$dr/dt = (2\pi r)^{-1}dA/dt$. We are given that when r=5, dA/dt = 30.
Thus $dr/dt = (10\pi)^{-1}(30) = 3/\pi$ km/hr.

53. $dR/dt = (dR/dT)(dT/dt) = \dfrac{1}{2\sqrt{T}} \cdot \dfrac{3(t+2) - (3t+1)\cdot 1}{(t+2)^2}$

$$= \dfrac{1}{2}(\dfrac{t+2}{3t+1})^{1/2}\cdot\dfrac{5}{(t+2)^2} = \dfrac{5}{2}(3t+1)^{-1/2}(t+2)^{-3/2}.$$

EXERCISES - 13.3

1. $y' = (d/dx)(7e^x) = 7(d/dx)(e^x) = 7e^x.$

5. $y' = (d/dx)(e^{x^2}) = e^{x^2} \cdot (d/dx)(x^2) = e^{x^2} \cdot 2x.$

9. $y = xe^x$ gives $y' = x\cdot e^x + e^x\cdot 1 = (x+1)e^x$, by product rule.

13. $y = (x+1)e^{-x}$ gives $y' = (x+1)\cdot(-e^{-x}) + e^{-x}\cdot 1 = (1-x)e^{-x}.$

17. $y = e^x/(x+2)$. By quotient rule, we have:

$y' = \dfrac{(x+2)\cdot e^x - e^x\cdot 1}{(x+2)^2} = (x+1)e^x/(x+2)^2.$

21. $y' = (1/7)(d/dx)(\ln x) = (1/7)(1/x) = 1/7x.$

25. $y' = (1/\ln 7)(d/dx)(\ln x) = (1/\ln 7)(1/x) = 1/(x \ln 7)$, because ln 7 is a constant.

29. $y' = 5(\ln x)^4 \, d/dx(\ln x) = 5(\ln x)^4 \cdot (1/x)$.

33. $y = (\ln x)^{-1/2}$ gives $y' = (-1/2)(\ln x)^{-3/2} \cdot (1/x)$.

37. By product rule, $y' = x^2\{\dfrac{1}{x^2+1} \cdot 2x\} + \{\ln(x^2+1)\}2x$.

41. By quotient rule, $y' = \dfrac{x \cdot 1/x - \ln x \cdot 1}{x^2} = (1 - \ln x)/x^2$.

45. $y = \ln(3^{x^2}) = x^2 \ln 3$ gives $y' = (\ln 3) \cdot 2x$, because $\ln 3$ is a const.

49. $y = \log(e^x) = x \log e$ gives $y' = (\log e) \cdot (d/dx)(x) = \log e \cdot 1$, because $\log e$ is simply a constant.

53. $y = \ln(\dfrac{\sqrt{x+1}}{x^2+4}) = \ln (x+1)^{1/2} - \ln(x^2+4) = (1/2) \ln(x+1) - \ln(x^2+4)$.

Thus, $y' = (1/2) \cdot \dfrac{1}{x+1} \cdot 1 - \left[1/(x^2+4)\right](2x) = \dfrac{1}{2(x+1)} - \dfrac{2x}{x^2+4}$.

57. $y = \log_a x = \dfrac{\ln x}{\ln a}$ gives $y' = (1/\ln a) \cdot (d/dx)(\ln x) = 1/x \ln a$,
because $1/\ln a$ is simply a constant.

61. $y = (\log_3 x)(\log_x 2) = (\ln x/\ln 3)(\ln 2/\ln x) = \ln 2/\ln 3 = $ const.

gives $y' = 0$.

65. $y = x^2 \log x = x^2 \log_{10} x = x^2 \ln x/\ln 10 = (1/\ln 10)(x^2 \ln x)$.

Thus, $y' = (1/\ln 10) \cdot (x^2 \bullet 1/x + \ln x \cdot 2x)$.

69. $R = xp = x(5 - e^{0.1x}) = 5x - xe^{0.1x}$ gives

$R' = 5 - \{x \cdot e^{0.1x}(0.1) + e^{0.1x} \cdot 1\} = 5 - (1 + 0.1x)e^{0.1x}$.

73. $C'(x) = 1 + e^{-0.5x}(-0.5) = 1 - 0.5e^{-0.5x}$

$\overline{C}(x) = C(x)/x = 100x^{-1} + 1 + x^{-1}e^{-0.5x}$ gives

$\overline{C}'(x) = -100x^{-2} + \{x^{-1} \cdot (-0.5e^{-0.5x}) + e^{-0.5x}(-1x^{-2})\}$.

77. $c'(t) = -kCe^{-kt}$. Therefore,

$c'(t) - k\{c_s - c(t)\} = -kCe^{-kt} - k\{c_s - (c_s + Ce^{-kt})\} = 0$.

$c(0) = c_s + C$. Therefore $C = c(0) - c_s$.

81. $dy/dt = 3y_m(1 - Ce^{-kt})^2(kCe^{-kt})$.

Now $1 - Ce^{-kt} = (y/y_m)^{1/3}$, $Ce^{-kt} = 1 - (y/y_m)^{1/3}$. Therefore,

$dy/dt = 3y_m(y/y_m)^{2/3}k\{1 - (y-y_m)^{1/3}\} = 3ky^{2/3}(y_m^{1/3} - y^{1/3})$.

1. $y = 3x^5 + 7x^3 - 4x^2 + 2$ gives $y' = 15x^4 + 21x^2 - 8x$,

$y'' = 60x^3 + 42x - 8$, $y''' = 180x^2 + 42$, $y^{(iv)} = 360x$,

$y^{(v)} = 360 = $ const. and $y^{(n)} = 0$ if $n > 5$.

5. $y = \dfrac{x^2+1-1}{x^2+1} = 1 - (x^2+1)^{-1}$ gives $y' = 0 - (-1)(x^2+1)^{-2} \cdot 2x$ or

$y' = 2x(x^2+1)^{-2}$. $y'' = 2x\{-2(x^2+1)^{-3} \cdot 2x\} + (x^2+1)^{-2} \cdot 2$

$= -8x^2/(x^2+1)^3 + 2/(x^2+1)^2 = \{-8x^2 + 2(x^2+1)\}/(x^2+1)^3$.

9. $u = (x^2+1)^{-1}$ gives $u' = -1(x^2+1)^{-2} \cdot 2x = -2x(x^2+1)^{-2}$

$u'' = (6x^2-2)(x^2+1)^{-3}$. (Compare u' with y' of #5 above).

13. $y = xe^x$ gives $y' = x \cdot e^x + e^x \cdot 1 = (x+1)e^x$, $y'' = (x+1)e^x + e^x \cdot 1$

$= (x+2)e^x$; $y''' = (x+2) \cdot e^x + e^x \cdot 1 = (x+3)e^x$ and $y^{(4)} = (x+3)e^x + e^x \cdot 1$
$= (x+4)e^x$, where we have used the product rule.

17. $y = (x+1)e^{-x}$ gives $y' = (x+1)(-e^{-x}) + e^{-x} \cdot 1 = -xe^{-x}$.

$y'' = (-x)(-e^{-x}) + e^{-x} \cdot (-1) = (x-1)e^{-x}$.

REVIEW EXERCISES ON CHAPTER - 13

1. See answers in the text.

5. $y = (2x+1)^3(3x-1)^4$ gives $y' = (2x+1)^3\{4(3x-1)^3 \cdot 3\} + (3x-1)^4\{3(2x+1)^2 \cdot 2\}$

$= (2x+1)^2(3x-1)^3\{12(2x+1) + 6(3x-1)\} = (2x+1)^2(3x-1)^3(42x+6)$.

9. $y = x^{\sqrt{2}}\ln x$ gives $y' = x^{\sqrt{2}} \cdot (1/x) + \ln x(\sqrt{2} \ x^{\sqrt{2}-1}) = x^{\sqrt{2}-1}(1 + \sqrt{2} \ln x)$.

13. $y = (3x-7)^6(x+1)^4$ gives $y' = (3x-7)^6\{4(x+1)^3 \cdot 1\} + (x+1)^4\{6(3x-7)^5 \cdot 3\}$

$= (x+1)^3(3x-7)^5\{4(3x-7) + 18(x+1)\} = (x+1)^3(3x-7)^5(30x - 10)$

$y'' = \{3(x+1)^2 \cdot 1\}(3x-7)^5(30x-10) + \{5(3x-7)^4 \cdot 3\}(x+1)^3(30x-10)$

$+ 30(x+1)^3(3x-7)^5 = 30(3x-7)^4(x+1)^2(27x^2-18x-5)$.

17. $x = a - b\ln p$ gives $p = e^{(a-x)/b}$ and $R(x) = xp = xe^{(a-x)/b}$.

Thus, $R'(x) = (1 - x/b)e^{(a-x)/b}$.

21. $x + \ln(p+1) = 50$ gives $\frac{dp}{dx} = 1 + e^{50-x}$ or $dp/dx = -e^{50-x}$.

25. $R(x) = xp = 300xe^{-x/20}$ gives $R'(x) = 15(20-x)e^{-x/20}$

$C(x) = 500 + 20x$ and $P(x) = R(x) - C(x) = 300xe^{-x/20} - 500 - 20x$.

$P'(x) = 15(20-x)e^{-x/20} - 20$.

29. $f'(t) = a(pt^{p-1}e^{-t} - t^p e^{-t}) = at^{p-1}e^{-t}(p-t)$.

$f'(t) = 0$ when $t=p$.

REVIEW TEST ON CHAPTER   13

FILL IN THE BLANKS: (DO NOT SIMPLIFY ANSWERS).

1. $\frac{d}{dx}(x^2+1)^7 =$ _____ .

2. $\frac{d}{dx}\{\frac{3}{(x^2-1)^5}\} =$ _____ .

3. $\frac{d}{dx}\{(x^2+5)^7(3x-5)\} =$ _____ .

4. $\frac{d}{dx}\{(2x+5)^4(3x-1)^7\} =$ _____ .

5. $\frac{d}{dx}(e^7) =$ _____ .

6. $\frac{d}{dx}(e^{x^2}) =$ _____ .

7. $\frac{d}{dx}(e^{\log 7}) =$ _____ .

8. $\frac{d}{dx}(\ln 3) =$ _____ .

9. $\frac{d}{dx}(\ln x \ln 2) =$ _____ .

10. $\frac{d}{dx}\ln(x^2+1) =$ _____ .

11. $\frac{d}{dx}\{\ln(\ln x)\} =$ _____ .

12. $\frac{d}{dx}\{\ln(e^x/x)\} =$ _____ .

13. $\frac{d}{dx}(x^3\ln x) =$ _____ .

14. $\frac{d}{dx}(e^{3x}\ln x) =$ _____ .

15. $\frac{d}{dx}\{\ln x \cdot \ln(e^x)\} =$ _____ .

16. $\frac{d}{dx}(\ln x)^7 =$ _____ .

17. $\frac{d}{dx}(x + 3\ln x)^5 =$ _____ .

18. $\frac{d}{dx}\{\ln(e^x+x)\} =$ _____ .

19. $\frac{d}{dx}(\log_2 x) = \frac{d}{dx}(\ln x/\ln 2) =$ _____ .

20. $\frac{d}{dx}(5^{\sqrt{x}}) = \frac{d}{dx}(e^{\sqrt{x}\ln 5}) =$ _____ .

21. $\frac{d}{dx}\{(\log_7(x^2+1)\} =$ _____ .

22. $\frac{d}{dx}(3^{x^2-1}) =$ _____ .

23. If $f(x) = e^{x^2}$, then $f'(0) =$ _____ .

24. If $f(x) = xe^x$, then $f'(0) =$ _____ .

25. If $f(x) = x \ln x$, then $f'(e) = $ _____ .

26. If $y = (2x+3)^4$, then $y' = $ _____ and $y'' = $ _____ .

27. If $y = e^{3x-4}$, then $y' = $ _____ , $y'' = $ _____ and $y''' = $ _____ .

28. If $y = \ln(2x-5)$, then $y' = $ _____ , $y'' = $ _____ and $y''' = $ _____ .

SEE ANSWERS AT THE END OF THIS BOOK.

CHAPTER - 14

YOU SHOULD BE FAMILIAR WITH THE FOLLOWING TERMS:

Increasing/decreasing function ; local extremum.

Concave up, concave down ; point of inflection.

Critical point ; local maximum, local minimum.

First derivative test.

Second derivative test.

Optimization problem.

Inventory cost model.

Absolute maximum value, absolute minimum value of a function.

Limit (or limiting value) at infinity or minus infinity.

Horizontal asymptote, slant asymptote.

Vertical asymptote.

OBJECTIVES

AFTER READING THIS CHAPTER YOU SHOULD BE ABLE TO DO THE FOLLOWING:.

1. Use the first derivative to determine the intervals in which a given function is increasing or decreasing.

2. Use the second derivative to determine the intervals in which the graph of a given function is concave up or concave down.

3. Sketch the graphs of polynomial functions with the help of the first and second derivatives.

4. Find the critical points of both types for a given function.

5. When appropriate, use the second derivative test to determine if a critical point is a local maximum or local minimum or neither.

6. Use the first derivative test to determine if a critical point is a local maximum or local minimum or neither.

7. (Very important) Solve applied optimization problems by first expressing the given verbal problem in mathematical form and then using the appropriate method of calculus. In particular, apply calculus to solve problems involving minimizing a cost or maximizing

a profit or an output.

8. Calculate the absolute maximum and minimum values of a function in a given interval

9. Calculate the limit of a function (if it exists) as $x \to \infty$ or $x \to -\infty$. Find the horizontal asymptote(s) of the graph of the function.

10. Find the vertical asymptote(s) of the graph of a function and on which side of such asymptotes(s) the graph lies.

11. Sketch the graphs of rational functions and other functions having horizontal and/or vertical asymptotes and simple cases involving slant asymptotes.

SOLUTIONS TO ALTERNATE ODD PROBLEMS

EXERCISES - 14.1

1. $y = x^2-6x+7$ gives $y' = 2(x-3)$. $y' > 0$ for $x > 3$ and $y' < 0$ for $x < 3$. Thus y is increasing for $x > 3$ and decreasing for $x < 3$. Since $y'' = 2 > 0$, y is always conc. up. Since the concavity does not change, there is no point of inflection.

5. $f(x) = x + 1/x$ gives $f'(x) = 1 - 1/x^2 = (x^2-1)/x^2$ and $f''(x) = 2/x^3$.

    (a) $f(x)$ is incr. if $f'(x) = (x^2-1)/x^2 > 0$ if $x > 1$ or $x < -1$.

    (b) $f(x)$ is decr. if $f'(x) = (x^2-1)/x^2 < 0$ or $x^2-1 < 0$ and $x \neq 0$ i.e. $-1 < x < 1$ and $x \neq 0$ or $-1 < x < 0$ and $0 < x < 1$.

    (c) $f(x)$ is conc. up if $f''(x) = 2/x^3 > 0$ or if $x > 0$.

    (d) $f(x)$ is conc. down if $f''(x)$ $2/x^3 < 0$ or if $x < 0$. x=0 is <u>not</u> a point of inflection, because $f(0)$ is undefined.

9. $f(x) = x + \ln x$ gives $f'(x) = 1 + 1/x$, $f''(x) = -1/x^2$.

    a,b) $f'(x) > 0$ if $1 + 1/x > 0$ or if $x > 0$. Thus $f(x)$ is incr. for $x > 0$ $f'(x) = 1 + 1/x < 0$ if $x < -1$, but $f(x)$ is not defined fo $x < 0$. Thus $f(x)$ is not decreasing for any x.

    c,d) Since $f''(x) = -1/x^2 < 0$ for all $x \neq 0$, $f(x)$ is conc. down for all $x \neq 0$ and conc. up for no x. No point of inflection.

13. $y = x^5 - 5x^4 + 1$ gives $y' = 5x^3(x-4)$ and $y'' = 20x^2(x-3)$

    (a) y is incr. if $y' > 0$ or $5x^3(x-4) > 0$ i.e. $x < 0$ or $x > 4$.
    (b) y is decr. if $y' < 0$ or $5x^3(x-4) < 0$ i.e. $0 < x < 4$.
    (c) y is conc. up if $y'' > 0$ or $20x^2(x-3) > 0$ i.e. $x > 3$
    (d) y is conc. down if $y'' < 0$ or $20x^2(x-3) < 0$ i.e. $x < 3$.

    Since y changes concavity at x=3, we have infl. pt. at x=3.

17. $y' = 30x^4(x-1)$, $y'' = 150(x^3(x - 4/5)$.
Ans. (a) incr. for $x > 1$ (b) decr. for $x < 1$ (c) conc. up for $x < 0$ or $x > 4/5$ (d) conc. down for $0 < x < 4/5$. Inflection points at $x = 0, 4/5$.

21. $y = \ln x$ gives $y' = 1/x$ and $y'' = -1/x^2$
Ans. (a) incr. for $x > 0$ (b) decr. for no x (note: $\ln x$ is not defined for $x \leq 0$) (c) Conc. up for no x (d) Conc. down for all $x > 0$. No point of inflection.

25. $C(x) = 2000 + 10x$; $R(x) = px = 100x - (1/2)x^2$

$P(x) = R(x) - C(x) = 90x - 0.5x^2 - 2000$
$C'(x) = 10 > 0$; $R'(x) = 100 - x$, $P'(x) = 90 - x$.
(note that domain of $C(x)$, $R(x)$ and $P(x)$ is $x \geq 0$).

29. $C'(x) = 9 - 6x + 6x^2$, $C''(x) = -6 + 12x$.
C' is increasing when $C''(x)$ 0, i.e. $x > 1/2$
C' is decreasing when $C''(x)$ 0, i.e. $0 \leq x < 1/2$ (Note $x \geq 0$).

33. $C(x) = 6 + 2(x^2+4)/(x+1) = 2x + 12 - 6/(x-1)$ gives

$C'(x) = 2 + 6/(x+1)^2$ and $C''(x) = -6/(x+1)^3$

Since $C''(x) < 0$ for all $x > 0$, $C'(x)$ is decreasing.

$\overline{C}(x) = C(x)/x = 2 + 12/x - 6/x(x+1)$ gives

$\overline{C}'(x) = -12/x^2 + 6(2x+1)/x^2(x+1)^2 = -6(2x^2+2x+1)/x^2(x+1)^2$

Since $\overline{C}'(x) < 0$ for all $x > 0$, $\overline{C}(x)$ is decreasing.

37. We have, $C'(x) = 25 - 0.2x + 0.012x^2$; $C''(x) = -0.2 + 0.024x$.

$C(x)$ is conc. up if $C'' > 0$ or $-0.2 + 0.024x > 0$ or $x > 0.2/0.024$ i.e. $x > 25/3$. Similarly, $C(x)$ is conc. down if $0 < x < 25/3$ (Note x _ 0)

41. $H(0) = 0$. $H'(x) = A/(1+x) - B = (A-B) - Bx /(1+x)$. Since $x \geq 0$,

$H'(x) > 0$ for $x < (A-B)/B$ and $H'(x) < 0$ for $x > (A-B)/B$. H is greatest at $x = (A-B)/B$.

EXERCISES - 14.2

1. $y = x^2 - 6x + 7$ gives
$y' = 2x - 6$, $y'' = 2$. Thus y is increasing
for $x > 3$ and decreasing for $x < 3$. Also
the graph is always concave up.
When $x=3$, $y = -2$. The graph
meets the y-axis at $y=7$. The
graph is as shown in the figure.

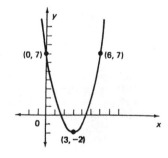

5. $y = x^3 - 3x + 2$ gives
$y' = 3(x^2-1) = 3(x-1)(x+1)$ and
$y'' = 6x$. The graph is incr.
for $x < -1$ or $x > 1$ and decr. for
$-1 < x < 1$. It is conc. up for $x > 0$
and conc. down for $x < 0$. Point of
inflection occurs at $x=0$. The
graph is as shown in figure.

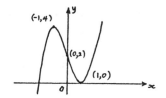

9. $y = x^5 - 5x^4 + 1$ gives $y' = 5x^3(x-4)$ and $y'' = 20x^2(x-3)$
The graph is increasing for
$x < 0$ or $x > 4$ and decreasing for
$0 < x < 4$. Also, the graph is
concave up for $x > 3$ and is
concave down for $x < 3$. There is
a point of inflection at $x=3$.
The graph meets y-axis at $y = 1$.
The graph is as shown in the figure.

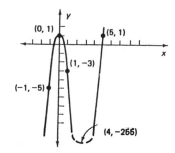

13. $C(x) = 1500 + 25x - 0.1x^2 + 0.004x^3$ gives

$C'(x) = 25 - 0.2x + 0.012x^2 = 0.012(x - 25/3)^2 + (72.5)/3$
Since $C' > 0$ for all x, $C(x)$ is increasing for all x.
$C''(x) = -0.2 + 0.024x = 0.024(x - 25/3)$
Thus the graph is concave up
for $x < 25/3$ and is concave down
for $0 < x < 25/3$. The graph is as
shown.

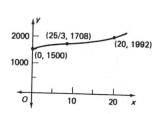

119

1. $f(x) = x^7$ gives $f'(x) = 7x^6 = 0$ when x=0. cr. pt. x=0.

5. $f(x) = 4 - x - 3x^2$ gives $f'(x) = -1 - 6x$. $f'(x) = 0$ when x = -1/6

    Ans. -1/6.

9. $f(x) = 2x^3 - 3x^2 - 36x + 1$ gives $f'(x) = 6(x^2-x-6) = 6(x-3)(x+2)$

    At cr. pt, $f'(x) = 0$ i.e. $6(x-3)(x+2) = 0$ or x = 3, -2   Ans. 3, -2.

13. $y = x^2(x-1)^3$ gives $y' = x^2 \cdot 3(x-1)^2 + (x-1)^3 \cdot 2x = x(x-1)^2(5x-2)$

    $y' = 0$ at x = 0, 1, 2/5. Thus, cr. pts. are x = 0, 1, 2/5.

17. $y = \dfrac{x-1}{x+1} = 1 - 2/(x+1)$ gives $y' = 2/(x+1)^2$. $y' \neq 0$ for any x.

    Also y' is undefined at x = -1, but x = -1 is not in the domain of

    y. Thus, there are no cr. pts.

21. $y = (x-1)^{1/5}/(x+1)$ gives $y' = (6-4x)/\{5(x+1)^2(x-1)^{4/5}\}$.

    $y' = 0$ when 6-4x = 0 i.e. x = 3/2. Also y' is undefined when x = -1

    or x = 1. But at x = -1, y is undefined whereas at x=1, y is

    defined. Thus, the cr. pts. are x = 3/2, 1.

25. $y = e^x/x$ gives $y' = \dfrac{(x-1)e^x}{x^2}$. $y' = 0$ when x=1

    (Note, e^x is never zero for any value of x). Thus, x=1 is the cr. pt.

    Also, y' is undefined at x=0, but y is not defined at x=0. Thus, x=0

    is not the cr. pt.   Ans. x=1.

29. $y = \ln x/x$ gives $y' = (1 - \ln x)/x^2 = 0$ when 1 - ln x = 0 or ln x = 1

    = ln e or x = e.   Ans. x = e.

33. The cr. pts. of functions involving absolute values are best found by sketching the graph of f(x). The graph of $f(x) = |x^2-4x-5|$ is as shown by the solid line in the figure. Clearly at the vertex (2,9), the tgt. is horizontal i.e. f'(x) = 0. Thus, x=2 is a cr. pt. Also, at x = -1, 5, f(x) is not differentiable. Thus, x = -1, 5 are also the cr. pts.   Ans. x = -1, 5, 2

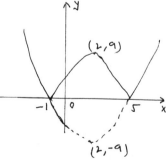

1. $f(x) = x^2 - 12x + 10$ gives $f'(x) = 2x - 12 = 0$ when x=6. Thus, cr. pt. is x=6. Also, since $f''(x) = 2 > 0$, $f(x)$ has a local min. at x=6.

5. $y = 2x^3 - 9x^2 + 12x + 6$; $y' = 6x^2 - 18x + 12$; $y'' = 12x - 18$
    $y' = 0$ gives the cr. pts. x=1, x=2. At x=1, $y'' = -6 < 0$ implies y has a rel. max. at x=1. At x=2, $y'' = 6 > 0$ implies rel. min. at x=2.

    <u>Ans.</u> rel. max. at x = -2 ; rel. min. at x = 1/2.

9. $y = x^5 - 5x^4 + 5x^3 - 10$; $y' = 5x^4 - 20x^3 + 15x^2 = 5x^2(x-1)(x-3)$.
    $y'' = 20x^3 - 60x^2 + 30x$. Critical points are x=0, 1, 3. At x=1, $y'' = -10 < 0$ implies local max. at x=1. At x=3, $y'' = 90 > 0$ implies local min. at x=3. At x=0, $y'' = 0$. The second derivative test (S.D.T.) fails at x=0. So, we use the first derivative test (F.D.T) for x=0. $y' > 0$ for x < 0 and for x > 0 slightly. Since y' does not change sign at x=0, we have inflection point at x=0.

    <u>Ans.</u> Max. at x=1, Min. at x=3; inflection point at x=0.

13. $f(x) = x^{4/3}$ gives $f'(x) = (4/3)x^{1/3}$
    cr. pt. is x=0. Since $f'(x) < 0$ for x < 0 and $f'(x) > 0$ for x > 0 i.e. $f'(x)$ changes sign from - to +, x=0 is a pt. of a local min.

17. $f(x) = 2x^3 + 3x^2 - 12x - 15$; $f'(x) = 6x^2 + 6x - 12$; $f''(x) = 12x + 6$
    cr. pts. are at x = 1, -2. $f''(1) = 18 > 0$ implies $f(x)$ has local min. at x=1 and the min. value is $f(1) = -22$.
    $f''(-2) = -18 < 0$ implies $f(x)$ has local max. at x = -2 and the max. value is $f(-2) = 5$.

    <u>Ans.</u> Max. value is 5 at x = -2; Min. value is -22 at x=1.

21. $f(x) = x^3(x-1)^{2/3}$; $f'(x) = (1/3)x^2(11x - 9)/(x-1)^{1/3}$
    $f'(x) = 0$ gives x=0, 9/11. $f'(x)$ is undefined at x=1 but $f(1)$ is defined. Thus, the cr. pts. are x=0, 9/11 and 1.
    Using the first derivative test, x=0 is a point of inflection; x = 9/11 is a pt. of local max. and the max. value is
    $f(9/11) = (9/11)^3(2/11)^{2/3}$; x=1 is a point of local min. and the min. value is $f(1) = 0$.

25. $f(x) = |x-1|$. The graph of $f(x)$ is as shown. $f(x)$ has a local minimum value of 0 at x = 1.

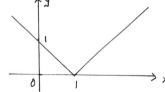

29. $f(x) = \begin{cases} e^x & \text{if } x \geq 0 \\ e^{-x} & \text{if } x < 0 \end{cases}$ Therefore, $f'(x) = \begin{cases} e^x & \text{if } x > 0 \\ -e^{-x} & \text{if } x < 0 \end{cases}$

    $f'(x)$ fails to exist at x=0. For x < 0, $f'(x) = -e^{-x} < 0$. For x > 0, $f'(x) = e^x > 0$. So x=0 is local minimum. $f(0) = 1$.

33. $f(x) = x^3 - 3x^2 + 3x + 7$, $f'(x) = 3x^2 - 6x + 3$, $f''(x) = 6x - 6$

$f'(x) = 0$ gives $x = 1$. Since $f''(1) = 0$, the second der. test fails. Since $f'(x) = 3(x-1)^2 > 0$ both for $x < 1$ and $x > 1$, $x=1$ is a pt. of inflection. Thus $f(x)$ has neither local max. nor local min. at $x=1$.

EXERCISES - 14.5

1. Let the two numbers be x and $10 - x$.
   $P = $ product of two numbers $= x(10-x) = 10x - x^2$
   $P''(x) = 10 - 2x = 0$ gives $x=5$. Since $p''(2) = -2 < 0$, the product P is max. when $x=5$. Thus the two numbers are x, $10-x$ or 5, $10-5$ i.e. 5 and 5.

5. Let x, y (cms) be the dimensions of the rectangle with area 100 cm^2.
   Thus, $xy = 100$ or $y = 100/x$ ... (i)
   $P = $ perimeter of rect. $= 2(x+y)$
   $\quad = 2x + 200/x$, on using   (i)

   $P' = 2 - 200/x^2 = 0$ gives $x=10$
   (Reject neg. value of x)
   $P''(x) = 400/x^3$ and $P''(10) = 0.4 > 0$
   implies the perimeter P is min.
   when $x=10$. When $x=10$,   (i)
   gives $y=10$. Thus, the rectangle
   is a square with side 10 cm.
   (because $x = y = 10$)

9. Here, $xy = 900$ ...(i)
   $C = $ Cost of fencing 3 sides
   $\quad = 15(x+2y) = 15x + 30(900/x)$
   $\quad = 15x + 27000/x$, on using   (i)

   $C'(x) = 15 - 27000/x^2 = 0$ gives

   $x = 30\sqrt{2}$ yds.
   Since $C'' = 54000/x^3 > 0$ when

   $x = 30\sqrt{2}$, C is min. at $x = 30\sqrt{2}$
   When $x = 30\sqrt{2}$,   (i)   gives $y = 15\sqrt{2}$.   Thus the dimensions are
   $30\sqrt{2}$ yds $\times$ $15\sqrt{2}$ yds.

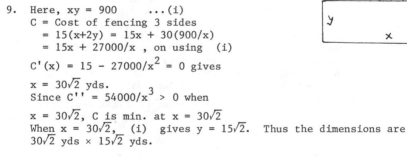

13. $\overline{C}(x) = 5 + 3x^2 + 48/x$ gives $\overline{C}'(x) = 6x - 48/x^2$.

   $\overline{C}'(x) = 0$ gives $x=2$, $\overline{C}''(x) = 6 + 96/x^3 > 0$ at $x=2$. Thus $\overline{C}(x)$ is min. when $x=2$ and the minimum value is $C_{min} = \overline{C}(2) = 5 + 12 + 48/2 = 41$.

17. (a) $C'(x) = 300 - 20x + x^2$. $C''(x) = -20 + 2x$. $C'''(x) = 2 > 0$
       $C''(x) = 0$ when $x=10$. $C'''(x) > 0$.   Therefore, C' is minimum when $x=10$.

    (b) $\overline{C}(x) = C(x)/x = 300 - 10x + x^2/3$. $\overline{C}'(x) = -10 + 2x/3$.

       $\overline{C}''(x) = 2/3 > 0$. $\overline{C}'(x) = 0$ when $x=15$.   Therefore, $\overline{C}$ is minimum when $x=15$.

21. $R(x)$ = rev. obtained by selling x units at \$4 each = 4x.

    (a) $P(x) = R(x) - C(x) = 4x - (50+1.3x + 0.001x^2) = 2.7x - 0.001x^2 - 50$

    (b) $P'(x) = 2.7 - 0.002x = 0$ gives $x = 1350$.

        Since $P''(x) = -0.002x < 0$, the profit P **is** max. when $x = 1350$ units are sold.

    (c) $P_{max.} = P(1350) = 2.7(1350) - 0.001(1350)^2 - 50 = \$1772.50.$

25. $R(x) = px = x(5 - 0.001x) = 5x - 0.001x^2$
$R'(x) = 5 - 0.002x = 0$ gives $x = 2500$. $R''(x) = -0.002 < 0$ implies the revenue R is max. when $x = 2500$.

$P(x) = R(x) - C(x) = (5x - 0.001x^2) - (2800 + x) = 4x - 0.001x^2 - 2800$
$P'(x) = 4 - 0.002x = 0$ gives $x = 2000$. Since

$P''(x) = -0.002 < 0$, the profit P is max. when $x = 2000$ and the max. value of the profit is

$P_{max.} = P(2000) = 4(2000) - 0.001(2000)^2 - 2800 = \$1200.$

29. (a) Total Cost C = cost of material + cost of replenishing + cost of inventory. ... (i)

    The cost of material for 10,000 units at \$2 each is \$20,000. There are $10,000/x$ numbers of orders of size x. The cost of replenishing these orders at \$40 each is $\$40(10,000/x)$ = \$400,000/x.
Value of the inventory $(x/2)$ at \$2 each = $2(x/2) = \$x$. The cost of inventory is 10% of the value of the inventory i.e. it is \$x/10. Then from (i) above it follows that:
    $C = 20,000 + 400,000/x + x/10.$

    (b) $C'(x) = -400,000/x^2 + 1/10 = 0$ gives $x = 2000$.
$C''(x) = 800,000/x^3 > 0$ at $x = 2000$ implies C is min. when $x=2000$. Thus the economic order quantity is $x = 2000$.

33. Let width of building = x, depth=y meters. Then width and depth of plot of land are x+40 and y+10. Area of land A = $(x+40)(y+10)$
Area of building = $xy = 6400$. Therefore, $y = 6400/x$, so
$A = xy + 10x + 40y + 400 = 6800 + 10x + 256000/x.$
$A'(x) = 10 - 256,000/x^2 = 0$ when $x=160$. Then $y=6400/160 = 40$ and
$A_{min.} = (200)(50) = 10,000$ sq. meters.

37. Volume $x(y-2x)^2 = 128$. Thus, $y - 2x = \sqrt{128/x}$ or $y = 2x + 8\sqrt{2}x^{-1/2}$.
Area $A = y^2 = (2x + 8\sqrt{2}x^{-1/2})^2 = 4x^2 + 32\sqrt{2}x^{1/2} + 128x^{-1}$.
$dA/dx = 8x + 16\sqrt{2}x^{-1/2} - 128x^{-2} = 0$, i.e. $x^3 + 2\sqrt{2}x^{3/2} - 16 = 0$.
This is a quadratic equation for $x^{3/2}$, $x^{3/2} = \frac{1}{2}(-2\sqrt{2} \pm \sqrt{8+64})$. The positive solution is $x^{3/2} = 2\sqrt{2}$, or $x=2$. Then $y = 2x + \sqrt{128/x} = 12$.

41. Solving the demand equation: $x = 100(5-p)$ and the supply equation $x = 200(p_1 - 1) = 200(p - t - 1)$ for x by eliminating p gives

$x = (200/3)(4-t)$
T = total tax for the govt. = (tax per unit)(No. of units sold x)
    = $tx = (200/3)(4t - t^2)$
$T'(t) = (200/3)(4-2t) = 0$ gives $t=2$. Since $T''(t) = -400/3 < 0$
T is max. when a tax of $t=2$ per unit is imposed.

45. $P(t) = S(1 + 0.2t)e^{-rt}$. $P'(t) = S\{0.2 - r(1 + 0.2t)\}e^{-rt}$

$P'(t) = 0$ when $t = r^{-1} - 5$. (Check that $P''(t) = -0.2rSe^{-rt}$ at this t).

49. (i) Let the size of the order be $x = 200 + n$, i.e. n units more than 200. Then the cost of each unit is $\$(10 - 0.02n)$. Then, the total revenue R to the manufacturer is given by:

$R(n) = (200 + n)(10 - 0.02n) = 2000 + 6n - 0.02n^2$
$R' = 6 - 0.04n = 0$ gives $n = 150$. Also $R'' = -0.04 < 0$ implies the revenue R is max. when $n = 150$. i.e. when the order size is $x = 200 + n = 200 + 150 = 350$ units.

(ii) The profit per unit is $\$(10 - 0.02n) - \$5 = \$(5 - 0.02n)$

$P = $ total profits $= (5 - 0.02n)(200 + n) = 1000 + n - 0.02n^2$

$P' = 1 - 0.04n = 0$ gives $n=25$. Also, $P'' = -0.04 < 0$ implies the profits P are max. when $n = 25$ or when the size of the order is $x = 200 + n = 200 + 25 = 225$.

(iii) In this case, the profit per unit is $\$(10 - 0.02n) - \$7 =$
$= \$(3 - 0.02n)$
$P = $ total profits $= (3 - 0.02n)(200+n) = 600 - n - 0.02n^2$
$P' = -1 - 0.04n = 0$ gives $n = -25$. But $n \geq 0$. Thus $n=0$, i.e. the size of the order for max. profits is $x = 200 + n = 200+0$ $= 200$.

53. $R_1 = te^{-t}$. $R_1' = (1-t)e^{-t} = 0$ when $t=1$. $(R_1)_{max} = R_1(1) = e^{-1} \approx 0.37$

$R_2 = te^{-2t^2}$. $R_2' = (1-4t)e^{-2t^2} = 0$ when $t=1/4$. $(R_2)_{max} = R_2(1/4)$

$= 0.25e^{-1/8} \approx 0.22$. So R_1 has greater maximum value.

EXERCISES - 14.6

1. $f(x) = x^2 - 6x + 7$; $1 \leq x \leq 6$. $f'(x) = 2x - 6 = 0$ gives the cr. pt. $x=3$ which is within the given interval $1 \leq x \leq 6$. Now $f(3) = -2$; $f(1) = 2$ and $f(6) = 7$. Thus the absolute max. is $f(6) = 7$ and the absolute min. is $f(3) = -2$.

5. $f(x) = x^3 - 18x^2 + 60x$; $-1 \leq x \leq 5$

$f'(x) = 3x^2 - 36x + 60 = 0$ gives $x=2$, 10. but $x=10$ is <u>outside</u> the given interval so it is rejected. Now, $f(2) = 56$, $f(-1) = -79$ and $f(5) = -25$. Thus, the abs. max. is $f(2) = 56$. and abs. min. is $f(-1) = -79$

9. $f(x) = xe^{-x}$; $1/2 \leq x \leq 2$

$f'(x) = (1-x)e^{-x} = 0$ gives $x=1$. Now $f(1) = e^{-1} \approx 0.3679$; $f(1/2) = 0.5e^{-0.5} \approx 0.3033$ and $f(2) = 2 e^{-2} \approx 0.2707$.

Thus, the abs. max. is $f(1) = 1/e$ and the abs. min. is $f(2) = 2e^{-2}$.

13. $f(x) = x \ln x$; $0 < x \le 0.9$.

$f'(x) = 1 + \ln x = 0$ gives $x = 1/3 \approx 0.368$ which is within the given interval. Now $f(1/e) = -(\ln e)/e = -1/e \approx -0.368$;

$f(0.9) = (0.9)\ln(0.9) \approx -0.0948$. As $x \to 0^+$, $f(x) = x \ln x \to 0$.

The abs. max. value is 0 as $x \to 0^+$ and abs. min. is
$f(0.9) = (0.9)\ln(0.9)$.
(Note, we cannot evaluate $f(x) = x \ln x$ at the end point 0, because $\ln x$ is not defined at $x = 0$. Therefore, we take limit as $x \to 0^+$).

17. (i) $R(x) = px = 12x - 0.0015x^2$; $0 \le x \le 3000$.
$R'(x) = 12 - 0.003x = 0$ gives $x = 4000$, which is outside the given interval and is thus rejected. The abs. max. and min. therefore occurs at the end points of the given interval

$0 \le x \le 3000$. Now $R(0) = 0$ and $R(3000) = 22,500$. Thus the revenue R is **max.** when $x = 3000$ units are produced and sold.

(ii) $P(x) = R(x) - C(x) = 6x + 0.0015x^2 - 10^{-6}x^3 - 1000$, $0 \le x \le 3000$,
$P'(x) = 6 + 0.003x - 3(10^{-6})x^2 = 0$ gives $x = 2000$, $x = -1000$.
Rejecting $x = -1000$, because $x \ge 0$, we have $x = 2000$.
Now, $P(2000) = 9000$, $P(0) = -1000$ and $P(3000) = 3500$.
Thus, the profit P is max. when $x = 2000$ units are produced and sold.

21. Let base have side x and height be h. $x^2 h = 50$. $x \le 5$, $h \le 5$.
Thus $x^2 \ge 10$ or $x \ge 10^{1/2} \approx 3.16$. Area of bottom and 4 sides
$A = x^2 + 4xh = x^2 + 200/x$. $A'(x) = 2x - 200/x^2 = 0$ when $x = 100^{1/3}$
≈ 4.64. $A(5) = 65$. $A(4.64) = 64.6$. $A(3.16) = 73.3$. A is minimum when $x = 4.64$ and $h = 50/x^2 = 2.32$

25. $y' = \frac{-1}{2} ae^t(1 + \frac{1}{2} e^t)^2$. $y'' = \frac{-1}{2} ae^t(1 - e^t/2)/(1 + e^t/2)^3$
$y'' = 0$ when $t = \ln 2$. $y'(0) = -2a/9$, $y'(\ln 2) = -a/4$
$y'(2) = \frac{-1}{2} ae^2/(1 + e^2/2)^2 \approx -0.168a$
Maximum y' is $-0.168a$ at $t=2$. Minimum is $-a/4$ at $t = \ln 2 \approx 0.69$

EXERCISES - 14.7
_____

1. $\lim_{x \to \infty} (1 - 2/x) = 1 - 0 = 1$.

5. $\lim_{x \to -\infty} \frac{5-2x}{3x+7} = \lim_{x \to -\infty} \frac{(5-2x)/x}{(3x+7)/x} = \lim_{x \to -\infty} \frac{5/x - 2}{3 + 7/x} = \frac{0-2}{3+0} = -2/3$.

9. $\lim_{x \to -\infty} \frac{5+3x-2x^2}{3x^2+4} = \lim_{x \to -\infty} \frac{(5+3x-2x^2)/x^2}{(3x^2+4)/x^2} = \lim_{x \to -\infty} \frac{5/x^2 + 3/x - 2}{3 + 4/x^2} = \frac{0+0-2}{3+0} = \frac{-2}{3}$.

13. See at the end of review exercises.

17. $\lim_{x \to -\infty} \frac{3x^2+5}{(2x-3)^3} = \lim_{x \to -\infty} \frac{(3x^2+5)/x^3}{(2x-3)^3/x^3} = \lim_{x \to -\infty} \frac{3/x + 5/x^3}{(2 - 3/x)^3} = \frac{0+0}{(2-0)^3} = 0$.

125

21. $\lim\limits_{x\to\infty} (x - \dfrac{x^2}{x+1}) = \lim\limits_{x\to\infty} \dfrac{x(x+1) - x^2}{x+1} = \lim\limits_{x\to\infty} \dfrac{x}{x+1} = \lim\limits_{x\to\infty} \dfrac{1}{1 + 1/x} = \dfrac{1}{1+0} = 1.$

25. As $x \to \infty$, $e^{-x} \to 0$. Thus, $\lim\limits_{x\to\infty} (1 + 2e^{-x}) = 1 + 2(0) = 1.$

29. As $x \to -\infty$, $e^{-x} \to \infty$ whereas $e^{x} \to 0$. Thus, we multiply top and bottom by e^{x} to obtain,

$$\lim\limits_{x\to -\infty} \dfrac{(3e^{-x} + 4)e^{x}}{(2e^{-x} - 1)e^{x}} = \lim\limits_{x\to -\infty} \dfrac{3 + 4e^{x}}{2 - e^{x}} = \dfrac{3+0}{2-0} = 3/2.$$

33. $\dfrac{5 - 2\ln x}{2 + 3\ln x} = \dfrac{(5 - 2\ln x)/\ln x}{(2 + 3\ln x)/\ln x} = \dfrac{(5/\ln x) - 2}{(2/\ln x) + 3} \to \dfrac{0-2}{0+3} = -2/3$ as $x \to \infty$.

37. $\lim\limits_{x\to 2^+} \dfrac{1}{x-2} = +\infty \qquad\qquad \lim\limits_{x\to 2^-} \dfrac{1}{x-2} = -\infty.$

41. $\lim\limits_{x\to 0^+} 1/x^2 = +\infty \qquad\qquad \lim\limits_{x\to 0^-} 1/x^2 = +\infty.$

45. For $x > 1$, $\dfrac{\sqrt{x^2-1}}{x-1} = \dfrac{\sqrt{(x-1)(x+1)}}{\sqrt{(x-1)^2}} = \dfrac{\sqrt{x+1}}{\sqrt{x-1}} \to +\infty$ as $x \to 1^+$

For $x < 1$, $\sqrt{x^2-1}$ is not defined so limit from below does not exist.

49. $y \to 1$ as $x \to \pm\infty$

$y \to +\infty$ $x \to 2^+$

$y \to -\infty$ as $x \to 2^-$

$y = -1/2$ when $x=0$

$y = 5/2$ when $x = 4.$

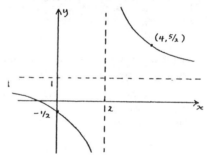

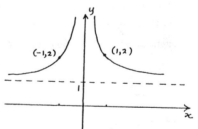

53. $y \to 1$ as $x \to \pm\infty$

$y \to +\infty$ as $x \to 0^{\pm}$

$y=2$ when $x = \pm 1$

$y = 1 + 1/x^2 \geq 1$ for all x.

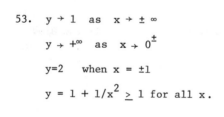

57. $y = (x^2+1)/(x^2-1) = 1 + 2/(x^2-1) \to 1$ as $x \to \pm\infty$. Thus $y = 1$ is the horizontal asymptote. The domain is all $x \neq \pm 1$.
The vertical asymptotes are $x=1$, $x = -1$. For $x < -1$ and $x > 1$, $2/(x^2-1) > 0$ and so $y > 1$, whereas for $-1 < x < 1$, $2/(x^2-1) < 0$ and so $y < 1$.

Also as $x \to 1^+$ or $x \to -1^-$, $y \to +\infty$

as as $\to 1^-$ or $x \to -1^+$, $y \to -\infty$. The graph meets y-**axis** at $y = -1$ and does not meet x-axis.

Now $y' = -4x/(x^2-1)^2$

and $y'' = (12x^2+4)/(x^2-1)^3$. Thus, the graph is increasing for $x < -1$ or $-1 < x < 0$, and is decreasing for $0 < x < 1$ and for $x > 1$. The graph is concave up for $x < -1$ or $x > 1$ and is concave down for $-1 < x < 1$. The graph is as shown in figure.

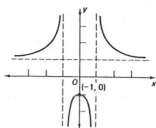

Horizontal asymptote: $y = 1$
Vertical asymptote: $x = \pm 1$

61. y defined for $x > 0$ only.

$y \to -\infty$ as $x \to \infty$

$y \to +\infty$ as $x \to 0^+$

$y = 0$ when $x = 1$

$y' = -1/x < 0$ for all $x > 0$

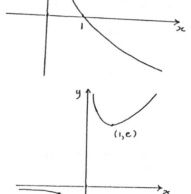

65. $y \to 0$ as $x \to -\infty$

$y \to \infty$ as $x \to \infty$

$y \to +\infty$ as $x \to 0^+$

$y \to -\infty$ as $x \to 0^-$

$y > 0$ for $x > 0$, $y < 0$ for $x < 0$.

$y' = (x-1)e^x/x^2$ so $y' > 0$ for $x > 1$,

$y' < 0$ for $x < 1$.

69. $P(t) \to 0$ as $t \to \infty$

$P'(t) = 5000(1 - 0.2t)e^{-0.2t} = 0$ when t=5.

$P' > 0$ when $t < 5$, $P' < 0$ when $t > 5$

Thus, $P_{max} = P(5) = 25,000e^{-1} \approx 9200$.

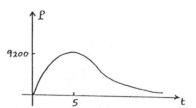

73. $\overline{C}(x) = C(x)/(x) = 2/x + 3$.
Note that the domain of $\overline{C}(x)$ is
all $x > 0$.

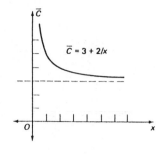

$\overline{C} = 3 + 2/x$

As $x \to +\infty$, $y = \overline{C}(x) \to 3$. Thus
$y=3$ is the horizontal asymptote.

Also as $x \to 0^{+}$, $y = 3 + 2/x \to +\infty$
Thus, $x=0$ is the vertical asymptote.

$\overline{C}'(x) = -2/x^2 < 0$ and

$\overline{C}''(x) = 4/x^3 > 0$ for all $x > 0$
imply that the graph of $\overline{C}$ is
always decreasing and is concave
up. The graph is as shown in figure.

77. $P(A) = 2x - A = 4000(1 - e^{-A}) - 1000A$
The domain of $P(A)$ is all $A \geq 0$;
There are no horizontal or
vertical asymptotes. Now,

$P'(A) = 4000e^{-A} - 1000$ and

$P''(A) = -4000e^{-A}$. P is increasing
if $4000e^{-A} - 1000 > 0$
i.e. $A < \ln 4 \simeq 1.4$ and is
decreasing for $A > \ln 4$. $P(A)$ has
a rel. max. at $A = \ln 4 \simeq 1.4$
Since $P'' < 0$ for all $A > 0$, the
graph is concave downwards.
The graph is as shown in figure.

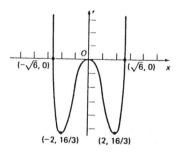

(1.4, 2614)

$P = 4000(1 - e^{-A}) - 1000A$

REVIEW EXERCISES ON CHAPTER - 14

1. See answers in the text book.

5. $y = (1/6)x^6 - x^4$; $y' = x^3(x^2-4)$; $y'' = 5x^2(x^2 - 12/5)$. Thus y is:
   (a) increasing for $x > 2$ and $-2 < x < 0$

   (b) decreasing for $x < -2$ and
           $0 < x < 2$
   (c) concave up for $x < -\sqrt{12/5}$ or

           $x > \sqrt{12/5}$
   (d) concave down for
           $-\sqrt{12/5} < x < \sqrt{12/5}$
   y has a local max. at $x=0$ and
   local min. at $x = \pm2$. Also y
   has points of inflection at
   $x = \pm12/5$. There are no
   horizontal or vertical asymptotes
   because $y = f(x)$ is a polynomial.
   The graph is as shown in the figure.

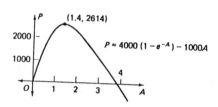

$(-\sqrt{6}, 0)$ $(\sqrt{6}, 0)$ x

$(-2, 16/3)$ $(2, 16/3)$

9. R = rev. = px = $200xe^{-x/20}$ gives R_m = marg. rev. = R'

$$= 200(1 - x/30)e^{-x/30}$$

and $R_m' = (2/9)(x - 60)e^{-x/30}$. Thus the marg. demand R_m is **increasing** for $x > 60$.

13. $f(t) = 2t^3 - 3t^2 + 1$. $f'(t) = 6t^2 - 6t = 0$, gives the cr. pts. $t=0$, $t=1$, $f''(t) = 12t - 6$. Since $f''(0) = -6 < 0$, $f(t)$ has local max. at $t=0$. Also, since $f''(1) = 6 > 0$, $f(t)$ has a local min. at $t=1$.

17. $f(x) = x^{2/3}(1 - x)^2$ gives $f'(x) = (2/3)(1-x)(1-4x)/x^{1/3}$. $f'(x) = 0$ gives $x=1$, $1/4$. Also $f'(x)$ is undefined at $x=0$ and $f(0)$ is defined. Thus the critical points are $x=1$, $1/4$ and 0. Since at $x=1$, $f'(x)$ changes from $(-)$ to $(+)$, $x=1$ is a point of local min. Also, at $x = 1/4$, $f'(x)$ changes from $(+)$ to $(-)$, $x = 1/4$ is a point of local max. Since at $x=0$, $f'(x)$ changes from $(-)$ to $(+)$, $x=0$ is a point of local min.

21. $f(x) = Ax^2 + Bx + C$ gives $f'(x) = 2Ax + B$ and $f''(x) = 2A$. Since $f(x)$ has a local min., $f''(x) = 2A > 0$ or $A > 0$.

25. $P(x) = R - C = 3x - (100 + 0.015x^2) = 3x - 0.015x^2 - 100$. $P'(x) = 3 - 0.03x = 0$ gives $x = 100$. Since $P''(x) = -0.03 < 0$, the profit P is max. when $x = 100$ and the max. profit is P_{max} = $P(100) = 50$. Also $P(120) = 44$.

29. $R = px = x(375 - 5x)/3 = 125x - (5/3)x^2$

$P = R - C = 125x - (5/3)x^2 - (500 + 13x + x^2/5) = 112x - (28/15)x^2 - 500$.

$P' = 112 - (56/15)x = 0$ gives $x = 30$. Also $P'' = -56/15 < 0$ implies the profits P are max. when $x = 30$ instruments are sold each week.

33. P = profits = $10x + 8y = 10x + 8\sqrt{25-2x^2}$, because $2x^2 + y^2 = 25$.

$P'(x) = 10 - 16x/\sqrt{25-2x^2} = 0$ gives $x = 2.341$. Also $P''(x) < 0$ for this value of x. Thus P is max. when $x = 2.341$.

Using this value of x in $2x^2 + y^2 = 25$ we get $y = 3.746$. Since x,y are in thousands, 2341 men's shoes and 3746 women's shoes must be produced to maximize the total profits.

37. (a) $dQ/dF = 40 + 6F - F^2 = (10-F)(4+F) = 0$ when $F = 10$

$dQ/dF > 0$ for $F < 10$, < 0 for $F > 10$.

(b) $d^2Q/dF^2 = 6 - 2F = 0$ when $F = 3$. $(dQ/dF)_{max} = 40 + 6.3 - 3^2 = 49$.

(c) $Q/F = 40 + 3F - F^2/3$. $(d/dF)(Q/F) = 3 - 2F/3 = 0$ when $F = 9/2$.

$(Q/F)_{max.} = 40 + 27/2 - 27/4 = 187/4$. When $F = 9/2$, the marginal product, $dQ/dF = 40 + 27 - 81/4 = 187/4$.

41. $P(0) = 100$.

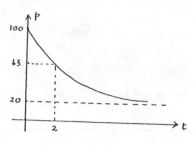

$P(2) = (180 + 20e)/(1+e) = 63.3$

$P(t) \to 20/1 = 20$ as $t \to \infty$

$P'(t) = -80e^{0.5t}/(1 + e^{0.5t})^2 < 0$

for all t.

45. Yield Y (peaches per acre) $= n(840 - 6n) = 840n - 6n^2$

$dY/dn = 840 - 12n = 0$ when $n = 70$.

$d^2Y/dn^2 = -12$. Thus Y is maximum when $n=70$.

49. Let the dimensions (in ft.) be x, x and y as shown. Then the volume

is $x^2y = 486$ (given) or $y = 486/x^2$.

T = total cost in dollars
   = 2(area of roof + area of 3 vertical sides)

$= 2(x^2 + 3xy) = 2x^2 + 6x(486/x^2) = 2x^2 + 2916/x$, because $y = 486/x^2$.

$T'(x) = 4x - 2916/x^2 = 0$ gives

$x^3 = 729$ or $x = 9$.

$T''(x) = 5832/x^3 > 0$ at $x=9$

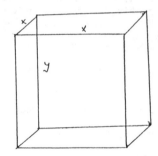

implies T is min. when $x=9$.

When $x=9$, we have

$y = 486/x^2 = 486/81 = 6$. Thus the dimensions are 9 ft. by 9ft. by 6 ft.

53. For $x > 0$, $y = e^{x-x} = e^0 = 1$

For $x < 0$, $y = e^{x-(-x)} = e^{2x}$

$y \to 0$ as $x \to -\infty$. $y(0) = 1$

$y' = 2e^{2x} > 0$ for $x < 0$.

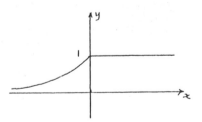

EXERCISES - 14.7

13. $\displaystyle \lim_{x\to\infty} \frac{x^2+4}{3x+7} = \lim_{x\to\infty} \frac{(x^2+4)/x}{(3x+7)/x} = \lim_{x\to\infty} \frac{x+4/x}{3+7/x} = \frac{\infty + 0}{3 + 0} = \infty$

FILL IN THE BLANKS:

1. If f'(x) > 0 then f(x) is a (an) _____ (increasing or decreasing) function of x.

2. If f'(x) < 0, then f(x) is a (an) _____ (increasing or decreasing) function of x.

3. f(x) = mx + b is an increasing or decreasing function of x according as _____ or _____ .

4. If f'(x) = $x^2 + e^x$, then f(3) _____ f(1).   (> , <)

5. If f'(x) = $-e^{-x}$, then f(2) _____ f(1).   (> , <)

6. If f"(x) = $x^2 + e^x$, then the graph of f(x) is concave _____ (up, down).

7. If f"(x) = ln x, then the graph of f(x) is concave up for x_____ and concave down for _____ .

8. If f'(c) = 0 and f"(c) < 0, then f(x) has a local _____ at x=c.

9. If f'(c) = 0 and f"(c) > 0, then f(x) has a local _____ at x=c.

10. f(x) = x^4 has a point of local _____ at x=0.

11. f(x) = 3 - |x| has a point of local _____ at x=0.

12. f(x) = x^3 has a point of _____ at x=0.

13. The absolute extrema of f(x) in a ≤ x ≤ b always occurs at _____ .

14. If a continuous function f(x) has no local maximum in a ≤ x ≤ b and f(a) < f(b), then the absolute maximum occurs at x = _____ .

15. If a continuous function f(x) has no local minimum in c ≤ x ≤ d and f(c) < f(d), then the absolute minimum of f(x) occurs at _____ .

16. If f(x) is continuous and does not have a local extrema in a ≤ x ≤ b and f(a) > f(b), then f(x) has an absolute minimum at x = _____ and an absolute maximum at x = _____ .

17. $\lim\limits_{x \to -\infty} x^{-7}$ = _____ .   18. $\lim\limits_{x \to \infty} \dfrac{3x^2+7}{2-3x^2}$ = _____ .

131

19. $\lim\limits_{x\to\infty} 1/\sqrt{7-x}$ = _____.   20. $\lim\limits_{x\to\infty} \sqrt{4-x^2}$ = _____.

21. $\lim\limits_{x\to-\infty} \sqrt{x^2-9}$ = _____.   22. $\lim\limits_{x\to\infty} \dfrac{|x-2|}{2-x}$ = _____.

23. $\lim\limits_{x\to-\infty} \dfrac{|x+7|}{x+7}$ = _____.   24. $\lim\limits_{x\to-\infty} e^{-x^2}$ = _____.

25. $\lim\limits_{x\to 3^-} 1/(3-x)$ = _____.   26. $\lim\limits_{x\to 2^+} 1/(x^2-4)$ = _____.

27. $\lim\limits_{x\to 3^+} \dfrac{1-x}{x^2-9}$ = _____.   28. $\lim\limits_{x\to 0^+} 1/\sqrt{\ln x}$ = _____.

29. The horizontal asymptotes of

    (a) $f(x) = 3/x$ are _____.   (b) $f(x) = 3x/(2x-1)$ are _____.

    (c) $f(x) = \dfrac{x-3}{x^2-9}$ are _____.   (d) $f(x) = \dfrac{x^2-4}{x^2+4}$ = _____.

    (e) $f(x) = e^x$ are _____.   (f) $f(x) = e^{-x^2}$ are _____.

30. The vertical asymptotes of

    (a) $f(x) = 3x/(2x-1)$ are _____.   (b) $f(x) = \dfrac{x-2}{4-x^2}$ are _____.

    (c) $f(x) = \dfrac{x+3}{x^2+9}$ are _____.   (d) $f(x) = \ln x$ are _____.

    (e) $f(x) = 1/(1 - \ln x)$ are _____.

    (f) $f(x) = e^x/(1 - e^x)$ are _____.

SEE ANSWERS AT THE END OF THIS BOOK.

CHAPTER - 15

YOU SHOULD BE FAMILIAR WITH THE FOLLOWING TERMS:

Differentials.

Linear model.

Error, relative error, percentage error.

Implicit differentiation.

Logarithmic differentiation ; logarithmic derivative.

Elasticity of demand ; elastic, inelastic, unit elasticity.

OBJECTIVES

AFTER READING THIS CHPATER YOU SHOULD BE ABLE TO DO THE FOLLOWING:

1. Calculate the differential of a dependent variable in terms of the value and the differential of the independent variable.

2. Use differentials to calculate the approximate values of functions.

3. Use differentials to estimate the errors and percentage errors in quantities computed from erroneous data.

4. Use implicit differentiation to complete derivative from an implicit relation. Apply this to find the tangent line to an implicit relation at a given point.

5. Calculate second derivatives from an implicit relation.

6. Use logarithmic differentiation to calculate the derivatives of appropriate functions.

7. Calculate the elasticity of demand for a given demand relation.

8. Use elasticity of demand

    (a) to estimate percent change in demand for a given percentage change in price.

    (b) to conclude whether revenue will increase or decrease given a change in price.

EXERCISES - 15.1

1. $y = f(x) = x^2+7x+1$ gives $dy = f'(x)dx = (2x+7)dx$.

5. $y = f(x) = \ln(z^2+1)$ gives $dy = f'(z)dz = \dfrac{2z}{z^2+1}\, dz$.

9. $y = f(x) = (x^2-3x)^{1/2}$ gives $dy = f'(x)dx = (1/2)(x^2-3x)^{-1/2} \cdot (2x-3)dx$.

13. $t = \ln(y^2+1)$ gives $dt = \dfrac{2y}{y^2+1}\, dy$. When y=0, we have dt = 0.

17. $x = f(y) = y \ln y$ gives $dx = f'(y)dy = (1 + \ln y)dy$.

When y=1, dy = 0.003, we have dx = (1 + ln 1)(0.003) = 0.003.

21. $y = \ln u$ gives $dy = \dfrac{1}{u}\, du = \dfrac{1}{3} \cdot (0.06) = 0.02$ when u=3, du = 0.06.

$\Delta u = f(u+\Delta u) - f(u) = \ln(3+0.06) - \ln 3 = \ln(1.02) = 0.0198$.

25. In the formula, $f(x+dx) \simeq f(x) + f'(x)dx$, take $f(x) = x^{1/5}$,

x = 32 and dx = -1 to obtain $(31)^{1/5} = f(x+dx) \simeq 1.9875$.

29. Given that when x=400, $dx/x = 5\% = 0.05 \Rightarrow dx = 0.05x = (0.5)(400) = 20$

$dR/R = (10 - 0.02x)dx/(10x - 0.01x^2)$. When x=400, dx = 20,

dR/R = 5/300 = 5/3 %.

33. D = 10,000, s = 0.2, a = 10 and b = 0.1 gives

$x = \sqrt{2aD/s} = 1000$ and C = 1200. If true value of s is 0.22, then

s = 0.2 and ds = 0.02.

$dx = \sqrt{2aD}\ (-1/2)s^{-3/2}ds = \sqrt{200000}(-1/2)(0.2)^{-3/2}(0.02) = -50$

$dC = \sqrt{2aD}(1/2)s^{-1/2}ds = \sqrt{200,000}(1/2)(0.2)^{-1/2}(0.02) = 10$

EXERCISES - 15.2

1. Differentiating both sides with respect to x gives

$2x + 2yy' + 2y' = 0$ or $y' = -x/(y+1)$.

5. $(y-x)(y+2x) - 12 = 0$ gives $y^2 + xy - 2x^2 - 12 = 0$. Differentiating:

$2yy' + (xy' + y \cdot 1) - 4x = 0$ or $y' = (4x-y)/(2y+x)$.

9. $x^5 + y^5 = 5xy$ gives $5x^4 + 5y^4 y' = 5(xy' + y \cdot 1)$

 Solving for y' gives $y' = (y - x^4)/(y^4 - x)$.

13. $xy + \ln x + \ln y = -1$ gives $(xy' + y \cdot 1) + 1/x + y'/y = 0$.

 or $y' = -y(xy + 1)/x(xy + 1) = -y/x$ because from given equation

 $xy + 1 \neq 0$. (If $xy + 1 = 0$, then from given equation $\ln (xy) = 0$

 or $xy = 1$ which contradicts that $xy + 1 = 0$.)

17. Differentiating $x^3 \div y^3 = xy$ with respect to y gives

 $3x^2\, dx/dy + 3y^2 = x \cdot 1 + y\, dx/dy$ or $dx/dy = (x - 3y^2)/(3x^2 - y)$.

21. $2y/x - x/y = 1$ or $2y^2 - x^2 = xy$ gives

 $4yy' - 2x = xy' + 1 \cdot y$.   Put $x = 2$, $y = -1$.

 $-4y' - 4 = 2y' - 1$ or $y' = -1/2$.

 Tangent at $(2, -1)$ is $y + 1 = (-1/2)(x - 2)$, $y = -x/2$.

25. $x^2 + y^2 = xy + 12$.   Differentiating w.r.t. x, gives

 $2x + 2yy' = (xy' + y)$ or $y' = dy/dx = (y - 2x)/(2y - x)$

 $dy/dx = 0$ when $y = 2x$.   Using this, the given equations becomes,

 $x^2 + (2x)^2 = x(2x) + 12$ or $x = \pm 2$.   Then $y = 2x = 2(\pm 2) = \pm 4$.

 Horizontal tangents at $(2, 4)$, $(-2, -4)$.

 $dx/dy = 1/(dy/dx) = (2y - x)/(y - 2x) = 0$ when $x = 2y$.   Using this, the

 given equation becomes $(2y)^2 + y^2 = (2y) \cdot y + 12$ or $y = \pm 2$, **then**

 $x = 2y$ gives $x = 2(\pm 2) = \pm 4$.   Tangents vertical at $(4, 2)$, $(-4, -2)$.

29. $x^3 + y^3 = 3xy$ gives $3x^2 + 3y^2 y' = 3(xy' + y \cdot 1)$ or $y' = (y - x^2)/(y^2 - x)$

 At $x = 1$, $y = 2$, we have $y' = 1/3$.

 Differentiating y': $y'' = \dfrac{(y^2 - x)(y' - 2x) - (y - x^2)(2yy' - 1)}{(y^2 - x)^2}$

 Using $x = 1$, $y = 2$, $y' = 1/3$, gives $y'' = -16/27$.

33. $xy + y^2 = 3$ gives $x\, dy + y\, dx + 2y\, dy = 0$ or $dy = -y\, dx/(x + 2y)$

 OR $xy + y^2 = 3$ gives $(xy' + y) + 2yy' = 0$ or $y' = -y/(x + 2y)$.

 By definition: $dy = (dy/dx)dx = -y\, dx/(x + 2y)$.

37. $p = \sqrt{100-9x^2}$. Differentiating with respect to p gives:

$1 = \frac{1}{2}(100-9x^2)^{-1/2} \cdot (-18x\ dx/dp)$ or $dx/dp = -(9x)^{-1}\sqrt{100-9x^2}$.

41. $P = 6p - p^2$ gives $dP/dp = 6 - 2p$.

$P = 6p - p^2$ or $p^2 - 6p + P = 0$ gives $p = 3 \pm \sqrt{9-P}$ and

$dp/dP = \mp \frac{1}{2}(9-P)^{-1/2} = \frac{-1}{2}(p-3)^{-1} = \frac{-1}{2(p-3)} = 1/(6-2p)$

$$= (6-2p)^{-1} = (dP/dp)^{-1}.$$

45. $y^q - x^p = 0$ gives $qy^{q-1} - px^{p-1} = 0$.

$dy/dx = (p/q)x^{p-1}/y^{q-1} = (p/q)x^{p-1}/x^{(p/q)(q-1)} = (p/q)x^{(p/q)-1}$.

EXERCISES - 15.3

1. $y = (x^2+1)(x-1)^{1/2}$ gives $\ln y = \ln(x^2+1) + (1/2)\ln(x-1)$.

Differentiating, we have: $(1/y)y' = \frac{2x}{x^2+1} + (1/2)\cdot\frac{1}{x-1}$ or

$y' = y\left[\frac{2x}{x^2+1} + (1/2)\cdot\frac{1}{x-1}\right]$.

5. $y = (\frac{2x^2+5}{2x+5})^{1/3}$ gives $\ln y = (1/3)\ln(2x^2+5) - (1/3)\ln(2x+5)$.

Thus, $y'/y = \frac{1}{3} \cdot \frac{1}{2x^2+5} \cdot 4x - \frac{1}{3} \cdot \frac{1}{2x+5} \cdot 2$

or $y' = \frac{y}{3}\left[\frac{4x}{2x^2+5} - \frac{2}{2x+5}\right]$.

9. $y = x^{x^2}$ gives $\ln 7 = \ln x^{x^2} = x^2 \ln x$. Thus, $y'/y = x^2 \cdot 1/x + \ln x(2x)$

or $y' = y(x + 2x \ln x)$.

13. $y = x^{\ln x}$ gives $\ln y = \ln(x^{\ln x}) = \ln x \cdot \ln x = (\ln x)^2$.

Thus, $y'/y = 2(\ln x)\cdot 1/x$ or $y' = (2y/x)\ln x$.

17. $x = kp^{-n}$ gives $dx/dp = -nkp^{-n-1}$. Thus,

$\eta = \frac{p}{x}\frac{dx}{dp} = \frac{p}{kp^{-n}} \cdot (-nkp^{-n-1}) = -n$.

21. $x = 400 - 100p$ gives $dx/dp = -100$. Thus, $\eta = \frac{p}{x}\frac{dx}{dp} = \frac{p}{400 - 100p}(-100)$

or $\eta = \dfrac{p}{p-4}$. (a) p = 1 gives η = -1/3 (b) p=2 gives η = -1.

(c) p=3 gives η = -3.

25. x = 200 - 100$\sqrt{p}$ gives dx/dp = -50/$\sqrt{p}$. Thus, $\eta = \dfrac{p}{x}\dfrac{dx}{dp}$

   $= \dfrac{p}{200 - 100\sqrt{p}} \cdot (-50/\sqrt{p}) = \dfrac{\sqrt{p}}{2(\sqrt{p}-2)}$. Note p $\geq$ 0. Hence,

(a) the demand is elastic if n < -1 i.e. $\dfrac{\sqrt{p}}{2(\sqrt{p}-2)}$ < -1   ...-(i)

   Assuming $\sqrt{p}$ > 2 or p > 4, (i) gives $\sqrt{p}$ < -2($\sqrt{p}$-2) or

   3$\sqrt{p}$ < 4 or p < 16/9

   But p can't be > 4 and < 16/9 at the same time. Thus, no

   solution. Next assume 0 < $\sqrt{p}$ < 2. Then (i) gives $\sqrt{p}$ > -2($\sqrt{p}$-2)

   or 3$\sqrt{p}$ > 4 or p > 16/9. Thus 0 $\leq$ $\sqrt{p}$ < 2 or p < 4 and p > 16/9

   together imply 16/9 < p < 4. Hence, the demand is elastic if

   16/9 < p < 4.

(b) The demand is inelastic if -1 < η < 0 or -1 < $\dfrac{p}{2(\,p-2)}$ <0.

   Solving as in (a) part above, this gives 0 < p < 16/9.

29. p = 250 - 0.5x gives x = 500 - 2p. η = (p/x)(dx/dp) = (p/x)(-2)

                                     = -(500-x)/x.

η < -1 if (500-x)/x > 1, i.e. x < 250 (note that x > 0).

(Revenue is increasing function) as in Ex. 8 of this section).

-1 < η < 0 if 0 < (500-x)/x < 1 i.e. 250 < x < 500 (Revenue is

decreasing). Note: it can also be verified directly that R'(x) > 0

for x < 250 etc.

33. p = 300 - 0.5x gives dp/dx = -0.5 = -1/2 or dx/dp = -2. Thus,

η = (p/x)(-2) = -(600-x)/x

(a) When x=200, η = -2: elastic demand. Thus, R decreases if p

   increases.

(b) When x = 400, η = -1/2: inelastic demand. Thus, R increases if

   p increases.

137

REVIEW EXERCISES ON CHAPTER - 15

1. See answers in the text book.

5. In the formula, $f(x+dx) \simeq f(x) + f'(x)dx$, take $f(x) = x^2\sqrt{x} = x^{5/2}$,

   $x=4$ and $dx=0.1$, we get $(4.1)^2\sqrt{4.1} = f(x+dx) \simeq 34$.

9. From #8, $x^3y^2 + xy^3 - x^3 - xy - x^2 - y = 0$ gives

   $(x^3 \cdot 2yy' + y^2 \cdot 3x^2) + (x \cdot 3y^2y' + y^3 \cdot 1) - 3x^2 - (xy' + y) - 2x - y' = 0$.

   or $y' = (3x^2 - y^3 - 3x^2y^2 + y + 2x)/(2x^3y + 3xy^2 - x-1)$

   At $x = -1$, $y = 0$, $y' = 5/0$ which is undefined. Thus, $dy = y'\ dx$ is

   undefined.

13. $y = \left[\dfrac{x^2-4}{x(x+1)^2}\right]^{1/3}$ gives $\ln y = (1/3)\{\ln (x^2-4) - \ln x - 2 \ln (x+1)\}$

   Thus, $y'/y = (1/3) \{\dfrac{2x}{x^2-4} - 1/x - \dfrac{2}{x+1}\}$ or $y' = \dots\dots$

17. $x/600 + p/12 = 1$ or $x = 600 - 50p$ gives $dx/dp = -50$.

   $\eta = (p/x)(dx/dp) = \left(p/(600-50p)\right)(-50) = p/(p-12)$

   (a) $\eta = -1$ or $p/(p-12) = -1$ gives $p=6$.

   (b) $\eta = -2$ or $p/(p-12) = -2$ gives $p=8$.

   (c) $\eta = -1/3$ or $p/(p-12) = -1/3$ gives $p=3$.

21. $R'(x) = p(1 + 1/\eta)$ gives $25 = p(1 + 1/(-2)) = p/2$ or $p=50$.

25. $x^y = e^x$ gives $\ln x^y = \ln e^x$ or $y \ln x = x$ or

   $y = x/\ln x$. Thus, $dy = y'\ dx = \dfrac{\ln x - 1}{(\ln x)^2} dx$.

REVIEW TEST ON CHAPTER - 15

FILL IN THE BLANKS:

1. If $y = f(x)$, then Δx _____ dx and Δy _____ dy $(=\ ,\quad \neq)$

2. If $y = g(t)$, then by definition dy = _____.

3. If $y = f(x)$ is linear function, then Δy _____ dy $(=\ ,\quad \neq)$

138

4. $d(x^7)$ = _____   5. $d(1/t^3)$ = _____   6. $d(e^{u^2})$ = _____

7. $d(\ln 2)$ = _____   8. $d(\ln x)$ = _____

9. $d(1/e^y)$ = _____   10. $d\{(x^2+1)^5\}$ = _____

11. $d(e^{\sqrt{x}})$ = _____   12. $d(\ln \sqrt{x})$ = _____

13. If $y = f(x)$, then corresponding to small error dx in x,

    (a) the error in y is given approximately by _____

    (b) the relative error in y is given approximately by _____

    (c) the percentage error in y is given approximately by _____.

14. $\frac{d}{dx}(x^2+y^2)$ = _____   15. $\frac{d}{dx}(e^{xy})$ = _____

16. $\frac{d}{dx}\{(\ln (xy))$ = _____   17. $\frac{d}{dx}(x^3 + y^3 - 3xy)$ = _____

18. $\frac{d}{dx}(e^x/e^y)$ = _____   19. $\frac{d}{dx}(y/x)$ = _____

20. $d(e^{xt})$ = _____   21. $d(y \ln x)$ = _____

22. If $p = f(x)$ is the demand relation, then the elasticity of demand is given by η = _____

23. The demand is elastic if _____ and inelastic if _____

24. Percentage change in demand $\approx$ (_____). percentage change in price.

25. If the demand is elastic, then the percentage change in demand _____ percentage change in price   (> , < or =)

26. If the demand is inelastic, then the percentage change in demand _____ percentage change in price   (> , < , =)

27. If the revenue $R(x)$ is a decreasing function of x, then the demand is _____ (elastic or inelastic).

28. If $y = (x+1)^x$, then $\ln$ = _____ and differentiation of this w.r.t.

    x gives _____ or y' = _____.

SEE ANSWERS AT THE END OF THIS BOOK.

CHAPTER - 16

YOU SHOULD BE FAMILIAR WITH THE FOLLOWING TERMS:

Antiderivative or indefinite integral ; integration.

Constant of integration.

Integrand, integral sign.

Method of substitution.

Table of integrals.

Integration by parts.

OBJECTIVES

AFTER READING THIS CHAPTER YOU SHOULD BE ABLE TO DO THE FOLLOWING:

1. Apply integration to find a function given its derivative.

2. Use the basic integration formulas to find the antiderivatives of x^n for all n, e^x, and multiples and combinations of these terms.

3. Use linear substitutions to find the antiderivative of $f(ax+b)$ if the antiderivative of $f(x)$ is known.

4. (Very important and difficult) Apply the substitution method to evaluate appropriate antiderivatives.

5. Find appropriate antiderivatives by using a table of integrals, possibly more than once and possibly in conjuction with a substitution.

6. Use integration by parts in cases where the integrand consists of
   (a) an exponential function multiplied by a polynomial or
   (b) a logarithmic function multiplied by a polynomial.

SOLUTIONS TO ALTERNATE ODD PROBLEMS

EXERCISES 16.1

1. $\int x^7 \, dx = \frac{x^{7+1}}{7+1} + C = x^8/8 + C.$

5. $\int 7x \, dx = 7 \int x^1 dx = 7 \, \frac{x^{1+1}}{1+1} + C = (7/2)x^2 + C.$

9. $\int \frac{1}{x \ln 2} \, dx = (1/\ln 2)\int \frac{1}{x} \, dx = (1/\ln 2) \ln |x| + C$, because $1/\ln 2$ is a constant.

13. $\int (e^2-2^e)e^x\,dx = (e^2-2^e)\int e^x\,dx = (e^2-2^e)e^x + C$, because (e^2-2^e) is a constant.

17. $\int (x^7+7x+7/x+7)\,dx = \int x^7 dx + 7\int x^1 dx + 7\int (1/x)\,dx + 7\int 1\,dx$

$= x^8/8 + 7x^2/2 + 7\ln |x| + 7x + C.$

21. $\int (x+2)(x+3)\,dx = \int (x^2+5x+6)\,dx = x^3/3 + 5x^2/2 + 6x + C.$

25. $\int (x+2)^2\,dx = \int (x^2+4x+4)\,dx = x^3/3 + 4x^2/2 + 4x + C.$

29. $\int (2x-3/x)^2\,dx = \int (4x^2-12+9x^{-2})\,dx = 4x^3/3 - 12x + 9x^{-1}/(-1) + C$

$= (4/3)x^3 - 12x - 9/x + C.$

33. $\int x^3(x+1)(x+2)\,dx = \int (x^5+3x^4+2x^3)\,dx = x^6/6 + 3x^5/5 + 2x^4/4 + C.$

37. $\int (\dfrac{\ln x^3}{\ln x^2})\,dx = \int \dfrac{3\ln x}{2\ln x}\,dx = \int (3/2)\,dx = (3/2)x + C.$

41. $\int \dfrac{e^x}{\ln 2}\,dx = (1/\ln 2)\int e^x dx = (1/\ln 2)e^x + C$, because $1/\ln 2$ is a const.

45. $\int (\sqrt{x}+3)^2\,dx = \int (x + 6x^{1/2} + 9)\,dx = x^2/2 + 6\,x^{3/2}/(3/2) + 9x + C$

$= x^2/2 + 4x^{3/2} + 9x + C.$

49. $\int x\,e^{\ln(x+1)}\,dx = \int x(x+1)\,dx = \int (x^2+x)\,dx$ $\qquad\Big|\ e^{\ln t} = t$

$= x^3/3 + x^2/2 + C.$

53. $\int (4x^3 + 3x^2 + 2x + 1 + 1/x + x^{-3})\,dx = 4\cdot x^4/4 + 3\cdot x^3/3 + 2\cdot x^2/2 + x$

$+ \ln |x| + x^{-2}/(-2) + C$

$= x^4 + x^3 + x^2 + x + \ln |x| - 1/2x^2 + C.$

57. $\int \sqrt{x}(x+1)(2x-1)\,dx = \int \sqrt{x}(2x^2+x-1)\,dx = \int (2x^{5/2} + x^{3/2} - x^{1/2})\,dx$

$= 2\cdot x^{7/2}/(7/2) + x^{5/2}/(5/2) - x^{3/2}/(3/2) + C$

$= (4/7)x^{7/2} + (2/5)x^{5/2} - (2/3)x^{3/2} + C.$

61. $\int (3\theta^2 - 6\theta + \dfrac{9}{\theta} + 4e^\theta)\,d\theta = 3\theta^3/3 - 6\theta^2/2 + 9\ln |\theta| + 4e^\theta + C$

65. Distance $= s = \int (t + \sqrt{t})^2\,dt = t^3/3 + (4/5)t^{5/2} + t^2/2 + C.$

At time t=0, distance travelled s=0. This gives C=0. Thus

$s = t^3/3 + (4/5)t^{5/2} + t^2/2.$

69. $C(x) = \int (3 + 0.001x)\,dx = 3x + 0.0005x^2 + K$, where K = constant of integragion. $C(100) = 305 + K = 1005$. Thus, K = 700. $C(200) = 620 + K = 1320.$

P = R - C. R = 5x gives $\Delta R = 5\Delta x = 5(2000 - 1000) = 5000$.
$\Delta C = C(2000) - C(1000) = 8700 - 4200 = 4500$. Therefore,
$\Delta P = \Delta R - \Delta C = 5000 - 4500 = 500$.

73. $P(x) = \int P'(x)dx = \int (5 - 0.002x)dx = 5x - 0.001x^2 + K$

x = 100, P = 310 gives K = -180. Thus $P(x) = 5x - 0.001x^2 - 180$.

EXERCISES - 16.2   (I = GIVEN INTEGRAL)

1. By Theorem 1, $\int (2x+1)^7 dx = \dfrac{(2x+1)^8}{8 \cdot 2} + C$
    $\overset{\curvearrowleft}{\text{coeff. of x in (2x+1)}}$

5. $\int \dfrac{1}{2y-1} dy = \dfrac{\ln|2y-1|}{2} + 2$
    $\overset{\curvearrowleft}{\text{coeff. of x}}$

9. $\int e^{3x+2} dx = \dfrac{e^{3x+2}}{3} + C$
    $\overset{\curvearrowleft}{\text{coeff. of x}}$

13. $\int \dfrac{e^{2x+3}}{e^{1-x}} dx = \int e^{2x+3-(1-x)} dx = \int e^{3x+2} dx = \dfrac{e^{3x+2}}{2} + C$ (see #9 above)

17. $u = x^2+3x+1$ gives $I = \int \dfrac{1}{u^3} du = \int u^{-3} du = \dfrac{u^{-2}}{-2} + C$

     $= (-1/2)(x^2+3x+1)^{-2} + C$.

21. $u = x^2+1$ gives $I = \int \dfrac{1}{u} \cdot (1/2)du = (1/2)\ln|u| + C = (1/2)\ln|x^2+1|+C$

25. $u = \sqrt{x}+7$ gives $I = \int u^5(2du) = 2u^6/6 + C = (1/3)(\sqrt{x}+7)^6 + C$

29. $u = t^2$ gives $I = \int e^u \cdot (\tfrac{1}{2} du) = (1/2)e^u + C = (1/2)e^{t^2} + C$.

33. $u = 3/x$ gives $I = (-1/3) \int e^u du = (-1/3)e^u + C = (-1/3)e^{3/x} + C$.

37. $u = x^3$ gives $I = (1/3) \int e^u du = (1/3)e^u + C = (1/3)e^{x^3} + C$.

41. $u = e^x+1$ gives $I = \int \dfrac{du}{(u+1)^2} = \int (u+1)^{-2} du = \dfrac{(u+1)^{-1}}{-1 \cdot 1} + C$.

     $= C - (e^x+1)^{-1}$

45. $u = e^x - e^{-x}$ gives $du = (e^x + e^{-x}) dx$. Thus,

     $I = \int \dfrac{e^x+e^{-x}}{e^x-e^{-x}} du = \int \dfrac{du}{u} = \ln|u| + C = \ln|e^x-e^{-x}| + C$

49. $\ln x = u$ gives $I = \int \sqrt{u} du = \int u^{1/2} du = u^{3/2}/(3/2) + C$

     $= (2/3)(\ln x)^{3/2} + C$.

53. $u = 1 + \ln x$ gives $I = \int \frac{1}{u} du = \ln |u| + C = \ln |1 + \ln x| + C$

57. $u = x^2+4x+1$ gives $I = \int u^{1/2} \cdot (\frac{du}{2}) = (1/2)\frac{u^{3/2}}{3/2} + C$

   $= (1/3)(x^2+4x+1)^{3/2} + C.$

65. $g(x) = \int \frac{x}{\sqrt{x^2+1}} dx.$ Put $x^2+1 = u.$ $2x\ dx = du.$

   $g(x) = \int \frac{1}{2} \frac{du}{\sqrt{u}} = \sqrt{u} + C = \sqrt{x^2+1} + C$

   $g(0) = 1 + C = 2$ gives $C = 1.$ Thus, $g(x) = \sqrt{x^2+1} + 1$

69. Put $\sqrt{x} = u$, $\frac{1}{2\sqrt{x}} dx = du.$ $\int \frac{g(\sqrt{x})}{\sqrt{x}} dx = \int 2g(u)\ du = 2f(u) + C$

   $= 2f(\sqrt{x}) + C$

73. $C(x) = \int C'(x) dx = (1/2000) \int 2x(x^2+2500)^{1/2} dx$

   $= (1/2000)(x^2+2500)^{3/2}/(3/2) + K = (1/3000)(x^2+2500)^{3/2} + K$

   $x=0$, $C = 100$ gives $K = 175/3.$ Thus,

   $C(x) = (1/3000)(x^2+2500)^{3/2} + (175/3)$

77. Put $t+1600 = u$

   $P(t) = \int P'(t)\ dt = 1,200,000 \int u^{-3/2}\ du = -2,400,000(t+1600)^{-1/2} + C.$

   $P(0) = 0$ gives $C = 60,000$ and so $P(t) = 2.4 \times 10^6\{1/40 - (t+1600)^{-1/2}\}.$

   $\lim_{t \to \infty} P(t) = 2.4 \times 10^6(1/40 - 0) = 60,000.$

EXERCISES 16.3

1. In formula # 66, take a=1, b = -3, c=1 to get the answer.

5. $\int \frac{\sqrt{3x+1}}{x} dx = 2 \sqrt{3x+1} + 1 \int \frac{1}{x\sqrt{3x+1}} dx$ (formula #24)

   $= 2\sqrt{3x+1} + \ln| (\sqrt{3x+1} - 1)/(\sqrt{3x+1} + 1)| + C$ (formula # 22)

9. Use formula #45 with a=3.

13. Use formula #14 with a=2, b=3.

17. $\int x^3 e^{2x} dx = (x^3/2)e^{2x} - (3/2)\int x^2 e^{2x} dx$ (formula # 70)

    $= (x^3/2)e^{2x} - (3/2)\{(x^2/2)e^{2x} - (2/2)\int xe^{2x} dx\}$ (formula # 70)

    $= (x^3/2)e^{2x} - (3x^2/4)e^{2x} + (3/2)(1/4)(2x-1)e^{2x} + C$ (formula #69)

    $= (1/8)(4x^3 - 6x^2 + 6x - 3)e^{2x} + C$

21. Put $e^x = u$. Then given integral is:

$$\int \frac{1}{(1-u)(2-3u)} du = \int \frac{1}{(u-1)(3u-2)} du = -\ln|(3u-2)/(u-1)| + C$$

                                    (formula # 15)

    $= \ln|(u-1)/(3u-2)| + C = \ln|(e^x-1)/(3e^x-2)| + C.$

25. $u = \ln x$ gives $I = \int\{u/(3+2u)\}du = (1/2)u - (3/4)\ln|3+2u| + C.$

                                    (formula # 8)

EXERCISES - 16.4   (I = given integral)

1. Take $f(x) = \ln x$ and $g(x) = x$. Then,

$$\int x \ln x \, dx = (x^2/2)\ln x - \int (1/x)x^2/2 \, dx = (x^2/2)\ln x - (1/2)\int x \, dx$$

    $= (x^2/2)\ln x - x^2/4 + C.$

5. Take $f(x) = \ln x$ and $g(x) = 1$. Then $\int 1 \cdot \ln x \, dx = (\ln x)\cdot x - \int x\cdot\frac{1}{x} \, dx$

    $= x \ln x - x + C.$

9. $I = \int (1/2)x^{-1/2}\ln x \, dx$. Take $f(x) = \ln x$, $g(x) = x^{-1/2}$. Thus,

    $I = (1/2)\left[(2x^{1/2})\ln x - \int(1/x)(2x^{1/2})dx\right] = \sqrt{x} \ln x - \int x^{-1/2}dx$

    $= \sqrt{x} \ln x - 2 x^{1/2} + C.$

13. $\int \ln(ex) \, dx = \int(\ln e + \ln x) \, dx = \int(1 + \ln x) \, dx = x + \int \ln x \, dx$

    $= x + (x \ln x - x) + C = x \ln x + C$ (see #5 above.)

17. $\int \log x dx = \int \frac{\ln x}{\ln 10} \, dx = (1/\ln 10)\int 1\cdot\ln x \, dx = (1/\ln 10)(x \ln x - x) + C$

                        $\left[\text{See #5 for } \int \ln x \, dx.\right]$

21. Take $f(x) = x$ and $g(x) = e^x$. Then $I = \int x \, e^x \, dx = xe^x - \int 1\cdot e^x \, dx$

    $= xe^x - e^x + C = (x-1)e^x + C.$

25. Take $f(x) = 2x+1$ and $g(x) = e^{3x}$. Then $I = \int (2x+1) e^{3x} \, dx$

$= (2x+1) \cdot e^x/3 - \int 2 \cdot e^{3x}/3 \, dx = (2x+1) e^{3x}/3 - (2/9) e^{3x} + C$

29. Take $f(x) = x^2$, and $g(x) = e^x$. Then $I = \int x^2 e^x \, dx$

$= x^2 e^x - \int 2xe^x \, dx = x^2 e^x - (2xe^x - 2e^x \, dx)$

$= x^2 e^x - 2xe^x + 2e^x + C$, where we have integrated

$\int 2xe^x \, dx$ by parts again with $f(x) = 2x$, $g(x) = e^x$.

33. See at the end of this chapter.

37. $C(x) = (5000) \int (x+20)^{-2} \ln(x+20) \, dx = 5000 \int y^{-2} \ln y \, dy$ where $y = x+20$.

$= 5000(-1/y)(1 + \ln y) + K = -5000\{1 + \ln(x+20)\}/(x+20)\} + K$

$x=0$, $C = 2000$ gives $K = 2250 + 250 \ln 20$.

Thus, $C(x) = 2250 + 250 \ln 20 - 5000(x+20)^{-1}\{1 + \ln(x+20)\}$

REVIEW EXERCISES ON CHAPTER - 16

1. See answers in the text book.

5. $I = \int e^{x^2+1 - (x^2-1)} \, dx = \int e^2 \, dx = xe^2 + C$, because e^2 is a constant.

9. $\log x = \log_{10} x = \dfrac{\ln x}{\ln 10}$, so that $\log x/\ln x = 1/\ln 10$. Thus,

$I = \int (\dfrac{\log x}{\ln x}) \, dx = (\ln 10)^{-1} \int dx = x(\ln 10)^{-1} + C$, because $(\ln 10)^{-1}$ is

a constant.

13. $I = \int \dfrac{1}{x(1+\ln x)} \, dx = \ln |1 + \ln x| + C$. (For solution, see #53 in

Exercises 16.2)

17. $u = 1+x^3$ gives $I = \int u^{-1/3} \cdot (\dfrac{du}{3}) = (1/3)\dfrac{u^{2/3}}{(2/3)} + C = (1/2)(1+x^3)^{2/3} + C$.

21. $I = \int \dfrac{3x-1}{(x-1)(x+2)} \, dx = 3 \int \dfrac{x}{(x-1)(x+2)} \, dx - \int \dfrac{1}{(x-1)(x+2)} \, dx$.

Now, use formula #16 for the first integral and formula #15 for the

second integral. (Here a=1, b = -1, c=1, d=2).

25. $I = \int \sqrt{25t^2 + 9} \, dt = 5 \int \sqrt{t^2 + 9/25} \, dt$. Now use formula #56 with x=t and

a = 3/5.

29. $\int x^5 \log_x(x^3) \, dx = \int x^5 (3 \log_x x) \, dx = 3x^6/6 + C = x^6/2 + C$ $| \log_x x = 1$

33. $\int \dfrac{1}{x(x^3-1)} \, dx = (1/3) \int \dfrac{3x^2}{x^3(x^3-1)} \, dx = (1/3) \int \dfrac{1}{u(u-1)} du$, where $u = x^3$

$$= (1/3) \ln \left| (u-1)/u \right| + C = (1/3) \ln \left| (x^3-1)/x^3 \right| + C.$$

37. $u = 1/x^2 = x^{-2}$ gives $du = -2x^{-3}dx$ or $x^{-3}dx = (-1/2)du$. Thus,

$$I = \int \frac{e^{1/x^2}}{x^3} \, dx = \int x^{-3} e^{1/x^2} \, dx = \int e^u (-du/2) = (-1/2)e^u + C$$

$$= (-1/2)e^{1/x^2} + C.$$

41. $f(t) = \int \dfrac{\ln t}{t^2} \, dt = -t^{-1} \ln t - \int -t^{-1} \dfrac{1}{t} \, dt = -t^{-1} \ln t - t^{-1} + C$

$f(1) = -1 + C = 1$, so $C = 2$. $f(t) = 2 - t^{-1} \ln t - t^{-1}$.

$f(e) = 2 - 2e^{-1}$, because $\ln e = 1$.

45. $x = \int 10(1 - e^{-t/50})dt = 10t + 500 \, e^{-t/50} + K$

t=0, x=0 gives K = -500. Thus, $x = 10t + 500e^{-t/50} - 500$

$t = 50$ gives $x = 500 \, e^{-1} \simeq 184$.

t=100 gives $x = 500 + 500e^{-2} \simeq 568$.

Thus number of units produced during next 50 hours = 568-184 = 384.

49. $R(x) = 10 \int (20-x)e^{-x/20} \, dx = 200 \, xe^{-x/20} + K$ |Int. by parts

x=0, R=0 gives K=0. Thus, $R(x) = 200xe^{-x/20}$

$R = px$ gives the demand relation as : $p = 200 \, e^{-x/20}$

53. $\rho = \int 250(x+4)^{3/2} \, dx = 100(x-4)^{5/2} + K$

x=0, $\rho = 0$ gives K = -3200. Thus, $\rho = 100(x+4)^{5/2} - 3200$.

When x=5, $\rho = 24,300 - 3200 = 21,100$.

57. Let F(t) = total consumption since t=0. $F(t) = \int R(t) \, dt$.

For $0 \le t \le 4$, $F(t) = 365 \int (1 + 0.1t)dt = 365(t + 0.05t^2)$.

(Constant is zero since F(0) = 0.) F(4) = 365(4.8)

For $4 \le t \le 12$, $F(t) = 365 \int (1.68 - 0.07t)dt = 365(1.68t - 0.035t^2 + C)$

Putting t=4 we get C = -1.36, and $F(t) = 365(1.68t - 0.035t^2 - 1.36)$. F(12) = (365)(13.76). For $12 \le t \le 18$, $F(t) = 365 \int (0.24 + 0.05t) \, dt = 365(0.24t + 0.025t^2 + D)$. Putting t=12 we get D = 7.28 and so

$F(t) = 365(0.24t + 0.025t^2 + D)$. Putting t=12 we get D = 7.28 and so

$F(t) = 365(0.24t + 0.025t^2 + 7.28)$.

(a) F(5) = 365(8.4 - 0.875 - 1.36) = 2250.
(b) F(15) - F(10) = 365(16.51) - 365(11.94) = 1666
(c) F(18) = 365(19.7) = 7191.

FILL IN THE BLANKS:

1. $\int x^{-7} \, dx =$ _____   2. $\int (1/\sqrt{x}) \, dx =$ _____   3. $\int e^x \, dx =$ _____

4. $\int \log(3^x) \, dx =$ _____   5. $\int e^{2 \ln x} \, dx =$ _____

6. $\int e^3 \, dx =$ _____   7. $\int (2x+3)^7 \, dx =$ _____

8. $\int (1/\sqrt{5-2x}) \, dx =$ _____   *9. $\int \dfrac{1}{4x^2+4x+1} \, dx =$ _____

10. $\int \dfrac{1}{2x+3} \, dx =$ _____   11. $\int (3x+7)^{-1} \, dx =$ _____

12. $\int e^{2x-3} \, dx =$ _____

(13 - 21)

INTEGRAL = I	SUBSTITUTION	I IN TERMS OF u	AFTER INTEGRATION IN TERMS OF u	ANSWER IN TERMS OF X
13. $(2x+3)(x^2+3x+1)^7 dx$	$u = x^2+3x+1$	$\int u^7 du$	$u^8/8 + C$	$(x^2+3x+1)^8/8 + C$
14. $\int \dfrac{3x^2+1}{\sqrt{x^3+x}} \, dx$	$u =$ _____	$\int$ ___ du	_____	_____
15. $\int \dfrac{2x+3}{x^2+3x+7}$	$u =$ _____	$\int$ ___ du	_____	_____
16. $\int \dfrac{\ln x}{x} \, dx$	$u =$ _____	$\int$ ___ du	_____	_____
17. $\int \dfrac{1}{x \ln x} \, dx$	$u =$ _____	$\int$ ___ du	_____	_____
18. $\int \dfrac{x}{x^2-4} \, dx$	$u =$ _____	$\int$ ___ du	_____	_____
19. $\int \dfrac{e^{\sqrt{x}}}{\sqrt{x}} \, dx$	$u =$ _____	$\int$ ___ du	_____	_____
20. $\int x\sqrt{x^2+4} \, dx$	$u =$ _____	$\int$ ___ du	_____	_____
21. $\int e^x\sqrt{e^x+7} \, dx$	$u =$ _____	$\int$ ___ du	_____	_____

(22-26) If $G(x)$ is an integral of $g(x)$, then by integration by parts,
$$\int f(x) \cdot g(x) \, dx = f(x)G(x) - \int f'(x)G(x) \, dx.$$

22. Let $I = \int x^7 \ln x \, dx$. Here $f(x) =$ _____ , $g(x) =$ _____ , $G(x) =$ ___

Thus, $I = ($ _____ $) - \int($ _____ $) dx =$ _____ $+ C$

23. Let $I = \int xe^{-2x} \, dx$. Here $f(x) =$ _____ , $g(x) =$ _____ , $G(x) =$ _____

Thus, $I = ($ _____ $) - \int($ _____ $) dx =$ _____ $+ C$

24. Let $I = \int \ln(x^x) \, dx$. Here $f(x) =$ _____ , $g(x) =$ _____ , $G(x) =$ _____

Thus, $I = ($ _____ $) - \int($ _____ $) \, dx =$ _____ $+ C.$

25. Let $I = \int \{(3x+2)/e^x\} \, dx$. Here $f(x) =$ _____ , $g(x) =$ _____ , $G(x) =$ ___

Thus, $I = ($ _____ $) - \int($ _____ $) dx =$ _____ $+ C$

26. Let $I = \int \ln x \, dx$. Here $f(x) =$ _____ , $g(x) =$ _____ , $G(x) =$ _____

Thus, $I = ($ _____ $) - \int($ _____ $) \, dx =$ _____ $+ C.$

SEE ANSWERS AT THE END OF THE BOOK.

CHAPTER - 17

YOU SHOULD BE FAMILIAR WITH THE FOLLOWING TERMS:

Definite integral ; upper limit and lower limit of integration.

Fundamental theorem of Calculus.

Inproper integral.

Lorentz curve ; coefficient of inequality.

Learning curve.

Consumers' surplus ; producers' surplus.

Average value of a function.

Differential equation of order n. Solution of a differential equation.

General solution ; initial condition, particular solution.

Continuous random variable ; probability density function.

Uniform probability distribution ; exponential probability distribution.

Mean (or expected value) of a random variable.

Normal probability distribution ; standard deviation.

Numerical integration ; trapezoidal rule ; Simpson's rule.

OBJECTIVES

AFTER READING THIS CHAPTER YOU SHOULD BE ABLE TO DO THE FOLLOWING:

1. Evaluate a definite integral by using the antiderivative of the integrand.

2. Use a definite integral to evaluate (a) the area under the graph of a non-negative function.
    (b) the area between a graph and the x-axis when the graph lies partly above and partly below the axis.
    (c) the area between two graphs.
    (d) the area between a graph and the y-axis.

3. Compute an improper integral (with limit ∞, $-\infty$ or both) if it converges

4. Apply definite integrlas (a) to calculate the coefficient of inequality for a Lorentz curve

   (b) to calculate the number of work hours from a learning curve.

   (c) to calculate the total revenue, cost and profit and their present values given the revenue rate and cost rate of an operatinn.

   (d) to calculate the consumers' and producers' surpluses.

5. Calculate the average value of a function over a given interval.

6. Solve first-order differential equations of separable type ; find the particular solution from a given initial conditinn.

7. Use differential equations to model simple processes, for example population growth.

8. Compute probabilities for a continuous random variable with given probability density function.

9. Calculate the mean value of a continuous random variable.

10. Use the trapezoidal rule and Simpson's rule to calculate approximations to a definite integral.

SOLUTIONS TO ALTERNATE ODD PROBLEMS

EXERCISES - 17.1   (I = given integral)

1. $\displaystyle\int_0^1 x^2\,dx = \left[x^3/3\right]_0^1 = 1/3 - 0/3 = 1/3.$

5. $\displaystyle\int_0^8 x^{1/3}\,dx = \left[\frac{3}{4}x^{4/3}\right]_0^8 = \frac{3}{4}(16) - 0 = 12.$

9. $\displaystyle\int_1^2 \frac{(2x+1)(x-2)}{x}\,dx = \int_1^2 \frac{2x^2-3x-2}{x}\,dx = \int_1^2 (2x - 3 - 2x^{-1})\,dx$

   $\displaystyle = \left[x^2 - 3x - 2\ln|x|\right]_1^2 = (4-6-2\ln 2)-(1-3-0) = -2\ln2.$

13. Put $x^2+1 = u$, when x=0, u=1 and when x=1, u=2.

    $\displaystyle I = \int_1^2 \frac{1}{2}u^{1/2}\,du = \left[\frac{1}{3}u^{3/2}\right]_1^2 = (2\sqrt{2} - 1)/3$

17. Put $\ln t = u$. $\displaystyle I = \int_1^2 u\,du = \left[u^2/2\right]_1^2 = 2 - 1/2 = 3/2.$

21. 0, becuase $\displaystyle\int_a^a f(x)\,dx = 0$ 25. I = 0   (limits equal).

29. Since $y = 4 - x^2 \geq 0$ for $0 \leq x \leq 2$, the area is given by

$$A = \int_0^2 (4-x^2)\ dx = \left[(4x - x^3/3)\right]_0^2 = 16/3 \text{ sq. units.}$$

33. The curve $y = 2 + x - x^2 = (2-x)(1+x)$ crosses the x-axis where $x=2$ or $x = -1$. $y \geq 0$ for x in $-1 \leq x \leq 2$. Thus, the area is

$$A = \int_{-1}^2 (2+x-x^2)\ dx = \left[2x + x^2/2 - x^3/3\right]_{-1}^2 = 9/2 \text{ sq. units.}$$

37. $A = \int_0^1 x\ e^x\ dx$. Integrating by parts, we have:

$$A = \int_0^1 x\ e^x\ dx = \left[x\ e^x - e^x\right]_0^1 = \left[(x-1)e^x\right]_0^1 = 1 \text{ sq. units.}$$

41. $(e^x \ln x)/(1+x^2)$ in view of Theorem 2 of this section.

45. $\int_1^2 \frac{d}{dx}\ (x^2 e^{\sqrt{x}}\ \ln x)\ dx = \left[x^2\ e^{\sqrt{x}}\ \ln x\right]_1^2 = 4\ e^{\sqrt{2}}\ \ln 2$

49. Overall change in revenue $= \int_{100}^{80} R'(x)\ dx + \int_{80}^{150} R'(x)\ dx = \int_{100}^{150} R'(x)\,dx$

$$= \int_{100}^{150} (12.5 - 0.02x)\ dx = \left[12.5x - 0.01x^2\right]_{100}^{150} = 500.$$

EXERCISES - 17.2

1. Since $y = -x^2$ is ≤ 0 in $0 \leq x \leq 3$, the area A is given by
$$A = \int_0^3 -(-x^2)\ dx = \left[x^3/3\right]_0^3 = 9 \text{ sq. units.}$$

5. $y = x^2 - 4 \leq 0$ in $0 \leq x \leq 2$ and is ≥ 0 for $2 \leq x \leq 3$. Thus
$$A = \int_0^2 -(x^2-4)\ dx + \int_2^3 (x^2-4)\ dx = 23/3 \text{ sq. units.}$$

9. Since $y = 3x > y = x^2$ in $1 \leq x \leq 2$, the area is given by
$$A = \int_1^2 (3x-x^2)\ dx = \left[3x^2/2 - x^3/3\right]_1^2 = 13/6 \text{ sq. units.}$$

13. Since $e^x > x^2$ in $0 \leq x \leq 1$, $A = \int_0^1 (e^x-x^2)\ dx = (e - 4/3)$ sq. units.

17. The two curves $y = x^3$ and $y = x^2$ meet where $x^3 = x^2$ or $x = 0, 1$.

Also $x^3 \le x^2$ for all x in $0 \le x \le 1$. Thus,

$$A = \int_0^1 (x^2 - x^3) \, dx = 1/12 \text{ sq. units.}$$

21. $\displaystyle\int_2^\infty (1/x^3) \, dx = \lim_{h \to \infty} \int_2^h x^{-3} \, dx = \lim_{h \to \infty} \left[\frac{x^{-2}}{-2} \right]_2^h = \lim_{h \to \infty} \left(\frac{-1}{2h^2} + \frac{1}{8} \right) = 1/8.$

25. $\displaystyle\int_0^\infty \frac{x}{x^2+1} \, dx = \lim_{h \to \infty} \int_0^h \frac{x}{x^2+1} \, dx = \lim_{h \to \infty} \int_1^{h^2+1} \frac{1}{2u} \, du,$ where $u = x^2 + 1$

$$= \lim_{h \to \infty} \left[\frac{1}{2} \ln |u| \right]_1^{h^2+1} = \lim_{h \to \infty} \left[\frac{1}{2} \ln(h^2+1) - \frac{1}{2} \ln 1 \right] = \infty .$$

29. $\displaystyle\int_{-\infty}^\infty xe^{-x^2} \, dx = \lim_{\substack{a \to \infty \\ b \to -\infty}} \int_b^a x \, e^{-x^2} \, dx$ $\qquad\qquad$ | Put $-x^2 = u$

$$= \lim_{\substack{a \to \infty \\ b \to -\infty}} \int_{-b^2}^{-a^2} (-1/2) \, e^u \, du = \lim_{\substack{a \to \infty \\ b \to -\infty}} \left[\left(\frac{-1}{2} e^u \right) \right]_{-b^2}^{-a^2}$$

$$= \lim_{\substack{a \to \infty \\ b \to -\infty}} \frac{-1}{2} (e^{-a^2} - e^{-b^2}) = 0 - 0 = 0.$$

EXERCISES - 17.3

1. (a) $x = 0.2$ gives $y = 0.048$. Thus, 4.8% of the income is received by the poorest 20% of the people.

   (b) $L = 2 \displaystyle\int_0^1 \left[x - f(x) \right] dx = 2 \int_0^1 (x - 19x^2/20 - x/20) \, dx$

   $$= (19/10) \int_0^1 (x - x^2) \, dx = 19/60.$$

5. 200 calculators = 4 units of 50 calculators and 700 = 14 units of 50.

   $$\Delta T = \int_4^{14} 70 \, x^{-0.32} \, dx = \left[70 \, x^{0.68}/(0.68) \right]_4^{14} \simeq 356 \text{ hours.}$$

9. $P = 15-2x$ and $p = 3+x$ give one solution $P_0 = 7$, $x_0 = 4$

   $$\text{C.S.} = \int_0^{x_0} (15 - 2x) \, dx - P_0 x_0 = \int_0^4 (15-2x) \, dx - 28 = 44 - 28 = 16.$$

   $$\text{P.S.} = P_0 x_0 - \int_0^{x_0} (3+x) \, dx = 28 - \int_0^4 (3+x) \, dx = 28 - 20 = 8.$$

13. $p = 280/(x+2)$ and $p = 20 + 2.5x$ give on solving $x_0 = 6$, $P_0 = 35$.

C.S. $= \displaystyle\int_0^6 \{280/(x+2)\}\ dx - 6(35) = 280\ \ln 4 - 210 \approx 178.16$

P.S. $=\ 6(35) - \displaystyle\int_0^6 (20 + 2.5x)\ dx = 210 - 165 = 45.$

17. Present value of savings $= \displaystyle\int_0^5 160(5+t)e^{-0.08t}\ dt$ (integrate by parts)

$= \left[160(5+t)(-1/0.08)e^{-0.08t}\right]_0^5 - \displaystyle\int_0^5 160(-1/0.08)e^{-0.08t}\ dt.$

$= \left[-2000(5+t)\ e^{-0.08t} + 2000(-1/0.08)e^{-0.08t}\right]_0^5 = -45,000e^{-0.4} + 35,000$

$= 4835.60.$ The machine does not quite pay for itself.

21. Present value of first strategy $= P_1 = \displaystyle\int_0^{20}(20-t)e^{-0.1t}\ dt - 25$

$= \left[10(t-10)e^{-0.1t}\right]_0^{20} - 25$ (by parts)

$= 100(1+e^{-2}) - 25 = 88.53$ millions.

For second strategy, $P_2 = \displaystyle\int_0^{10}(40-4t)e^{-0.1t}\ dt - 60 = \left[40te^{-0.1t}\right]_0^{10} - 60$

$= 400e^{-1} - 60 = 87.15$ millions. P_1 is greater.

25. $A(t) = \displaystyle\int_0^5 2Ie^{0.1(10-t)}\ dt = \left[2I(-10e^{0.1(10-t)})\right]_0^5$

$= 20I(-e^{0.5} + e) = 21.39\ I.$

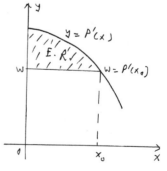

29. If T denotes the total profit per week, than we are given that $T(x) = P(x) - Wx$.

This gives $T'(x) = P'(x) - W$. For maximum profit, we have $T'(x) = 0$ or $P'(x) = W$. That is, if the maximum profit occurs at $x = x_0$, then $T'(x_0) = 0$ or $P'(x_0) = W$. Thus, $T'(x) = P'(x) - W = P'(x) - P'(x_0)$ Total weekly profit is then given by

$$T(x) = \int_0^{x_0} T'(x)\ dx = \int_0^{x_0}\left[P'(x) - P'(x_0)\right]dx \qquad \ldots \text{(i)}$$

This represents the area between the graph of the marginal productivity function, $y = P'(x)$ and the horizontal line $y = W$ as shown shaded in the figure. $T(x)$ given by (i) is known as the economic rent (E.R.) We are given that $P'(x) = 120(x + 400)^{-1/2}$.

(a) $P'(x) = W$ gives: $120(x + 400)^{-1/2} = 3$ or $x = 1200 = x_0$

Thus, E.R. $= \int_0^{x_0} \{P'(x) - P'(x_0)\} dx = \int_0^{1200} \{120(x+400)^{-1/2} - 3\} dx$

$= \$1200$

(b) Here $W=4$. Then $P'(x_0) = W$ gives $120(x_0 + 400)^{-1/2} = 4$ or $x_0 = 500$.

E.R. $= \int_0^{x_0} \left[P'(x) - W\right] dx = \int_0^{500} \left[120(x+400)^{-1/2} - 4\right] dx = \$400$

(c) Here $W=5$. Then $P'(x_0) = W$ gives $120(x_0 + 400)^{-1/2} = 5$ or $x_0 = 176$

E.R. $= \int_0^{176} \left[120(x + 400)^{-1/2} - 5\right] dx = \left[240\sqrt{x+400} - 5x\right]_0^{176} = \$80.$

EXERCISES - 17.4

1. $\bar{f} = \dfrac{1}{b-a} \int_a^b 3\,dx = \dfrac{1}{b-a} \left[3x\right]_a^b = \dfrac{1}{b-a}(3b - 3a) = 3.$

5. $\bar{f} = \dfrac{1}{2-0} \int_0^2 x^3\,dx = \left[\dfrac{1}{2}\cdot x^4/4\right]_0^2 = 2.$

9. $\bar{f} = \dfrac{1}{\ln 2 - 0} \int_0^{\ln 2} e^x\,dx = \dfrac{1}{\ln 2}\left[e^x\right]_0^{\ln 2} = \dfrac{1}{\ln 2}(e^{\ln 2} - 1) = \dfrac{1}{\ln 2}$

because $e^{\ln 2} = 2.$

13. $\bar{C} = \dfrac{1}{300-200} \int_{200}^{300} (5000 + 16x + 0.1x^2)\,dx = \dfrac{1}{100}\left[5000x + 8x^2 + \dfrac{x^3}{30}\right]_{200}^{300}$

$= 15,333$ dollars.

17. For $0 \le t < 4$, inventory $I(t) = 100 - 20t$. $I(4) = 20.$
For $4 \le t < 8$, $I(t) = 120 - 30(t-4) = 240 - 30t$

$\bar{I} = \dfrac{1}{8}\left(\int_0^4 (100-20t)\,dt + \int_4^8 (240-30t)\,dt\right) = \dfrac{1}{8}\left(\left[100t - 10t^2\right]_0^4\right.$

$\left. + \left[240t - 15t^2\right]_4^8\right) = \dfrac{1}{8}\{(240 - 0) + (960 - 720)\} = 60.$

21. (a) $\bar{v} = \dfrac{1}{1-0} \int_0^1 (64 - 32t)\,dt = \dfrac{1}{1}\left[64t - 16t^2\right]_0^1 = 48$

(b) $\bar{v} = \dfrac{1}{3-1} \int_1^3 (64 - 32t)\,dt = \dfrac{1}{2}\left[64t - 16t^2\right]_1^3 = \dfrac{1}{2}(48 - 48) = 0.$

EXERCISES - 17.5

1. $\dfrac{\text{x:}\quad 1\quad 5/4\quad 3/2\quad 7/4\quad 2}{\text{y:}\quad 1\quad 4/5\quad 2/3\quad 4/7\quad 1/2}$; $h = \dfrac{2-1}{4} = 1/4.$

Integral $\approx \dfrac{1}{8}\{1 + 2(4/5 + 2/3 + 4/7) + 1/2\} \approx 0.697.$

Exact answer $= \displaystyle\int_{1}^{2} \dfrac{1}{x}\, dx = \Big[\ln\, |x|\Big]_{1}^{2} = \ln\, 2 = 0.6931....$

5. $\dfrac{\text{x:}\quad 4\quad\ 4.5\quad\ 5\quad\ 5.5\quad\ 6\quad\ 6.5\quad\ 7\quad\ 7.5\quad\ 8}{\text{y:}\quad 1/4\ \ 2/9\ \ 1/5\ \ 2/11\ \ 1/6\ \ 2/13\ \ 1/7\ \ 2/15\ \ 1/8}$; $h = 1/2$

$\qquad\qquad y_1\quad\ y_2\quad\ y_3\quad\ y_4\quad\ y_5\quad\ y_6\quad\ y_7\quad\ y_8\quad\ y_9$

Integral $\approx \dfrac{h}{3}\ (X + 2O + 4E\ )$

$\approx \dfrac{1}{6}\ \{(1/4 + 1/8) + 2(1/5 + 1/6 + 1/7) + 4(2/9 + 2/11 + 2/13 + 2/15)\}$

$\approx \dfrac{1}{6}\ \{(0.375 + 1.0190 + 2.7649)\} = 0.693.$

9. $\dfrac{\text{x:}\quad -3\quad -2\quad -1\quad 0\quad 1\quad 2\quad 3}{\text{y:}\quad\ 81\quad\ 16\quad\ \ 1\quad\ \ 0\quad\ 1\quad 16\quad 81}$; $h = 1$

Integral $\approx \dfrac{1}{3}\{(81 + 81) + 2(1+1) + 4(16+0+16)\} = 98$

Exact integral $= \displaystyle\int_{-3}^{3} x^4\ dx = \Big[\dfrac{x^5}{5}\Big]_{-3}^{3} = 486/5 = 97.2$

13. Here h = interval length = 10

Area $\approx \dfrac{10}{3}\Big[(0+3) + 2(7+12+14)\ + 4(4+9+15+8)\Big] = 710.$

EXERCISES - 17.6

1. $y = t^{-4}$ gives $dy/dt = -4t^{-5}$. Thus, $t\ dy/dt + 4y = t(-4t^{-5}) + 4t^{-4} = 0.$

5. $dy/dt = t^2 + 1/t$ gives $y = \int(t^2 + 1/t)\ dt = t^3/3 + \ln|t| + C.$

9. $dy/dt - 2y = 1$ gives $dy/(2y+1) = dt$ or $\int dy/(2y+1) = \int dt.$
    or $(1/2)\ \ln\ |2y+1| = t + c_1$ or $\ln\ |2y+1| = 2t + 2c_1.$ This gives
    $2y + 1 = \pm\ e^{2t + 2c_1} = ce^{2t}$, where $c = \pm e^{2c_1}$ is another constant.
    Thus, $y = (ce^{2t} - 1)/2.$

13. $dy/dt = y(y-1)$ gives $\displaystyle\int \dfrac{1}{y(y-1)}\ dy = \int dt.$ Using integration
    formula # 12 in the table of integrals, we have:

$- \ln |y/(y-1)| = t + c_1$ or $y/(y-1) = \pm e^{-t-c_1} = c_2 e^{-t}$.

Thus, $y = (y-1)c_2 e^{-t}$ or $y = 1/(1 - ce^t)$.

where we have divided the top and bottom by $c_2 d^{-t}$ and $c = 1/c_2$.

17. $dy/dt + 2y = 0$ gives $y = ce^{-2t}$. $t=1$, $y=1$ gives $1 = ce^{-2}$ or $c = e^2$

Thus, $y = ce^{-2t} = e^2 e^{-2t} = e^{2-2t}$.

21. $dy/dt = te^{t+y} = te^t \cdot e^y$ or $\int e^{-y} dy = \int te^t dt$. Integration gives:

$-e^{-y} = (t-1)e^t + c$. $t=0$, $y=0$ gives, $-1 = -1 + c$ or $c=0$.

Thus, $-e^{-y} = (t-1)e^t$ or $e^{-y} = (1-t)e^t$. Taking natural logs:

$-y = \ln(1-t) + t$ or $y = -t - \ln(1-t)$.

25. $\eta = (p/x)/(dp/dx) = (x - 200)/x$ gives $\int dx/(x-200) = \int dp/p$

or $\ln |x-200| = \ln |p| + C$ or $\ln(200-x) = \ln p + C$, since $p > 0$

and $200 - x > 0$. Now $p = 5$, $x = 190$ gives $\ln 10 = \ln 5 + C$ or

$C = \ln(10/5) = \ln 2$. Thus, we have:

$\ln(200-x) = \ln p + \ln 2$ or $2p = 200 - x$ or $p = 100 - x/2$.

29. $(dy/dt)/y = \text{cost.} = k$ gives $\int(1/y)dt = \int k \, dt$ or $y = Ce^{kt}$,
where C is the constant of integration. At $t=0$, $y = 2$ (billion)

gives $C = 2$. Thus, $y = 2e^{kt}$.
In 1975, $t=45$ and $y=4$ (billion). This leads to:

$4 = 2e^{k(45)}$ or $k = (\ln 2)/45 \approx 0.0154$

Thus, $y = 2e^{0.0154t}$

In 1960, $t=30$. Thus $y = 2e^{(0.0154)(30)} \approx 3.17$ billion.

33. $dP/dA > 0$ when $A < C$, $dP/dA < 0$ when $A > C$. So P has a maximum when $A = C$. C is the optimal expenditure on advertising. Separate the variables: $dP = k(C-A) \, dA$. Integrate:

$P = k(CA - \frac{1}{2} A^2) + P_0$.
$P_0 = 100$. $P(100) = k(100C - 5000) + 100 = 1100$ gives $k(C-50) = 10$.
$\quad\quad\quad\quad\quad\quad\quad\quad\quad\quad\quad\quad\quad\quad\quad\quad\quad\quad$ .... (i)

$P(200) = k(200C - 20,000) + 100 = 1600$ gives $k(C-100) = 7.5$ ... (ii)

Divide (i) by (ii) to eliminate k: $C-50 = \frac{4}{3}(C - 100)$, i.e. $C = 250$.

37. $dA/dt = rA + I$. Separate: $(A + r^{-1}I)^{-1} dA = rdt$. Integrate:

$\ln(A + r^{-1}I) = rt + C$. $A(0) = 0$ so $C = \ln(r^{-1}I)$. Then

$\ln(A + r^{-1}I) = \ln(r^{-1}I) + rt$, or $rt = \ln(A+r^{-1}I)/(r^{-1}I) = \ln(\frac{Ar}{I} + 1)$

Thus, $\frac{Ar}{I} + 1 = e^{rt}$ or $A = Ir^{-1}(e^{rt} - 1)$.

For Ex. 24 in §17.3 put $r = 0.1$ and $t = 10$: $A = 10I(e-1)$.

41. Separate: $\frac{1}{y(2000-y)}$ dy = 0.002 dt. Using the hint, we re-write

first as $\frac{1}{2000} (\frac{1}{y} + \frac{1}{2000-y})$ dy = 0.002 dt.

or $(\frac{1}{y} + \frac{1}{2000-y})$ dy = 2000(0.002dt) = 4 dt. Now integrate:

$\ln y - \ln(2000-y) = 4t + C$. When t=0, y=2, so C = ln 2 - ln 1998

$$= -\ln 999$$

Therefore, $\ln y - \ln (2000-y) = 4t - \ln 999$. y = 1500 when

$\ln 1500 - \ln 500 + \ln 999 = 4t$, i.e. $t = \frac{1}{4} \ln (2997) = 2.00$

To solve for y, combine the logs: $\ln\{999y/(2000-y)\} = 4t$

i.e. $(2000-y)/y = 999e^{-4t}$ or $y = 2000/(1 + 999e^{-4t})$.

EXERCISES - 17.7

1. $1 = \int_0^3 f(x)\ dx = \int_0^3 C(3x-x^2)\ dx = \left[C(3x^2/2 - x^3/3)\right]_0^3 = 9C/2$ gives C = 2/9

$\mu = \int_0^3 x\ f(x)\ dx = \int_0^3 (2/9)(3x^2 - x^3)\ dx = (2/9)\left[(x^3 - x^4/4)\right]_0^3 = 27/4.$

5. $1 = \int_0^c (2/3)(x+1)\ dx = (2/3)\left[(x^2/2 + x)\right]_0^c = (2/3)(c^2/2 + c)$ gives

$c^2 + 2c - 3 = 0$ i.e. c = -3 or 1. Since $0 \le x \le c$ implies $c \ge 0$, we cannot have c = -3. Thus, c = 1.

$\mu = \int_0^1 (2/3)x(x+1)\ dx = (2/3)\left[(x^3/3 + x^2/2)\right]_0^1 = 2/3(1/3 + 1/2) = 5/9.$

9. $1 = \int_0^c f(x)\ dx = \int_0^c (2x-4)\ dx = c^2 - 4c$ gives $c = 2 \pm \sqrt{5}$,

Rejecting the negative value of $c = 2 - \sqrt{5}$, we have $c = 2 + \sqrt{5}$.
f(x) is <u>not</u> a p.d.f. because f(x) is not ≥ 0 for all x in $0 \le x \le c$.
(Note at x=1, f(x) = 2-4 = -2 < 0.)

13. (a) (i) $\int_{10}^{20} (1/60)\ dx = 1/6$ (ii) $1/4$ (iii) $1/3$

(b) Expected waiting time $= \int_{0}^{60} (x/60)\ dx = 30$ minutes.

17. (a) Prob. $= \int_{5}^{\infty} (0.4)e^{-0.4x}\ dx = \left[-e^{-0.4x}\right]_{5}^{\infty} = e^{-2} \approx 0.1353$.

(b) Prob. $= \int_{0}^{3} 0.4e^{-0.4x}\ dx = \left[-e^{-0.4x}\right]_{0}^{3} = 1 - e^{-1.2} \approx 0.6988$.

21. (a) $P(0 \le X \le 2) = \int_{0}^{2} 0.2e^{-0.2x}\ dx = 1 - e^{-0.4} \approx 0.33$ or 33% .

(b) $(10,000)(\int_{0}^{1} 0.2e^{-x/5}\ dx) = 10,000(1 - e^{-1/5}) \approx 1813$ sets.

25. $1 = \int_{0}^{\infty} cxe^{-(x/40)^2}\ dx = \left[-800ce^{-x^2/1600}\right]_{0}^{\infty} = 800c$ gives $c = 1/800$.

Prob. $= \int_{50}^{\infty} f(x)\ dx = \int_{50}^{\infty} (x/800)e^{-x^2/1600}\ dx = \left[-e^{x^2/1600}\right]_{50}^{\infty}$

$= e^{-25/16} \approx 0.2096$.

REVIEW EXERCISES ON CHAPTER 17

1. See answers in the text book.

5. $A = \int_{1}^{3} (1/x^2)\ dx = \left[-1/x\right]_{1}^{3} = 1 - 1/3 = 2/3$ sq. units.

9. Ans. $= \int_{10}^{15} p'(x)\ dx = \int_{10}^{15} (15-x)\ dx = 12.5$.

13. Solving $p = 25 - 3x$ and $p = 5 + 0.5x^2$, the equilibrium point is:

$x_0 = 4$, $p_0 = 13$.

C.S. $= \int_{0}^{x_0} f(x)\ dx - p_0 x_0 = \int_{0}^{4} (25-3x)\ dx - 52 = 76 - 52 = 24$.

P.S. $= p_0 x_0 - \int_{0}^{x_0} g(x)\ dx = 52 - \int_{0}^{4} (5 + 0.5x^2)\ dx = 52 - 92/3 = 64/3$.

17. $dy/dx = 2\sqrt{y}(2x+e^x)$ gives $\int \frac{1}{2\sqrt{y}}\ dy = \int (2x+e^x)\ dx$

or $\sqrt{y} = x^2 + e^x + c$. Now, $x=0, y=0$ gives $c = -1$.

Thus, $\sqrt{y} = x^2 + e^x - 1$ or $y = (x^2 + e^x - 1)^2$.

21. $Pe^{0.06(5)} = \$26,997$ gives $P \approx \$20,000$.

25. $f(t) = 1/15$ on $0 \leq t \leq 15$.

$P(t \leq 5) = \int_0^5 (1/15) \, dt = 5/15 = 1/3$.

$\mu = \int_0^{15} tf(t) \, dt = \int_0^{15} (t/15) \, dt = \left[t^2/30\right]_0^{15} = 15/2$ minutes.

29. $dy/dx = -ky$. $y = Ae^{-kx}$. When $x=0$, $y=100$, so $A = 100$ and $y = 100e^{-kx}$.

When $x = 2000$, $y = 60$, (because 60% survive), so $e^{-2000k} = 0.6$, or

$k = 2.55 \times 10^{-4}$. When $y=10$, $e^{-kx} = 0.1$, $x = (\ln 10)/k = 9015$ lb/mi.^{2}

33.

x:	0	1/2	1	3/2	2	5/2	3	7/2	4	; h = 1/2
y:	1	4/5	1/2	4/13	1/5	4/29	1/10	4/53	1/17	

$y_1 \quad y_2 \quad y_3 \quad y_4 \quad y_5 \quad y_6 \quad y_7 \quad y_8 \quad y_9$

Trapezoid rule: Integral $\approx \frac{1}{4} \{(1 + 2(4/5 + 1/2 + \ldots + 4/53) + \frac{1}{17}\} \approx 1.33$

Simpson's rule Integral $\approx \frac{h}{3} (X + 2O + 4E)$

$\approx \frac{1}{6} \{(1 + 1/17) + 2(1/2 + 1/5 + 1/10)$

$+ 4(4/5 + 4/13 + 4/29 + 4/53)\} \approx 1.32$.

REVIEW TEST ON CHAPTER - 17

FILL IN THE BLANKS:

1. $\int_0^1 (2x+1)^5 \, dx = \left[(\underline{\hspace{1cm}})\right]_0^1 = \underline{\hspace{2cm}}$.

2. $\int_1^0 \frac{1}{3-2x} \, dx = (\underline{\hspace{1cm}}) \Big]_1^0 = \underline{\hspace{2cm}}$.

3. If $u = \ln x$, then $\int_2^e \frac{1}{x \ln x} \, dx = \underline{\hspace{2cm}}$ (definite integral in terms of u).

4. $\int_2^2 (\ln x)^7 \, dx = \underline{\hspace{1.5cm}}$.   5. $\frac{d}{dx} \int_a^x f(t) \, dt = \underline{\hspace{1.5cm}}$.

6. $\frac{d}{dx} (\int_1^x e^{\sqrt{t}} \, dt) = \underline{\hspace{1.5cm}}$.   7. $\frac{d}{du} (\int_1^2 e^t \ln t \, dt) = \underline{\hspace{1.5cm}}$.

8. The area bounded by $y = 1/(x+2)$, x-axis and the lines $x=0$, $x=2$ is given by the integral $\underline{\hspace{3cm}}$.

9. The area between $y = 4-x^2$, axis and the lines $x=0$, $x=3$ is given by the integral $\underline{\hspace{3cm}}$.

10. If $f(x) \leq g(x)$ in $a \leq x \leq b$, then the area between the curves $y=f(x)$, $y=g(x)$ and the lines $x=a$, $x=b$ is given by the integral _____ .

11. In any Lorentz curve $y = f(x)$, we assume that $f(0) =$ _____ and $f(1) =$ _____ .

12. The coefficient L of inequality of a Lorentz curve $y=f(x)$ is given by the definite integral _____ .

13. If a Lorentz curve is $y = (x/16)(15x+1)$, then the lowest paid 40% of the people receive only _____% of the total income.

14. If p% of the lowest paid people receive p% of the total income for various values of p, then the income distribution is given by $y = f(x)$, where $f(x) =$ _____ .

15. $f(x) = e^x + 2e^{-x}$ _____ (is or is not) a solution of
$$f''(x) - f(x) = 0, \quad f(0) = f'(0) = 3.$$

16. $y = 2 + 3e^{2t}$ _____(is or is not) a solution of the diff. equn.
$$d^2y/dt^2 = 2\, dy/dt.$$

17. The diff. equation $t\, dy/dt - (2t+1)y = 0$ in the variable separable form can be written as _____ .

18. The general solution of the diff. equation $dy/dt = ky$, where k is a constant is given by $y =$ _____ .

19. If $f(x)$ is prob. density function (p.d.f.) on the interval $a \leq x \leq b$, then $f(x)$ _____ 0 and $\int_a^b f(x) =$ _____ .

20. If $f(x) = cx^2$, (c=const.) is a p.d.f. on the interval $1 \leq x \leq 2$, then $c =$ _____ .

21. If $f(x) = ce^{-2x}$, (c=const) is a p.d.f. on the interval $x \geq 0$, then $c =$ _____ .

22. If $f(x)$ is a p.d.f. of a continuous random variable X on the interval $a \leq X \leq b$ and c, d are any two numbers in $a \leq X \leq b$, then

(i) $P(c \leq X \leq d) =$ _____ .   (ii) $P(X \leq c) =$ _____ .

(iii) $P(X > d) =$ _____ .   (iv) $P(x = c) =$ _____ .

23. If $f(x) = Ke^{-Kx}$,(K = const) is an exponential p.d.f. on the interval $x \geq 0$, then the mean μ of this distribution is given by the definite integral _____ .

24. If $f(x) = (1/50)e^{cx}$ is an exponential p.d.f. on the interval $0 \leq x < \infty$, then $c =$ _____ .

SEE ANSWERS AT THE END OF THIS BOOK.

YOU SHOULD BE FAMILIAR WITH THE FOLLOWING TERMS:

Function of two variables ; function of several (or n) variables.

Domain, range of a function.

Graph of a function of two variables.

Sections ; contour lines (or level curve).

Partial derivatives.

Second-order partial derivatives ; mixed partial derivatives.

Production function ; production factors ; marginal productivities.

Marginal demands ; competitive and complementary products.

Elasticity : cross-elasticity of demand.

Extremum ; local maximum, local minimum, saddle point.

Critical point .

Lagrange multipliers ; constraints.

Method of least squares.

Error, mean square error.

OBJECTIVES

AFTER READING THIS CHAPTER YOU SHOULD BE ABLE TO DO THE FOLLOWING:

1. Find the domain of a function of several variables. In the case of two independent variables, represent the domain graphically.

2. Represent the graph of a function of two variables by drawing

    (a) contour lines (or level curves) or (b) vertical sections.

3. Calculate the partial derivatives of a function of two or more variables; calculate second and higher-order partial derivatives.

4. Apply partial derivatives
    (a) to calculate marginal productivity with respect to different production factors.

(b)   to calculate the elasticity of demand of a product with respect to its own price and the prices of related products.

(c)   to calculate approximate values of functions when the increments in the independent variables are small.

5.   Find the critical points of a smooth function of two variables. Use the Δ-test to find out if these points are local maxima or minima or saddle points.

6.   Apply this to practical word problems involving optimization.

7.   Use the method of Lagrange multipliers to find the critical points of a function when the independent variables are subject to one or more constraints.

8.   Use the method of least squares to find the best straight line to fit a given set of data points.

SOLUTIONS TO ALTERNATE ODD PROBLEMS.

EXERCISES - 18.1

1. $f(x,y) = x^2 + 2xy + y^2$ gives $f(3,-2) = 9 - 2(3)(-2) + 4 = 25$, $f(-4,-4)=0$

5. $f(1,2,3) = 36$, $f(-2,1,-4) = 54$.   9.   D = whole xy-plane.

13. $D = \{(x,t) \mid x-t > 0 \}$

17.

21.

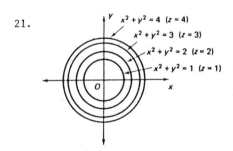

25.

29. Let the dimensions of the box be x, y and z (in feet) as shown in figure. Then volume of the box is

$x \cdot y \cdot z = 100$ (given) or $z = 100/xy$.

C = cost in dollars = 5(area of base) + 3(area of four walls)

= $5xy + 2(2yz + 2xz) = 5xy + 6z(x+y)$

= $5xy + 600(x+y)/xy = 5xy + 600(1/x + 1/y)$ $\left| z = 100/xy \right.$

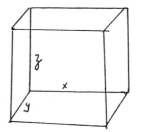

33. Let the pipeline consist of 3 straight segments AL, LM and MB as shown. Then the cost C is given by

$C = 2P(\text{length of AL}) + 3P(\text{length of LM})$

$\quad + P(\text{length of MB})$

$\quad = 2P\sqrt{x^2 + 200^2} + 3P\sqrt{y^2 + 100^2}$

$\quad + P\sqrt{200^2 + (500-x-y)^2}$

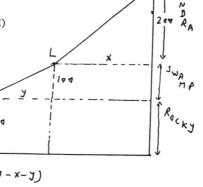

EXERCISES - 18.2
_____

1. $\partial z/\partial x = \partial/\partial x(x^2 + y^2) = 2x$; $\partial z/\partial y = \partial/\partial y(x^2 + y^2) = 2y$.

5. $\partial z/\partial x = \partial/\partial x(xe^y + ye^{-x}) = e^y\partial/\partial x(x) + y\partial/\partial x(e^{-x}) = e^y \cdot 1 + y(-e^{-x})$.

   $\partial z/\partial y = \partial/\partial y(xe^y + ye^{-x}) = x\partial/\partial y(e^y) + e^{-x}\partial/\partial y(y) = xe^y + e^{-x} \cdot 1$

9. $\partial z/\partial x = \partial/\partial x(e^{2x+3y}) = e^{2x+3y} \cdot \partial/\partial x(2x + 3y) = e^{2x+3y} \cdot 2$

   $\partial z/\partial y = \partial/\partial y (e^{2x+3y}) = e^{2x+3y} \cdot \partial/\partial y(2x+3y) = e^{2x+3y} \cdot 3$

13. $\partial z/\partial x = \partial/\partial x(x+2y^3)^{1/3} = (1/3)(x+2y^3)^{-2/3} \cdot \partial/\partial x(x+2v^3) = (1/3)(x+2y^3)^{-2/3} \cdot 1$

    $\partial z/\partial y = \partial/\partial y(x+2y^3)^{1/3} = (1/3)(x+2y^3)^{-2/3} \cdot \partial/\partial y(x+2y^3)$

    $\qquad = (1/3)(x+2y^3)^{-2/3} \cdot 6y^2$

17. $\partial z/\partial x = (1/y)\partial/\partial x(xe^{xy}) = y^{-1}\{x(e^{xy}\cdot y) + e^{xy}\cdot 1\} = (x + 1/y)e^{xy}$

$\partial z/\partial y = x\,\partial/\partial y(y^{-1}e^{xy}) = x\{y^{-1}\cdot(e^{xy}\cdot x) + e^{xy}\cdot(-1y^{-2})\} = (x^2/y - x/y^2)e^{xy}$.

21. $\partial z/\partial x = \dfrac{1}{e^x + xy^3}\cdot\dfrac{\partial}{\partial x}(e^x + xy^3) = (e^x + y^3)/(e^x + xy^3)$.

$\partial z/\partial y = \dfrac{1}{e^x + xy^3}\,\dfrac{\partial}{\partial y}(e^x + xy^3) = 3xy^2/(e^x + xy^3)$.

25. $z = x^4 + y^4 + 3x^2y^3$ gives $z_x = 4x^3 + 0 + 3y^3(2x) = 4x^3 + 6xy^3$;

$z_y = 0 + 4y^3 + 3x^2(3y^2) = 4y^3 + 9x^2y^2$; $z_{xx} = \partial/\partial x(4x^3 + 6xy^3)$

$= 12x^2 + 6y^3$; $z_{yy} = \partial/\partial y(4y^3 + 9x^2y^2) = 12y^2 + 18x^2y$;

$z_{xy} = \partial/\partial y(z_x) = \partial/\partial y(4x^3 + 6xy^3) = 6x(3y^2) = 18xy^2$.

29. $z_x = y^{-1/2}(5x^4) = 5x^4y^{-1/2}$; $z_y = x^5(-1/2)y^{-3/2} = (-1/2)x^5y^{-3/2}$.

$z_{xx} = 5y^{-1/2}(4x^3) = 20x^3y^{-1/2}$; $z_{xy} = \dfrac{\partial}{\partial y}(z_x) = (5x^4)(-1/2)y^{-3/2}$

$= (-5/2)x^4z^{-3/2}$

$z_{yy} = (-1/2)x^5\{(-3/2)y^{-5/2}\} = (3/4)x^5y^{-5/2}$.

33. $z_x = \dfrac{1}{x^2+y^2}\cdot\partial/\partial x(x^2+y^2) = 2x/(x^2+y^2)$;

$z_y = \dfrac{1}{x^2+y^2}\cdot\partial/\partial y(x^2+y^2) = 2y/(x^2+y^2)$;

$z_{xx} = \partial/\partial x(z_x) = \partial/\partial x\{2x/(x^2+y^2)\} = 2(y^2-x^2)/(x^2+y^2)^2$ – quotient rule.

$z_{yy} = \partial/\partial y(z_y) = \partial/\partial y\{2y/(x^2+y^2)\} = 2(x^2-y^2)/(x^2+y^2)^2$

$z_{xy} = \partial/\partial y(z_x) = \partial/\partial y\{2x/(x^2+y^2)\} = -4xy/(x^2+y^2)^2$.

37. $z_x = -y^2(x-y)^2$, $z_y = x^2(x-y)^2$

$z_{xx} = 2y^2(x-y)^{-3}$, $z_{xy} = -2xy/(x-y)^3$, $z_{yy} = 2x^2/(x-y)^3$.

41. $z = x^3+y^3$ gives $z_x = 3x^2$ and $z_y = 3y^2$. Thus,

$xz_x + yz_y = x(3x^2) + y(3y^2) = 3(x^3 + y^3) = 3z$.

45. $\dfrac{\partial c}{\partial t} = we^{kx+wt}$, $\dfrac{\partial^2 c}{\partial t^2} = w^2 e^{kx+wt}$, $\dfrac{\partial c}{\partial x} = ke^{kw+wt}$, $\dfrac{\partial^2 c}{\partial x^2} = k^2 e^{kx+wt}$

Thus, $\dfrac{\partial^2 t}{\partial t^2} - \dfrac{\partial^2 c}{\partial x^2} = (w^2 - k^2)e^{kt+wt} = 0$ if $w^2 = k^2$.

EXERCISES - 18.3

1. $P_L = 7 + 2K - 2L$, $P_k = 5 + 2L - 4K$. At L=3, K=10, we have:

$P_L = 21$, $P_K = 29$.

5. $P_L = 100K^{0.7}(0.3)L^{-0.7}) = 30(K/L)^{0.7}$; $P_K = 100L^{0.3}(0.7K^{-0.3}) = 70(L/K)^{0.3}$.

9. $\partial x_A/\partial p_A = -3$; $\partial x_A/\partial p_B = 1$; $\partial x_B/\partial p_A = 2$; $\partial x_B/\partial p_B = -5$.

Since $\partial x_A/\partial p_B > 0$, $\partial x_B/\partial p_A > 0$, the two products are competitive.

13. $x_A = 250 + 0.3p_B - 2p_A^2$ gives $\partial x_A/\partial p_A = -4p_A$, $\partial x_A/\partial p_B = 0.3$

At $p_A = 5$, $p_B = 40$, we have $x_A = 212$, $\partial x_A/\partial p_A = -20$, $\partial x_A/\partial p_B = 0.3$

Then, $\eta_{p_A} = (\partial x_A/\partial p_A) \big/ (x_A/p_A) = -20/(212/5) = -100/212 = -25/53$.

$\eta_{p_B} = (\partial x_A/\partial p_B)/(x_A/p_B) = 0.3/(212/40) = 12/212 = 3/53$.

17. $Q = 327 + 0.2I + 0.5p_B - 2p_A^2$ gives $\partial Q/\partial p_A = -4p_A$, $\partial Q/\partial p_B = 0.5$,

$\partial Q/\partial I = 0.2$. At $p_A = 3$, $p_B = 20$ and I = 200, we have:

$Q = 327 + 40 + 10 - 18 = 359$, $\partial Q/\partial p_A = -12$, $\partial Q/\partial p_B = 0.5$, $\partial Q/\partial I = 0.2$

(a) $\eta_{p_A} = (\partial Q/\partial p_A)/(Q/p_A) = -12/(359/3) = -36/359$.

(b) $\eta_{p_B} = (\partial Q/\partial p_B)/(Q/p_B) = 0.5/(359/20) = 10/359$.

(c) $\eta_I = (\partial Q/\partial I)/(Q/I) = 0.2/(359/200) = 40/359$.

21. $f(x,y) = \sqrt{x^2+y^2}$ gives $f_x(x,y) = x/\sqrt{x^2+y^2}$, $f_y(x,y) = y/\sqrt{x^2+y^2}$

At $(x_0,y_0) = (3,4)$, we have: $f(x_0,y_0) = 5$, $f_x(x_0,y_0) = 3/5$,

$f_y(x_0,y_0) = 4/5$. Here $x_0 + \Delta x_0 = 3.1$, $y_0 + \Delta y_0 = 4.1$, so that $\Delta x = 0.1$ $\Delta y = 0.1$.

$$f(x_0+\Delta x, \ y_0+\Delta y) = f(3.1, \ 4.1) \simeq f(x_0,y_0) + f_x(x_0,y_0)\Delta x + f_y(x_0,y_0)\Delta y$$

$$\simeq 5 + 3/5 + 4/5 = 5.14.$$

25. $f(x,y) = (x-y)/\sqrt{x+y}$ gives $f_x = (x+3y)/2(x+y)^{3/2}$, $f_y = -(3x+y)/2(x+y)^{3/2}$

   At $(x_0,y_0) = (2,2)$, we have $f(x_0,y_0) = 0$, $f_x(x_0,y_0) = 1/2$, $f_y = -1/2$.

   Here $\Delta x = 0.1$, $\Delta y = -0.05$, so that

$$f(2.1,1.95) = f(x_0+\Delta x,y_0+\Delta y) \approx f(x_0,y_0) + f_x(x_0,y_0)\Delta x + f_y(x_0,y_0)\Delta y$$

$$= 0 + (1/2)(0.1) + (-1/2)(-0.05) = 0.075.$$

29. $P(L,K) = 9L^{2/3}K^{1/3}$ gives $P_L = 6(K/L)^{1/3}$, $P_K = 3(L/K)^{2/3}$.

   Here $L_0+\Delta L = 1003$, $K_0+\Delta K = 28$. Chose $L_0 = 1000$, $K_0 = 27$, so that

   $\Delta L = 3$, $\Delta K = 1$. At $(L_0 , K_0) = (1000,27)$, we have: $P = 2700$,

   $P_L = 18/10$, $P_K = 100/3$. Thus,

$$P(1003, \ 28) = P(L_0+\Delta L, \ K_0+\Delta K) \simeq P + P_L\Delta L + P_K\Delta K$$

$$= 2700 + (18/10)(3) + (100/3)(1) \simeq 2738.73.$$

EXERCISES - 18.4

1. $f(x,y) = x^2 + y^2 - 2x + 4y + 7$ gives $f_x = 2x-2$, $f_y = 2y+4$.

   $f_x = 0$, $f_y = 0$ gives the critical point $x=1$, $y = -2$ i.e. $(1,-2)$.

   $f_{xx} = 2 > 0$, $f_{yy} = 2 > 0$ $f_{xy} = 0$. $\Delta = f_{xx}f_{yy} - f_{xy}^2 = 4 > 0$. Thus,

   since at $(1,-2)$, $\Delta > 0$, f_{xx}, $f_{yy} > 0$, $(1,-2)$ is a local minimum.

5. $f(x,y) = 2x^2 + xy + 2y^2$ gives $f_x = 4x+y$, $f_y = x + 4y$.

   $f_x = 0 = f_y$ gives $x = 0$, $y = 0$. Thus, the critical point is $(0,0)$.

   $f_{xx} = 4$, $f_{yy} = 4$, $f_{xy} = 1$ and $\Delta = f_{xx}f_{yy} - f_{xy}^2 = 15 > 0$. Since at $(0,0)$

   $\Delta > 0$, f_{xx}, $f_{yy} > 0$, $(0,0)$ is a point of local minimum.

9. $f_x = 3x^2-3 = 0$, $f_y = 2y-4 = 0$ gives $x = \pm 1$, $y = 2$.

   Thus, the critical points are $(1,2)$ and $(-1,2)$

   $f_{xx} = 6x$, $f_{yy} = 2$, $f_{xy} = 0$.

   At $(1,2)$ $f_{xx} > 0$, $f_{yy} = 2 > 0$ $\Delta = 12 > 0$, so $(1,2)$ is a local minimum.

   At $(-1,2)$, $f_{xx} = -6$, $f_{yy} = 2$ $\Delta = -12 < 0$, so $(-1,2)$ is a saddle point.

13. $f(x,y) = 2x^2y + 2xy^2 + x^2 + 2x$ gives $f_x = 4xy + 2y^2 + 2x + 2$

and $f_y = 2x^2 + 4xy$. Solving $f_x = 0$, $f_y = 0$ gives the critical points

as $(2, -1)$ and $(-2/3, 1/3)$.

$f_{xx} = 4y + 2$, $f_{yy} = 4x$, $f_{xy} = 4(x+y)$ and $\Delta = 8x(2y+1) - 16(x+y)^2$

At $(2,-1)$ and $(-2/3, 1/3)$, $\Delta < 0$. Thus these are the saddle points.

17. $f_x = (y-2)(2x+y-5)$, $f_y = (x-2)(x+2y-5) = 0$ gives x=2, x = -2y+5

If x=2, then $f_x = (y-2)(y-1) = 0$ when y = 1,2.

If x = -2y+5, then $f_x = (y-2)\{2(-2y+5)+y-5\} = (y-2)(-3y+5) = 0$

when y=2 or 5/3. When y=2, x=1 ; When y=5/3, x = 5/3.

Thus, the critical points are $(2,1)$, $(2,2)$, $(1,2)$ and $(5/3, 5/3)$

$f_{xx} = 2(y-2)$, $f_{yy} = 2(x-2)$, $f_{xy} = 2x + 2y - 7$.

(2,1): $f_{xx} = -2 f_{yy} = 0$, $f_{xy} = -1$, $\Delta < 0$; saddle point.

(2,2): $f_{xx} = 0$, $f_{yy} = 0$, $f_{xy} = 1$, $\Delta < 0$; saddle point.

(1,2): $f_{xx} = 0$, $f_{yy} = -2$, $f_{xy} = 1$, $\Delta < 0$; saddle point,

(5/3, 5/3): $f_{xx} = -2/3$, $f_{yy} = -2/3$, $f_{xy} = -1/3$, $\Delta > 0$; local max.

21. $f_x = (1-x)e^{-x}$, $f_y = (1 - 2y)e^{-2y}$

$f_x = 0$ when x=1, $f_y = 0$ when y = 1/2: critical point $(1,1/2)$.

(Note that e^{-x} and $e^{-2y} > 0$ for all values of x,y)

$f_{xx} = (x-2)e^{-x}$, $f_{yy} = (4y-4)e^{-2y}$, $f_{xy} = 0$

At $(1,1/2)$, $f_{xx} < 0$, $f_{yy} < 0$, $f_{xy} = 0$; $\Delta > 0$: local maximum.

25. $C(x,y) = 1500 - 7.5x - 15y - 0.3xy + 0.3x^2 + 0.2y^2$

$C_x = -7.5 - 0.3y + 0.6x$, $C_y = -15 - 0.3x + 0.4y$

$C_x = 0$, $C_y = 0$ gives x = 50, y = 75. Since $\Delta = 0.15 > 0$,

$C_{xx} > 0$, $C_{yy} > 0$ at $(50,75)$, $C(x,y)$ is minimum at x = 50, y = 75.

29. T = profit = revenue – cost = $15P - (5.10x + 1.80y)$

$= 15(0.52x + 0.48y + 0.12xy - 0.07x^2 - 0.06y^2) - (5.1x + 1.8y)$

$= 2.7x + 5.4y + 1.8xy - 1.05x^2 - 0.9y^2$

$T_x = 2.7 + 1.8y - 2.1x = 0$, $T_y = 5.4 + 1.8x - 1.8y = 0$ gives $x = 27$,

$y = 30$. Since $T_{xx} = -2.1 < 0$, $T_{yy} = -1.8 < 0$, $\Delta = 0.54 > 0$, the profit

T is maximum when $x = 27$ units of X and $y = 30$ units of Y are used.

33. P = net profit = revenue - cost - cost of advertising

$= px - 2x - A = 30(1 - e^{-0.001A})(p-2)(22-p) - A$

$\partial P/\partial p = 30(1 - e^{-0.001A})(24-2p) = 0$ gives $p = 12$ or $A = 0$

But $A = 0$ is not admissible, thus, $p = 12$

$\partial P/\partial A = 30(0.001)e^{-0.001A}(p-2)(22-p) - 1.$

$p = 12$, $\partial P/\partial A = 0$ gives $3e^{-0.001} = 1$ or $A = 1000 \ln 3$.

Thus, $p = 12$ and $A = 1000 \ln 3$. It can be checked that for these

values of p and A, the net profit P is maximum.

37. T = total weight of fish stock

$= x(3 - \alpha x - \beta y) + y(4 - \beta x - 2\alpha y)$

$T_x = 3 - 2\alpha x - 2\beta y$ and $T_y = 4 - 2\beta x - 4\alpha y$

$T_x = 0$, $T_y = 0$ gives $x = (3\alpha - 2\beta)/(2\alpha^2 - \beta^2)$,

$y = (4\alpha - 3\beta)/(4\alpha^2 - 2\beta^2)$

$T_{xx} = -2\alpha$, $T_{yy} = -4\alpha$ and $T_{xy} = -2\beta$

$\Delta = T_{xx} T_{yy} - T_{xy}^2 = 8\alpha^2 - 4\beta^2 = 4(2\alpha^2 - \beta^2)$

For T to be maximum, $\Delta > 0$ i.e. $2\alpha^2 - \beta^2 > 0$. Then to make the values

of x,y in the critical point positive, we must have

$3\alpha - 2\beta > 0$ and $4\alpha - 3\beta > 0$. When $4\alpha > 3\beta$, $3\alpha - 2\beta > 0$.

Thus, T is maximum when $x = (3\alpha - 2\beta)/(2\alpha^2 - \beta^2)$ and

$y = (4\alpha - 3\beta)/(4\alpha^2 - 2\beta^2)$, provided $4\alpha > 3\beta$.

41. (a) $y_t = x(a-x)\{ \frac{1}{2} t^{-1/2}e^{-xt} + t^{1/2}(-xe^{-xt})\} = 0$ when $t = 1/2x$.

(b) $y_x = (a-2x)t^{1/2}e^{-xt} + x(a-x)(-t^{3/2}e^{-xt}) = 0$ when

$(a-2x) - x(a-x)t = 0$. Putting $t = 1/2x$ we get

$(a-2x) - \frac{1}{2}(a-x) = 0$. i.e. $x = a/3$, $t = 3/2a$.

1. $f(x,y) = x^2 + y^2$, $g(x,y) = 2x + 3y - 7 = 0$.

$F(x,y,\lambda) = x^2 + y^2 - \lambda(2x + 3y - 7)$

$F_x = 2x - 2\lambda = 0$, $F_y = 2y - 3\lambda = 0$, $F_\lambda = -2x - 3y + 7 = 0$ gives

$\lambda = 14/13$, $x = 14/13$, $y = 3\lambda/2 = 21/13$.

Answers: $(x,y) = (14/13, 21/13)$.

5. $F(x,y,z,\lambda) = x^2 + y^2 + z^2 - \lambda(2x + 3y + 4z - 29)$

$F_x = 2x - 2\lambda = 0$, $F_y = 2y - 3\lambda = 0$, $F_z = 2z - 4\lambda = 0$ and

$F_\lambda = -2x - 3y - 4z + 29 = 0$ give the solution x=2, y=3 and z=4.

Thus the critical point is $(x,y,z) = (2,3,4)$.

9. $F(x,y,z,\lambda_1,\lambda_2) = x^2 + 2y^2 - 3z^2 - \lambda_1(x + 2y - 3z - 5) - \lambda_2(2x-3y+6z+1)$

$F_x = 2x - \lambda_1 - 2\lambda_2$, $F_y = 4y - 2\lambda_1 + 3\lambda_2$, $F_z = -6z + 3\lambda_1 - 6\lambda_2$

$F_{\lambda_1} = -(x+2y-3z-5)$ and $F_{\lambda_2} = -(2x-3y+6z+1)$

$F_x = 0$, $F_y = 0$, $F_z = 0$ gives $x = (\lambda_1+2\lambda_2)/2$, $y = (2\lambda_1-3\lambda_2)/4$ and

$z = (\lambda_1 - 2\lambda_2)/2$. Using these values of x,y,z in the equations

$F_{\lambda_1} = 0$, $F_{\lambda_2} = 0$ we get : $5\lambda_2 = 10$ and $10\lambda_1 - 7\lambda_2 = 0$

Solving, we get: $\lambda_1 = 1$, $\lambda_2 = 2$. Then $x = (\lambda_1+2\lambda_2)/2 = 5/2$,

$y = (2\lambda_1 - 3\lambda_2)/4 = -1$ and $z = (\lambda_1 - 2\lambda_2)/2 = -3/2$. Thus, the

critical point is $(x,y,z) = (5/2, -1, -3/2)$.

13. (a) We want to maximize $P(L,K) = 80L^{3/4}K^{1/4}$ subject to

$60L + 200K = 40,000$.

$F(L,K,\lambda) = 80 L^{3/4}K^{1/4} - \lambda(60L + 200K - 40,000)$

$F_L = 60(K/L)^{1/4} - 60$, $F_K = 20(L/K)^{3/4} - 200$,

$F_\lambda = -(60L + 200K - 40,000)$ $F_L = 0$, $F_K = 0$ give

$\lambda = (K/L)^{1/4} = (1/10)(L/K)^{3/4}$ or $L = 10K$

Solving this with $F_\lambda = 0$ gives L = 500, K = 50

Then $\lambda = (K/L)^{1/4} = (10)^{-1/4} \approx 0.5623$

Answer: L = 500, K = 50.

(b) $P_L/P_K = \{60(K/L)^{1/4}\}/\{20(L/K)^{3/4}\} = 3\ K/L$

When $L = 500$, $K = 50$, $P_L/P_K = 3K/L = 150/500 = 3/10 = 60/200$

$$= \text{(unit cost of labor)/(unit cost of capital).}$$

(c) If ΔL units of labor and ΔK units of capital can be bought with the extra \$1 available, then

$$60\Delta L + 200\Delta K = 1$$

$\Delta P = P(500 + \Delta L,\ 50 + \Delta K) - P(500,50)$

$\quad \approx P_L(500,50)\ \Delta L + P_K(500,50)\Delta K$

From the equations of F_L and F_K in part (a), it follows that at the maximum $F_L = P_L - 60\lambda = 0$ and $F_K = P_K - 200\lambda = 0$

i.e. $P_L(500,50) = 60\lambda$, $P_K(500,50) = 200\lambda$. Thus,

$\Delta P \approx 60\lambda\ \Delta L + 200\lambda\ \Delta K = \lambda(60\Delta L + 200\Delta K) = \lambda(1) = \lambda$.

17. (a) The cost of using L units at \$64 each and K units at \$108 each is $C(L,K) = 64L + 108K$. We want to minimize $C(L,K)$ subject to $P(L,K) = 60\ L^{2/3}K^{1/3} = 2160$.

$F(L,K,\lambda) = 64L + 108K - \lambda(60L^{2/3}K^{1/3} - 2160)$

$F_L = 64 - 40\lambda(K/L)^{1/3} = 0$, $F_K = 108 - 20\lambda(L/K)^{2/3} = 0$, and

$F_\lambda = 2160 - 60L^{2/3}K^{1/3} = 0$ give the solution $L = 54$, $K = 16$.

(b) $P_L = 40(K/L)^{1/3}$ and $P_K = 20(L/K)^{2/3}$, so that

$P_L/P_K = \{40(K/L)^{1/3}\}/\{20(L/K)^{1/3}\} = 2\ K/L = 2(16)/54$.

$\quad = 32/54 = 64/108$ when $L = 54$, $K = 16$.

Thus at the optimum level of production (i.e.) when $L = 54$, $K=16$;

$P_L/P_K = 64/108 = \text{(unit cost of labor)/(unit cost of capital)}$.

21. Let the radii be x,y,z. Sum of weights $= (4\pi x^3/3)(1) + (4\pi y^3/3)(2) + (4\pi z^3/3)(3) = 10$. So take $g(x,y,z) = x^3 + 2y^3 + 3z^3 - 15/2$.

Surface area $= 4\pi x^2 + 4\pi y^2 + 4\pi z^2$. We take $f(x,y,z) = x^2 + y^2 + z^2$

At the extremum: $2x - \lambda 3x^2 = 0$, $2y - \lambda 6y^2 = 0$, $2x - \lambda 9z^2 = 0$. i.e.

$x = 2/3\lambda$, $y = 1/3\lambda$, $z = 2/9\lambda$. Then $x^3 + 2y^3 + 3z^3 = \dfrac{294}{(9\lambda)^3} = 15/2\pi$

so $\dfrac{1}{9\lambda} = (5/196\pi)^{1/3}$. Therefore, $x = 6(5/196\pi)^{1/3}$

$y = 3(5/196\pi)^{1/3}$, $z = 2(5/196\pi)^{1/3}$.

EXERCISES - 18.6

1. $n = 6$, $\Sigma x = 37$, $\Sigma y = 33$, $\Sigma x^2 = 299$ and $\Sigma xy = 237$
    Then the equation $\Sigma y = a\Sigma x + nb$ and $\Sigma xy = a\Sigma x^2 + b\Sigma x$ give:
    $37a + 6b = 33$, $299a + 37b = 237$. Solution is
    $a = 0.47$, $b = 2.58$. Thus $y = ax + b$ or $y = 0.47x + 2.58$.

5. $n = 6$, $\Sigma x = 21$, $\Sigma y = 179$, $\Sigma xy = 693$, $\Sigma x^2 = 91$; $a = 3.8$, $b = 16.53$
    Thus, $y = 3.8x + 16.53$.

9. $n = 6$, $\Sigma x = 96$, $\Sigma y = 346$, $\Sigma xy = 5816$, $\Sigma x^2 = 1634$; $a = 2.86$, $b = 11.95$.
    Thus, $y = 2.86x + 11.95$. When $x = 24$, $y = 80.59$ i.e. 8059 units will be
    sold, since y is in hundreds.

13. $n = 5$, $\Sigma x = 15$, $\Sigma y = 50$, $\Sigma x^2 = 55$ and $\Sigma xy = 173$ gives
    $a = 2.3$; $b = 3.1$. Thus, $y = ax + b$ or $y = 2.3x + 3.1$. When
    $x = 6$, $y = 2.3(6) + 3.1 = 16.9$ and at $x = 7$, $y = 19.2$.

REVIEW EXERCISES FOR CHAPTER - 18

1. See answers in the text book.

5. $D = \{(x_1, x_2, x_3) \mid x_1 + x_2 + x_3 > 0$ and $x_1 - x_2 > 0\}$.

9. $z = \ln(x^2 + y^2) + e^{y\sqrt{x}}$ gives $\partial z/\partial x = 2x/(x^2+y^2) + e^{y\sqrt{x}} \cdot y(1/2)x^{-1/2}$

    $\partial z/\partial y = 2y/(x^2+y^2) + e^{y\sqrt{x}} \cdot \sqrt{x}$; $\partial^2 z/\partial x\partial y = \partial/\partial x(\partial z/\partial y)$

    $$= \partial/\partial x\left(\frac{2y}{x^2+y^2} + \sqrt{x}\, e^{y\sqrt{x}}\right)$$

    $= -4xy/(x^2+y^2)^2 + (y/2 + 1/2\sqrt{x})e^{y\sqrt{x}}$ and

    $\partial^2 z/\partial y^2 = \partial/\partial y(\partial z/\partial y) = 2(x^2-y^2)/(x^2+y^2)^2 + xe^{y\sqrt{x}}$.

13. $x_A = 100\sqrt{P_A P_B}$ gives $\partial x_A/\partial P_A = 50\sqrt{P_A P_B}$, $\partial x_A/\partial P_B = 50\sqrt{P_A/P_B}$

    (a) $P_A(\partial x_A/\partial P_A) + P_B(\partial x_A/\partial x_{P_B}) = 50\sqrt{P_A P_B} + 50\sqrt{P_A P_B} = 100\sqrt{P_A P_B} = x_A$.

(b) $\eta_{p_A} = (p_A/x_A)(\partial x_A/\partial p_A) = (p_A/100\sqrt{p_A p_B})(50\sqrt{p_A/p_B}) = 1/2.$

$\eta_{p_A} = (p_B/x_A)(\partial x_A/\partial p_B) = (p_B/100\sqrt{p_A p_B})(50\sqrt{p_A/p_B}) = 1/2$

$\eta_{p_A} + \eta_{p_B} = 1/2 + 1/2 = 1.$

17. $g(u,v) = uv + u^{-1} - 8v^{-1} + 7$ gives $g_u = v - u^{-2}$, $g_v = u + 8v^{-2}$. $g_u = 0$

$g_v = 0$ gives the cr. pt. $u = -1/2$, $v = 1/4$. $g_{uu} = 2/u^3$, $g_{vv} = -16/v^3$

$g_{uv} = 1$. At $(-1/2, 1/4)$, we have: g_{uu}, $g_{uv} < 0$, $\Delta > 0$. Thus $g(u,v)$

is a local maximum at $(-1/2, 1/4)$.

21. $R = px + qy = x(40.5 - 0.03x - 0.004y) + y(25.4 - 0.005x - 0.02y)$

$= 40.5x + 25.4y - 0.009xy - 0.03x^2 - 0.02y^2$

R is maximum when $x = 600$ and $y = 500$ i.e. the revenue is maximum

when 600 lbs. of beef and 500 lbs. of pork are sold.

25. (a) $F(L,K,\lambda) = P(L,K) - \lambda(pL + qK - C)$

where p, q, C are given constants.

For maximum of $F(L,K,\lambda)$ or of $P(L,K)$, we have:

$F_L = P_L - \lambda p = 0$, $F_K = P_K - q\lambda = 0$, $F_\lambda = (pL + qK - C) = 0 \ldots (1)$

From the first two equations, we have

$P_L/p = P_K/q$ or $P_L/P_K = p/q$

i.e. ratio of marginal productivities of labor and capital is equal to the ratio of their unit costs.

(b) Suppose extra \$1 can buy ΔL units of labor and ΔK units of capital. Then,

$$p\Delta L + q\Delta K = 1 \qquad\qquad \ldots(2)$$

Let (L_0, K_0) be the solutions of the system (1) above. Then the first two equations in (1) give:

$P_L(L_0, K_0) = \lambda p$, $P_K(L_0, K_0) = \lambda q$.

The increase in production when the labor used is increased from

L_0 to $L_0 + \Delta L$, and the capital is increased from K_0 to $K_0 + \Delta K$

is given by:

(b) Suppose extra \$1 can by ΔL units of Labor and ΔK units of capital. Then,

$$p\Delta L + q\Delta K = 1 \qquad \ldots\ldots \quad (2)$$

Let (L_0, K_0) be the solutions of the system (1) above. then L_0 to $L_0 + \Delta L$, and the capital is increased from K_0 to $K_0 + \Delta K$, is given by:

$$\Delta P = P(L_0 + \Delta L, K_0 + \Delta K) - P(L_0, K_0)$$

$$\simeq P_L(L_0, K_0)\,\Delta L + P_K(L_0, K_0)\Delta K$$

$$= (\lambda p)\Delta L + (\lambda q)\Delta K = \lambda(p\Delta L + q\Delta K) = \lambda(1) = \lambda$$

on using equation (2) above.

29. $\dfrac{\partial C}{\partial x} = \dfrac{c}{\sqrt{t}} \cdot \dfrac{-2(x-vt)}{at}\, e^{-(x-vt)^2/at}$

$\dfrac{\partial^2 C}{\partial x^2} = \dfrac{-2c}{2t^{3/2}} \left\{1 - \dfrac{2(x-vt)^2}{at}\right\}\, e^{-(x-vt)^2/at}$

$\dfrac{\partial C}{\partial t} = \dfrac{-c}{2t^{3/2}}\, e^{-(x-vt)^2/at} + \dfrac{c}{\sqrt{t}}\, e^{-(x-vt)^2/at} \left[\dfrac{(x-vt)^2}{at^2} + \dfrac{2v(x-vt)}{at}\right]$

Then $\dfrac{\partial C}{\partial t} + v\,\dfrac{\partial C}{\partial x} = \left\{\dfrac{-c}{2t^{3/2}} + \dfrac{c(x-vt)^2}{at^{5/2}}\right\} e^{-(x-vt)^2/at} = \dfrac{a}{4}\cdot\dfrac{\partial^2 C}{\partial x^2}$

33. See answer in the text.

REVIEW TEST ON CHAPTER - 18

FILL IN THE BLANKS:

1. If $f(x,y) = x/y$, then $f(0,4) =$ _____ , $f(9,0) =$ _____ and

   $f(-8,-2) =$ _____ .

2. If $g(x,y) = \ln (x/y)$, then $g(4,1) =$ _____ , $g(-8,-2) =$ _____

   and $g(0,4) =$ _____ .

3. If $f(x,y) = \ln x + e^y$, then $f(1,0) =$ _____ , $f(e,1) =$ _____

   and $f(0,0) =$ _____ .

4. If $f(x,y) = \sqrt{x^2+y^2-4}$, then the domain of f is _____ and the range

   of f is _____ .

5. If the point (p,q,r) lies on the

   (a) xy-plane, then _____ .   (b) zx-plane, then _____ .

   (b) yz-plane, then _____ .   (d) x-axis, then _____ .

   (e) y-axis, then _____ .   (f) z-axis, then _____ .

6. If $z = f(x,y)$, then by definition,

   $$\partial z/\partial x = \underline{\hspace{2cm}} \quad \text{and} \quad \partial z/\partial y = \underline{\hspace{2cm}}.$$

7. If $f(x,y) = \ln(x^2+3y)$, then $f_x =$ _____ and $f_y =$ _____

8. If $g(x,y) = x^2 \ln y$, then $f_x =$ _____ and $f_y =$ _____

9. If $z = f(x+2y)$, then $z_x/z_y =$ _____

10. If $z = \ln (x^3+y^3)$, then $z_x/z_y =$ _____

11. If $f(x,y) = x^5 + y^5 - 5xy$, then $f_x =$ _____ , $f_y =$ _____

    $f_{xy} =$ _____ $f_{xx} =$ _____ and $f_{yy} =$ _____

12. If x_A units of product A can be sold at a price p_A each and x_B units

    of a related product B can be sold at a price p_B each, then

    $x_A = f(p_A,p_B)$ and $x_B = g(p_A,p_B)$.

    (a) The marginal demand of the product A with respect to price p_A is

        given by _____ and with respect to price p_B is given by _____

    (b) The two products A and B are competitive if _____ and

        complementary if _____

176

13. If $x_A = f(p_A, p_B)$ and $x_B = g(p_A, p_B)$ are the demand functions for two products A and B, then the price elasticity of demand for A is given by

_____

14. If Δx and Δy are small, then

$$f(x_0 + \Delta x, \ y_0 + \Delta y) \simeq f(x_0, y_0) + \underline{\hspace{2cm}}$$

15. The critical points of

(a) $f(x,y) = x^2 + y^2 - 4x + 6y + 7$ are given by _____

(b) $f(x,y) = (x+y)(x-2)^3(y-2)^3$ are given by _____

(c) $f(x,y) = xy \ e^{x+y}$ are given by _____

(d) $f(x,y) = (\ln x)/x + (\ln y)/y$ are given by _____

16. If $\Delta = f_{xx} f_{yy} - f_{xy}^2 < 0$ at the critical point (a,b) then (a,b) is a _____ point of $f(x,y)$.

17. If $\Delta > 0$ at the critical point (a,b), then $f(x,y)$ has a local maximum at (a,b), if at (a,b) _____

18. If $f(x,y)$ has a local minimum at (a,b), then at (a,b) _____

19. If at the critical point (a,b), f_{xx} and f_{yy} are of opposite signs, then $f(x,y)$ has a _____ at (a,b)

20. The critical points of $f(x,y) = x^2 + 5y^2$ subjects to $x + 2y = 7$ are given by _____

SEE ANSWERS AT THE END OF THIS BOOK.

TEST ON CHAPTER - 1

1. non-negative   2. negative   3. $1 ; \neq 0$ 4. $p \neq 0$

5. $a ; \neq 0$ 6. $1 , \neq 0$ 7. $2x$ 8. p/qr 9. xz/y

10. d/b 11. $8/x$ 12. $8a/15$ 13. $(a-bc)/c$ 14. $(ad+bc)/bd$

15. cannot be simplified (It is <u>incorrect</u> to say that $p/(q+r) = \dfrac{p}{q} + \dfrac{p}{r}$).

16. $|a|$ 17. $-x$ 18. $1, \neq 0$ 19. $x/2$ 20. 1   21. 0

22. $1/5$ 23. a^2b^2 24. $-ba^5$ 25. 6   26. $36/25$ 27. 8

28. -0.2 29. $x^2+2xy+y^2$ 30. $a^2-2ab+b^2$ 31. x^2-y^2

32. b^2-a^2 33. $4x^2-9$ 34. $4a^2-12ab+9b^2$ 35. $(3x-y)(3x+y)$

36. $(2x-3y)(2x+3y)$ 37. $(x+3)(x+1)$ 38. $(x-2)(x-1)$

39. $(x-6)(x+1)$ 40. $(x+2)(x-1)$ 41. $(a-b)(a^2+ab+b^2)$

42. $(x+y)(x^2-xy+y^2)$ 43. $(x-2)(x^2+2x+4)$ 44. $(3a+1)(9a^2-3a+1)$

45. $3y/2x ; x \neq 2$ 46. $x-2 ; x \neq -2$ 47. $\neq$ 48. $\neq$ 49. $\neq$

50. $\sqrt{3} + \sqrt{2} ; \sqrt{3} + \sqrt{2}$

TEST ON CHAPTER - 2

1. $\neq 0$ 2. is not   3. 3   4. 4   5. -2 6. 0   7. 3

8. 0   9. $\neq$ 10. one   11. no ; one ; two   12. $2, -3/2$

13. ± 3 14. $0, 5$ 15. $0, \pm 3$ 16. no solution   17. $(x+4)(x-3)$;

$-4, 3$ 18. $9x+14 ; 0, -9$ 19. $(-b \pm \sqrt{b^2-4ac})/2a$ 20. b^2-4ac

21. equal   **22.** unreal   23. $x+3$ 24. $x-5$ 25. $(x/2 + 3)$

TEST ON CHAPTER - 3

1. negative ; positive   2. $= ; >$ 3. $x < y ; y < z$ 4. set

5. elements or members   6. (a) $\{1, 2, 3, \ldots , 9\}$ (b) $\{a, b, c, \ldots, z\}$

(c) $\{a, e, i, o, u\}$ 7. (a) x is a positive odd integer

(b) $x = n/(n+1)$, where n is a natural number   (c) $x = -3y$, where y

is any integer   8. member or element   9. empty or void ; $\emptyset$

10. subset ; $\subseteq$ 11. subset   12. $\subseteq$ 13. =   14. > ; > ; <

15. <   16. $x > 5$ 17. $x > -3/2$ 18. $2 < x < 7$

19. $-3 < x < 4$ 20. -3 ; 1   21. 5 ; -2   22. All values of x

23. all x   24. No x   25. $x = -5$ 26. x ; -x   27. $\geq$

28. < 0 ; $\geq$ 0   29. -1 ; 1   30. $|x|$ 31. =   32. $\pm c$

33. $\pm b$ 34. $\pm(x+5)$; 8, -2/3   35. No x   36. $-c < x < c$

37. $x < -c$ or $x > c$ 38. all x   39. No x   40. all $x \neq 2$

41. all x   42. no x   43. $x = -2$ 44. $|x|$ 45. $|x|$

TEST ON CHAPTER - 4

1. $\sqrt{(x_2-x_1)^2 + (y_2-y_1)^2}$ 2. $|b-a|$ 3. second or fourth

4. slope   5. $(y_2-y_1)/(x_2-x_1)$ 6. zero ; no   7. b=d   8. a=c

9. $y - y_1 = m(x - x_1)$ 10. $y = mx + c$ 11. 1/3 ; -6 ; 2

12. y = q ; x = p   13. y-   14. a, b are not both zero

15. p, q are not both zero   16. $m_1 = m_2$; $m_1 m_2 = -1$

17.   x = 3, y = 2   18. x = 1 , y = -1   19. p = 2 , q = 3

20. x = 1, y = 2 , z = 1   21. No   22. infinite   23. variable

cost per unit ; fixed   24. 500 ; 3   25. total cost

26. > ; <   27. p = 10, x = 14   28. p = 4 + 0.5x , p = 38-2x ,

p = 10.8 , x = 13.6   29. p + 2x = 38 , p = 2.5 + 0.5x ; p = 9.6

x = 14.2   30. fixed costs ; variable cost per unit

TEST ON CHAPTER - 5

1. $2x^2 + 3$, $2x + 2h + 3$ 2. 5, 5, 5   3. 3/2 ; undefined

4. -3   5. all $x \neq \pm 2$ 6. all x 7. all $x \geq 3/2$

8. all $x \leq 3/2$ 9. parabola ; up ; (2, -3)   10. Maximum,

$x = 2$ 11. all x ; all $y \geq -1$ 12. $-x$, x 13. all $x \neq 3$

{1, -1}   14. $(x-a)^2 + (y-b)^2 = r^2$ 15. $(x+3)^2 + (y-3)^2 = 9$

16. $f[g(x)]$ 17. 3 ; 7   18. $2x^2 + 3$; $(2x+3)^2$

19. x , $|x|$ 20. x 21. 9 ; 3   22. 3, 3   23. $\neq$

24. (i) $70x - 2x^2$ (ii) $35p - 0.5p^2$

25. (i) $R(x) = 20x - (2/3)x^2$; $P(x) = 17x - 70 - (2/3)x^2$

(ii) $R(p) = 30p - 1.5p^2$; $P(p) = 34.5p - 1.5p^2 - 160$

26. at least   27. horizontal , atmost one   28. $f^{-1}(y)$ 29. $\dfrac{x-7}{3}$

30. $x^{1/5}$ 31. $-\sqrt{x-3}$ 32. does not exist   33. $y = x$

34. =   35. $\neq$ 36. vertical ; atmost   37. 15   38. 10

39. (i) $x^2 - 1 \pm (x-1)/(x-2)$; $(x+1)(x-2)$

(ii) all $x \neq 2$ (iii) all $x \neq 2$ (iv) all $\neq 2, 1$

40. $y = (1 - \sqrt{x})^2$

TEST ON CHAPTER - 6

1. $a > 0, \neq 1$ 2. > 1 ; $0 < a < 1$ 3. all x ; all $y > 0$

4. all x, all $y < 3$ 5. (0,1)   6. (a) $P(1+i)^n$

(b) $P(1 + i/2)^{2n}$ (c) $P(1 + i/4)^{4n}$ (d) $P(1 + i/k)^{nk}$ (e) Pe^{in}

7. $\log_a y$ 8. $\log y$ 9. $\ln x$ 10. p^u 11. 0 ;$> 0, \neq 1$

12. 1 ; $> 0, \neq 1$ 13. 1, 0   14. xy 15. x/y 16. x 17. x

18. 3/2   19. $(\log x)^n$, cannot be simplified. (it is <u>incorrect</u> to

write $(\log x)^n = n \log x$)   20. n 21. x 22. > 0 ; $> 0 , \neq 1$

23. $\log_2 y$ 24. $-\log_3 x$ 25. e^x 26. $(2 + 10^t)/3$ 27. 27^x ; $3x$;

4/3   28. $Pe^{0.1x}$; 10 ln 2   29. $e^{R/100} = 1.12$; 100 ln(1.12)

30. $1 + R/100 = (1.02)^4$; $100\{(1.02)^4 - 1\} \approx 8.24$

31. $(3-y)/2y$; $-\ln\{(3-y)/2y\}/\ln 3$

32. $(1-P)/CP$; $(-1/k)\ln\{(1-P)/Cp\}$.

33. $\log_a y$; $\log y$; $\ln y$ 34. $\log e$; $\ln 10$ 35. 1   36. $\log x$

37. e   38. $Pe^{5R/100}$; $20\ln 2$ 39. $P(1 + R/100)^7$; $100(2^{1/7} - 1)$

40. $P(1 + R/400)^{40}$; $400(3^{1/40} - 1)$

TEST ON CHAPTER - 7

1. (a) $T_2 - T_1 = T_3 - T_2 = T_4 - T_3 = \ldots\ldots$

    (b) $T_2/T_1 = T_3/T_2 = T_4/T_3 = \ldots\ldots$

2. (a) $a + (n-1)d$ (b) $(n/2)\{2a + (n-1)d\}$; $\frac{n}{2}(a + \ell)$

3. (a) $a r^{n-1}$ (b) $a(1 - r^n)/(1-r)$ (c) $a/(1-r)$; < 1

4. (a) 26, 3n-1   (b) 345   (c) $3p^2/2 + 3p/2$ 5. 25 ; 1225

6. (a) 256 ; $(-2)^{p-1}$ (b) -341   (c) $(1/3)\{1-(-2)^p\}$

7. 6 ; 378   8. (a) 17, 14, 11, ...   (b) $p(37 - 3p)/2$

9. (a) 6, 3, 3/2, 3/4, ...   (b) $12(1 - 2^{-n})$ (c) 12

10. (a) $T_n = S_n - S_{n-1} = (n^2 + 3n) - \{(n-1)^2 + 3(n-1)\} = 2n + 2$

     (b) 4, 6, 8, 10, ...   (c) is

11. (a) $T_n = 2n-1 + 2^{n-1}$ (b) 2, 5, 9, 15, ...   (c) neither

12. 4/3   13. 1/3   14. 5   15. $S = \$500\, s_{\overline{8}|\,0.06}$

16. $P = \$150,000/a_{\overline{15}|\,0.08}$ 17. $\dfrac{n(n+1)}{2}$; $\dfrac{n(n+1)(2n+1)}{6}$

18. 23   19. $a = -3/2$, $b = -7$, $c = -25/2$ 20. p=18 , q=6

1. Sample space, sample point   2. $\{$HH, HT, TH, TT$\}$.

3. 36   4. event   5. impossible   6. certain

7. mutually exclusive   8. $P(E_1) + P(E_2) - P(E_1 \cap E_2)$

9. independent   10. Mutually exclusive   11. $P(E_1 \cap E_2)/P(E_2)$;

$P(E_1 \cap E_2)$ 12. 1 ; 0 ; 1   13. 0.85   14. 0.65

15. 0.25   16. (a) $P(E_1)$ (b) $P(E_1')$

17. (a) 0.24   (b) 0.26   (c) 0.64

    (d) 0.76   (e) 18/25   (f) 3/5

    (g) 12/25   (h) 7/20   (i) 13/25

    (j) 2/5

	A	A'	
B	0.36	0.14	0.5
B'	0.24	0.26	0.5
	0.6	0.4	1

18. independent, because $P(A \cup B) = P(A) + P(B)P(A')$ implies

    $P(A) + P(B) - P(A \cap B) = P(A) + P(B)\{1 - P(A)\}$ or $P(A \cap B) = P(A)P(B)$

19. $P(B)/P(A)$ 20. (a) $1 \cdot 2 \cdot 3 \cdot \ldots \cdot n$ (b) $n(n-1)(n-2) \ldots (n-r+1)$

    $= n!/(n-r)!$ (c) $n!/\{n!(n-r)!\}$ (d) $n-r$ (e) 1   (f) 1

        21. (a) 1 (b) 6   (c) 8   (d) 56   (e) 8   (f) 28

(g) 2   (h) 1   22. $\binom{n}{r} p^r q^{n-r}$ 23. 1/2 , 1/2 (a) 10/32 (b) $\frac{1}{2}$

24. (a) $a^n + \binom{n}{1} a^{n-1}b + \binom{n}{2} a^{n-2}b^2 + \ldots + \binom{n}{n} b^n$ (b) $\binom{n}{r} a^{n-r}b^r$

(c) n+1   25. $x^5 - 5x^4y + 10x^3y^2 - 10x^2y^3 + 5xy^4 - y^5$.

1. q ; p   2. x=4 , y = 2 , u=3, v=2   3. $\begin{bmatrix} 0 & 5 \\ -3 & 6 \end{bmatrix}$

4. $\underline{B}$; $\underline{A}$ 5. n=p ; m × q   6. n × m   7. $\neq$ 8. n × n

9. $\underline{A}\,\underline{B} = \begin{bmatrix} 2 & 3 \\ 0 & 6 \end{bmatrix}$; $\underline{B}\,\underline{A} = \begin{bmatrix} 2 & 1 \\ 0 & 6 \end{bmatrix}$ 10. $\begin{bmatrix} 1 & 4 \\ 0 & 1 \end{bmatrix}$

11. $\underline{B}\,\underline{A}$ 12. $\begin{bmatrix} 2 & -3 & 4 \\ 3 & 1 & 1 \\ 1 & 1 & -1 \end{bmatrix}\begin{bmatrix} x \\ y \\ z \end{bmatrix} = \begin{bmatrix} 5 \\ 7 \\ 4 \end{bmatrix}$ 13. $2x + 5y = 1$, $3x-y = 2$

14. $\begin{bmatrix} 2 & -3 & | & 7 \\ 5 & 1 & | & 8 \end{bmatrix}$ 15. at least one   16. no   17. infinite

solutions   18. either one, or none or more than one

19. either no solution or more than one

20. more than one

TEST ON CHAPTER - 10

1. $\underline{A}\,\underline{B} = \underline{B}\,\underline{A} = \underline{I}$ 2. does not exist   3. exists   4. n = m

5. 3×3 6. $\underline{A}^{-1}\underline{B}$; $\underline{A}^{-1}$ exists   7. $\underline{I}$; $\underline{A}^{-1}$ exists   8. $\underline{A}$

9. does not exist   10. $\underline{A}$ 11. $\underline{X} = \underline{A}\,\underline{X} + \underline{D}$; $\underline{X} = (\underline{I}-\underline{A})^{-1}\underline{D}$,

provided $(\underline{I}-\underline{A})^{-1}$ exists.   12. probability ; j ; i   13. row

14. ≥ 0 15. (a) $p_{13} = 0.3$,   (b) $p_{32} = 0.2$ (c) $p_{33} = 0.2$

16. is not (because one of the probabilities viz. $p_4 = -1/4$ is negative).

17. is not, (because $\underline{P}^2$ is an identity matrix and $\underline{P}^n = \underline{P}$ for all $n \geq 3$

and so $\underline{P}^n$ contains zero elements for all $n \geq 1$).

18. (a) 78   (b) 13   (c) 6   19. x=1, 3 or -2   20. $|\underline{A}| \neq 0$

21. $\begin{bmatrix} 3 & 1 \\ 7 & -3 \\ 2 & 4 \end{bmatrix}$ 22. $\begin{bmatrix} 4 & -3 \\ 1 & 2 \end{bmatrix}$; $\begin{bmatrix} 4 & 1 \\ -3 & 2 \end{bmatrix}$ 23. $(1/|\underline{A}|)$adj. $\underline{A}$

24. $\neq 0$ 25. $\begin{bmatrix} 7 & -3 \\ -2 & 1 \end{bmatrix}$; $\begin{bmatrix} 7 & -2 \\ -3 & 1 \end{bmatrix}$; 1 ; $\begin{bmatrix} 7 & -2 \\ -3 & 1 \end{bmatrix}$

TEST ON CHAPTER - 11

1. right   2. above   3. above   4. on or below

5. on or above   6. below   7. on or below ; $5y - x = 4$

8. $2x + y = 4$ and $2x - 3$; $x + 2y = 4$ 9. $x + y = 1$, $y=x$ and

$x - 2y = 1$; $x + y = 4$.   10. constraints ; objective

11. (i) feasible (ii) vertex or vertices.   12. equations ; slack ;

13. $x + y - u = 4$ and $x + 2y + v = 10$ or $(x + y - v = 4$ and

$x + 2y + u = 10)$

14. (a) $x + y + z + t = 5$, $2x + y + 3z + u = 7$ and $2x + 4z + v = 13$

(b)
$$
\begin{array}{c}
\,\,\begin{array}{cccccc} x & y & z & t & u & v \end{array} \\
\begin{array}{c} t \\ u \\ v \\ \end{array}
\left[\begin{array}{cccccc|c}
1 & 1 & 1 & 1 & 0 & 0 & 5 \\
2 & 1 & 3 & 0 & 1 & 0 & 7 \\
2 & 3 & 4 & 0 & 0 & 1 & 13 \\
3 & 1 & 2 & 0 & 0 & 0 & Z
\end{array} \right]
\end{array}
$$

(c) indicators

(d) (x, y, z) ; (t, u, v) ;

$Z = 0$

(e) departing ; entering   (g) u ; x ; (t, x, v)

(f) entering   (h) positive.

TEST ON CHAPTER - 12

1. 0.2   2. -3/4   3. $\dfrac{f(x+\,x) - f(x)}{x}$ 4. 3   5. 1/(e-1)   6. =

7. $\neq$ 8. 3   9. -2/3   10. 0   11. no limit   12. 1, -1, does not exist.

13. 2, 5, 10, 1, does not exist   14. is not necessarily   15. may

not exist   16. $\lim\limits_{h \to 0} \dfrac{f(x+h) - f(x)}{h}$ 17. $-6x^{-7}$ 18. $-5x^{-6}$

19. $\dfrac{-1}{2} t^{-3/2}$ 20. $1 - x^{-2}$ 21. $3(\ln 2) x^2$ 22. $2e^5 x$

23. $f(c)$ and $\lim\limits_{x\,c} f(x)$ both exist and are equal to one another.

24. 2, -1   25. 3, -2

TEST ON CHAPTER - 13

1. $14x(x^2+1)^6$ 2. $-30x(x^2-1)^{-6}$ 3. $14x(x^2+5)^6(3x-5) + 3(x^2+5)^7$

4. $8(2x+5)^3(3x-1)^7 + 21(2x+5)^4(3x-1)^6$ 5. 0   6. $2x\,e^{x^2}$

7. 0   8. 0   9. $(\ln 2)/x$ 10. $2x(x^2+1)^{-1}$ 11. $1/(x \ln x)$

12. $(x-1)/x$ 13. $3x^2 \ln x + x^2$ 14. $e^{3x}/x + 3e^{3x} \ln x$

15. $(\ln x) + 1$ 16. $7(\ln x)^6/x$ 17. $5(x + 3\ln x)^4(1 + 3/x)$

18. $\dfrac{e^x+1}{e^x+x}$ 19. $1/(\ln 2)x$ 20. $(\dfrac{1}{2\sqrt{x}} \ln 5)(5^{\sqrt{x}})$ 21. $2x(\ln 7)(x^2+1)$

22. $(\ln 3)(2x)3^{x^2-1}$ 23. 0   24. 1   25. 2

26. $8(2x+3)^3$, $48(2x+3)^2$ 27. $3e^{3x-4}$, $9e^{3x-4}$, $27e^{3x-4}$

28. $1/(2x-5)$, $-2/(2x-5)^2$, $8(2x-5)^{-3}$

TEST ON CHPATER - 14

1. increasing   2. decreasing   3. $m > 0$, $m < 0$ 4. $>$ 5. $<$

6. up   7. $x > 1$, $0 < x < 1$ 8. maximum   9. minimum   10. minimum

11. minimum   12. inflection   13. either at the critical point

which lies in $a < x < b$ or at the end point of interval.

14. b   15. c   16. b, a   17. 0   18. -1 19. does not exist

20. no limit   21. $+\infty$ 22. -1 23. -1 24. 0   25. $+\infty$

26. $+\infty$ 27. $-\infty$ 28. does not exist   29. (a) $y=0$ (b) $y = 3/2$

(c) $y=0$ (d) $y = 1$ (e) $y = 0$ (f) $y = 0$ 30. (a) $x = 1/2$

(b) $x = -2$ (c) no vertical asymptotes   (d) $x = 0$ (e) $x = e$

(f) $x = 0$

TEST ON CHAPTER - 15

1. $=$, $\neq$ 2. $g'(t)\ dt$ 3. $=$ 4. $7x^6\ dx$ 5. $(-3/t^4)\ dt$

6. $2ue^{u^2}\ du$ 7. 0   8. $(1/x)\ dx$ 9. $-e^{-y}\ dy$

10. $10x(x^2+1)^4\ dx$ 11. $\dfrac{1}{2\sqrt{x}}\, e^{\sqrt{x}}\ dx$ 12. $\dfrac{1}{2x}\ dx$

13. (a) dy (b) dy/y (c) $(dy/y)(100)$

14. $2x + 2y\dfrac{dy}{dx}$ 15. $(y + x\dfrac{dy}{dx})\, e^{xy}$ 16. $\{y + x(dy/dx)\}/xy$

17. $3x^2 + 3y^2\dfrac{dy}{dx} - 3(y + x\dfrac{dy}{dx})$ 18. $e^{x-y} - e^{x-y}\dfrac{dy}{dx}$

19. $\dfrac{-y}{x^2} + \dfrac{1}{x}\dfrac{dy}{dx}$ 20. $e^{xt}(x\ dt + t\ dx)$ 21. $\dfrac{1}{x}\, y\ dx + \ln x\ dy$

22. $\dfrac{p}{x}\dfrac{dx}{dp}$ 23. $\eta < -1$, $-1 < \eta < 0$.   24. η (percentage change in price)

25. > 26. < 27. inelastic

28. $x \ln(x+1)$, $y'/y = \frac{x}{x+1} + \ln(x+1)$, $\left[\frac{x}{x+1} + \ln(x+1) \right](x+1)^x$

TEST ON CHAPTER - 16

1. $-x^{-6}/6 + C$ 2. $2\sqrt{x} + C$ 3. $e^x + C$ 4. $(\log 3)(x^2/2) + C$

5. $x^3/3 + C$ 6. $e^3 x + C$ 7. $\frac{(2x+3)^8}{16} + C$ 8. $-\sqrt{5-2x} + C$

9. $\frac{-1}{2}(2x+1)^{-1} + C$ 10. $\frac{1}{2} \ln |2x+3| \cdot + C$ 11. $\frac{1}{3} \ln |3x+7| + C$

12. $\frac{1}{2} e^{2x-3} + C$ 14. x^3+x , $1/\sqrt{u}$, $2\sqrt{u} + C$, $2\sqrt{x^3+x} + C$

15. x^2+3x+7 , $1/u$, $\ln |u| + C$, $\ln |x^2+3x+7| + C$

16. $\ln x$, u $u^2/2 + C$, $\frac{(\ln x)^2}{2} + C$

17. $\ln x$, $1/u$, $\ln |u| + C$, $\ln |\ln x| + C$

18. x^2-4 , $1/2u$, $(1/2) \ln |u| + C$, $(1/2) \ln |x^2-4| + C$

19. $\sqrt{x}$, $2e^u$, $2e^u + C$, $2e^{\sqrt{x}} + C$

20. $x^2 + 4$, $\sqrt{u}/2$, $u^{3/2}/3 + C$, $\frac{(x^2+4)^{3/2}}{3} + C$

21. $e^x + 7$, $\sqrt{u}$ $(2/3) u^{3/2} + C$, $(2/3) (e^x + 7)^{3/2} + C$

22. $\ln x$, x^7 , $x^8/8$, $(x^8/8)\ln x$, $x^7/8$, $(x^8/8)\ln x - x^8/64$

23. x , e^{-2x} , $\frac{-1}{2} e^{-2x}$, $\frac{-x}{2} e^{-2x}$, $\frac{-1}{2} e^{-2x}$, $\frac{-1}{2}xe^{-2x} - \frac{1}{4} e^{-2x}$

24. $\ln x$, x , $x^2/2$, $\frac{x^2}{2} \ln x$, $x/2$, $\frac{x^2}{2} \ln x - \frac{x^2}{4}$

25. $3x + 2$, e^{-x} , $-e^{-x}$, $-e^{-x}(3x+2)$, $-3e^{-x}$, $-e^{-x}(3x+2) - 3e^{-x}$

26. $\ln x$, 1 , x , $x \ln x$, 1 , $x \ln x - x$

186

TEST ON CHAPTER - 17

1. $\frac{1}{12}(2x+1)^5$, $(3^6 - 1)/12$ 2. $(-1/2) \ln |3-2x|$; $\frac{-\ln 3}{2}$

3. $\int_{\ln 2}^{1} (1/u) \, du$ 4. 0   5. $f(x)$ 6. $e^{\sqrt{x}}$ 7. 0

8. $\int_{0}^{2} \frac{1}{x+2} \, dx$ 9. $\int_{0}^{2} (4-x^2) \, dx + \int_{2}^{3} (x^2-4) \, dx$ 10. $\int_{a}^{b} \{g(x)-f(x)\} \, dx$

11. 0 , 1   12. $\int_{0}^{1} \{x - f(x)\} \, dx$ 13. 17.5   14. x   15. is not

16. is   17. $y^{-1} \, dy = \{(2t+1)/t\} \, dt$ 18. ce^{kt} where c is the

constant of integration.   19. $\geq$, 1   20. 3/7   21. 2

22. (i) $\int_{c}^{d} f(x) \, dx$ (ii) $\int_{a}^{c} f(x) \, dx$ (iii) $\int_{d}^{b} f(x) \, dx$

(iv) 0   23. $\mu = 1/K$ 24. $-1/50$

TEST ON CHAPTER - 18

1. 0 , not defined , 4   2. ln 4 , ln 4 , not defined

3. 1 , 1+e , not defined

4. $\{(x,y) \mid x^2+y^2 \geq 4\}$ = set of all points (x,y) on or outside the circle

$x^2 + y^2 = 4$; $f(x,y) \geq 0$ 5. (a) r=0   (b) q=0   (c) p=0

(d) q=r=0   (e) p=r=0   (f) p=q=0

6. $\lim_{h \to 0} \frac{f(x+h, y) - f(x,y)}{h}$; $\lim_{h \to 0} \frac{f(x, y+h) - f(x,y)}{h}$

7. $-\frac{2x}{x^2+3y}$, $\frac{3}{x^2+3y}$ 8. $2x \ln y$; x^2/y 9. 1/2

10. x^2/y^2 11. $5x^4 - 5y$; $5y^4 - 5x$; -5 ; $20x^3$; $20y^3$

12. (a) $(\partial x_A/\partial p_A)$, $(\partial x_A/\partial p_B)$ (b) $\partial x_A/\partial p_B > 0$ and $\partial x_B/\partial p_A \gtrless 0$;

$\partial x_A/\partial p_B < 0$ and $\partial x_B/\partial p_A < 0$ 13. $(\partial x_A/\partial p_A)/(x_A/p_A)$

14. $\Delta x \, f_x(x_0,y_0) + \Delta y f_y(x_0,y_0)$ 15. (a) (2,-3)   (b) (2,2), (2,-1),

(-1,2)   (c) (0,0) , (-1,-1)   (d) (e,e)   16. saddle

187

17. $f_{xx} < 0$, $f_{yy} < 0$ 18. $f_{xx} > 0$, $f_{yy} > 0$ and $\Delta > 0$

19. saddle point   20. (5,2)

GOOD LUCK

"HOPE IS A BETTER COMPANION THAN FEAR"

- DR. J.C. ARYA.